THE GOTHIC
CATHEDRAL

CHRISTOPHER WILSON

THE GOTHIC CATHEDRAL

The Architecture of the Great Church
1130~1530

With 220 illustrations

THAMES AND HUDSON

To my parents
Eldred and Kathleen Wilson

1 (*on the half-title page*) Florence Cathedral, coloured drawing showing the original scheme for the bell tower, *c.* 1334 [cf. *203*]. The increase in the number of openings in successive storeys is a long-established feature of Italian towers [cf. *197*], but the gradual transition from square panelling to upright windows is unique.

2 (*frontispiece*) Sées Cathedral, choir looking east, begun *c.* 1270. The decorative gables over the main arcades and the extensions of the clearstorey mullions below the base of the triforium are unique in the main elevations of a 13th-century church; they are closely modelled on the interior face of the south transept façade at Notre-Dame in Paris. The richly but repetitively moulded arches of the main arcade derive from early 13th-century Norman Gothic [cf. *79*].

Printed and bound in Singapore

Contents

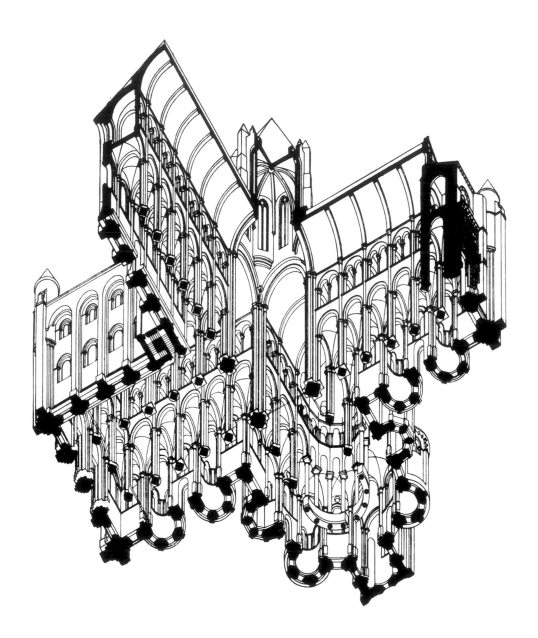

3 Santiago de Compostela Cathedral, 1075–1211. This is the biggest and best preserved of the 'Pilgrimage Churches', a type apparently disseminated from the Loire valley during the 11th century. Except in its lack of a clearstorey in the regular, straight-sided bays, this scheme can be regarded as the epitome of the northern French Romanesque great church.

Introduction

THIS BOOK is both more and less than a history of Gothic cathedral architecture. It is less in the sense that it excludes the modest cathedrals of the poorer dioceses, and it is more because an important minority of the buildings discussed are splendid churches created to serve wealthy corporate bodies other than cathedral chapters – monasteries, collegiate foundations and city parishes. Since the buildings which form this uppermost stratum of Gothic architecture include hardly any features specific to their different institutional functions, and since influences passed freely between them, it is logical and appropriate that they be considered as a single category, namely the 'great church'.

The historical reality embodied in this category is that virtually all Gothic great churches inherited the basic premises of their design from the most highly evolved traditions of Romanesque architecture, those developed in northern France during the 11th century [3, 5]. The constituent elements of the great church type may be enumerated as follows: a cruciform plan, with a nave* longer than the other three arms; a nave and possibly also other arms built to the basilican scheme, that is with side aisles and a higher and wider central vessel receiving direct lighting from a clearstorey; a middle storey of some kind between the clearstorey and the arcades separating central vessel from aisles; masonry vaulting over all or most of the aisles and central vessels; longitudinal division of the arms into a series of (in theory) uniform spatial units or 'bays' articulated as a system of linked arches and cylindrical shafts; an eastern termination of complex plan, most commonly an apse with an ambulatory and radiating chapels; and one or more towers integrated into the main body of the church, usually over the centre of the cross (the crossing) or on the west façade of the nave. Many of the churches discussed possess all these features, and all possess most of them.

Size is not in itself a qualification for inclusion in the great church category. If it were, one would have to include the largest of the severely plain vaulted basilicas built by the orders of friars in Central Europe and Italy. Some of the Italian and German cathedrals considered here are internally not much closer than the most ambitious friars' churches to the norms of great church architecture, but they compensate for their lack of elaborate articulation by incorporating other features of equivalent value as display. A few churches of less ambitious types are mentioned in order to trace

---

* Architectural terms are explained in the Glossary, pp. 292–4.

developments which originated outside the sphere of great church architecture [*14, 140, 200, 216*] or to give some sense of the context of the great churches built in milieux where the concept did not gain general acceptance [*112, 117, 194*].

Every medieval church was an evocation of the heavenly Jerusalem, the abode of the saved to be established after the completion of the Last Judgment (Revelation, chapters 21 and 23). That this was the primary meaning of church buildings is clear from the service for their consecration, where frequent allusions are made to St John's vision. There were of course other meanings (see, for example, pp. 65, 220, 262–3), and the fact that these overlapped or even appeared incompatible with the primary meaning was a merit rather than otherwise, for no one symbol could yield more than a partial and imperfect glimpse of that ultimate, transcendental reality which mankind sees only as if distorted in a mirror (1 Corinthians 13:12). Obviously, literal portrayal of the heavenly city was never attempted, and the great church remained in essence a very large hall for worship, its fundamental simplicity always apparent however numerous the layers of meaning in which it became enveloped. The cruciform plan, the most important of the symbolic features which did not arise from the heavenly city metaphor, was easily reconciled to this meaning, since the cross was the sign of Christ's triumph which he himself predicted would appear in heaven at the end of the world (Matthew 24:30).

The great church type created in 11th-century northern France surpassed earlier Western churches in symbolic as well as architectural terms, for its complex and systematic use of arches and vaulting made it a far richer evocation of the heavenly Jerusalem than the flat-ceilinged naves of the Early Christian and early medieval basilicas or the less fully articulated interiors of other Romanesque traditions. Since Antiquity, the circle and sphere, by virtue of their having no beginning and no end, were associated with eternity and by extension with immortality and heaven; hence arches and vaults which are part-circular or part-spherical in shape and which rise high over our heads also function as symbols of heaven. The visual support of compartments of vaulting is the primary function of the bay divisions which are so distinctive a feature of the walls of Romanesque and Gothic churches, and the design of the bay unit, including its vault, tended to be far more highly considered than either the overall proportioning of a church or the total number of bays included in it, for these could often be the outcome of a change of plan or of some accident of fortune such as lack of space or money. The indeterminate aspect of churches conceived as successions of many identical or near-identical bays is a most powerful evocation of heaven's infinite vastness [*71, 213*].

As symbols, arches and vaults were interchangeable with the many other arched forms which proliferated in Gothic architecture and art, for all of them signify heaven both as an entity and as the sum of innumerable small heavens, the dwelling places of the saved in the house of the Lord alluded to by Christ (John 14:2). In this sense the tracery of Reims [67], the panelled elevations of Gloucester [154], the arch mouldings of Lincoln [124], the vaults of Salamanca [219], the aedicular towers of Laon [37], the statue-populated niches of Wells [126, 151], and even the clergy-sheltering choir stalls of Albi [194] are all as one. Of course this visual diversity reflects the huge margins of creative freedom which architects were allowed when giving physical form to what remained after all very general symbolic concepts, yet it would be a mistake to imagine that the didactic function of great church architecture was ever forgotten. In Chapter III it is tentatively suggested that the most dramatic revolution in architectural taste during the late Middle Ages was successful partly on account of the enhanced symbolic value of the new style (see p. 212). The symbolic poverty of such lesser building types as hall churches and aisleless churches is no less a justification for their exclusion from the 'great church' category than their architectural simplicity, for though they are sometimes very impressive aesthetically, the utilitarian premise underlying the design of these efficient space-enclosers drastically reduces their capacity to evoke the heavenly city.

The ritual and devotional use of medieval churches is a subject of great intrinsic interest but it can be given only a small amount of space here since the functions and architectural forms of the Gothic great churches showed remarkably little interaction. Obviously, every major church had to make certain basic provisions – a presbytery or sanctuary area round the high altar; a liturgical choir near the presbytery and together with it forming what was almost the private chapel of the clergy who staffed the church; spaces for and access to subordinate altars; routes for processions on Sundays and feast days; an accessible area behind the high altar for a shrine if the church possessed a relic which was the focus of a popular cult – yet it is also obvious that this does not amount to an architectural specification. As was noted above, the Gothic church interior is essentially an assemblage of uniform bays, and at almost all the many great churches where the original screens and walls defining the liturgical choir have been taken away, the former choir-containing bays retain nothing to show that they were once a privileged area. The only major part of a great church other than the crossing which is usually not in the form of regular bays is the main apse, but even here there is hardly ever anything in the architecture to signal whether it was built to accommodate a major shrine as well as the high altar which normally stood in this position. That different functions could be fulfilled by identically shaped spaces is evident from the case of the only T-plan east ends in Gothic architecture, the Nine Altars Chapels at Durham Cathedral and Fountains Abbey, the former housing an important relic, the latter not. Conversely, the same kind of activity could take place in totally different architectural settings, for the shrine of the Three Kings at Cologne was installed in the axial chapel of the chevet, which pilgrims reached via the ambulatory [84, 111], whereas at Lincoln the shrine of St Hugh was the centrepiece of a purpose-built rectangular extension which actually superseded a chevet with an ambulatory and axial chapel [*119, 135*].

It seems certain that the general lack of correspondences between the main architectural divisions of lofty and uniformly built Gothic churches and the ground-level barriers separating the laity in the nave from the clergy installed near the high altar was in itself a sign that the separation was temporal only and would be transcended in heaven. The virtual impossibility of perceiving the interiors of the great churches as architectural entities while they retained their original furnishings mirrored mankind's inability to comprehend the whole of the Creator's plan. Externally, there was a still sharper contrast between the ideal quality of the house of God and the low, cramped, irregular and impermanent character of men's earthly dwellings [*64*].

Symbolic readings apart, contemporary attitudes to Gothic architecture do not emerge clearly from the written sources. In the Middle Ages, as in Antiquity, there was no continuous tradition of writing about the visual arts, and most of the minority of philosophers and theologians who considered them at all did so within the context of discussions of aesthetic theory or the religious status of images. A 'Lives of the Artists' on the lines of Vasari's work was quite inconceivable since biography was by tradition edifying in intent and hence reserved for exceptionally important individuals, usually saints. The only work of Gothic great church architecture built under the auspices of a saint, the eastern parts of Lincoln Cathedral, was a beneficiary of this tradition in that the writer of the *Metrical Life of St Hugh* (*c.* 1220–35) felt obliged to include a passage on the church of which his subject was (albeit only technically) the patron. As a document of the contemporary response to Gothic architecture this text is extremely disappointing since it is mostly couched in traditional symbolic-allegorical terms, with the occasional fanciful touches such as the likening of the high vaults to the wings of hovering birds. There is nothing to indicate that the writer realized or cared that he was in the presence of one of the strangest and most innovatory churches of his time. Indeed there is no sign that he possessed any kind of conceptual framework in which to situate the individual work of art. Like virtually all medieval writers who discuss buildings, the author of the *Metrical Life* was content to marvel. His disability was in fact not just a medieval one, for most post-medieval generations have also experienced difficulty when trying to discuss Gothic architecture analytically. One of the main reasons for this must be that Gothic designs, unlike Classical ones, are not assembled from elements whose form is relatively constant and which are therefore easy to isolate and identify.

The virtual impossibility that non-expert contemporaries would have been able to gain any intellectual purchase on Gothic great church architecture must have discouraged patrons from making detailed interventions in the design process such as were common from the Renaissance onwards. Italy, in so many ways the great exception to Western medieval norms, did develop a tradition of lay involvement in architectural decision-making, but there the designs were far simpler than in the North and hence more susceptible to discussion by non-architects. One of our very few authentic glimpses of architect–patron relations in Northern Europe during the Gothic period, Gervase's account of the rebuilding of the choir of Canterbury Cathedral from 1174, reveals the architect William of Sens skilfully manoeuvring his hesitant clients into letting him do what he wanted. It is tempting to think that this was a fairly common situation, for the fact that few of the higher clergy would have found themselves in the position of patronizing great church architecture more than once in their lifetimes must have tended to give architects the tactical and psychological advantage. No doubt when a design was in process of being formulated the patron would normally have had rights of veto in matters of size, richness of treatment or anything else which directly affected the cost; and a bishop or abbot or dean would probably have felt no compunction about rejecting a design out of hand, although, as we know from a report of an incident which took place in the mid-13th century, he would then run the risk of losing the services of a sought-after architect (see p. 142).

When a patron was assessing his architect's proposals [101], we can be sure that he would have been pondering how well they measured up to the churches owned by peer institutions. This competitive aspect is in fact the most recoverable part of the patron's 'input', for many major churches include features derived from buildings that would probably not have seemed obvious sources to their architects. These 'extraneous' elements are particularly prominent in churches such as St-Denis or Barcelona Cathedral which were the first great churches in their respective regions. In cases like these, or in the cases of buildings which represent a reaction against a well-established tradition – Chartres or the eastern parts of Gloucester, for example – the cultural context has to be explored carefully if one is to reach an understanding of why the church in question came to be the fountainhead of a new tradition. 'Cultural context' can range from momentous developments such as the rise of the French monarchy to the iconography of fittings, the latter often very revealing of a corporate patron's self-image and hence its motivation for building. Unlike the universal meaning of the great church as symbol of heaven, special local meanings tended to become submerged if the features which conveyed them were widely imitated and thereby absorbed into the current stock of fashionable motifs. Such short-lived meanings are often difficult to detect, and one can be sure that some have not yet been identified.

However much the Gothic great churches bear the imprint of the milieux in which they originated, they are also the product of individual intelligences. Sadly, the cathedral architects are not knowable now as personalities, yet some of their creative processes can be retrieved through reconstructing the situations of constraint and choice in which they worked. By treating each major design as an exercise in aesthetic and practical problem-solving one can hope to recapture something of the urgency of the moment and also to dispel any impression that designing great churches was normally a matter of realizing an already formed artistic vision. For architects faced with having to draw up designs within the few months which were usually all that separated their appointment from the start of work, the process must often have become one of precipitate self-revelation.

4 Paris, St-Germain-des-Prés, nave looking north-east, after *c.* 1025 (high vault, 17th-century). The width of the main vessel was dictated by that of the 6th-century nave on whose foundations it stands.

5 Caen, St-Etienne, interior looking east: nave, mostly *c.* 1066–77; choir, *c.* 1190–1200. The high vault added in the early 12th century is the oldest extant example of the sexpartite type later adopted in the Early Gothic period [cf. *30*]. As in most French medieval churches, the solid screen originally separating the nave from the liturgical choir has been removed; here, it stood under the eastern arch of the crossing.

CHAPTER I

Early Gothic

IN THE EARLY 1130s it would not have been obvious that Paris was about to become the birthplace of a new kind of architecture. None of the small number of churches built in the city since 1100 was specially large or impressive, and the surrounding area, the Ile-de-France, was among the few regions of northern France where church building had not flourished during the past hundred years. The root of this failure was the enfeebled state of the Capetian kings, who lacked the resources to found monasteries, the medieval ruler's most effective means of displaying both his piety and his power. Admittedly the one assertive 11th-century king, Robert II (996–1031), had been an enthusiastic patron of monastic and other church building in the then more favoured southern part of the Royal Domain around Orléans, but in the Ile-de-France his only important achievement was the refoundation of St-Germain-des-Prés in Paris. The nave at St-Germain [4], which probably dates from the reign of his successor Henry I (1031–60), is hardly more ambitious than the 6th- and 8th-century churches built in the city under earlier and more vigorous royal dynasties, and it cannot begin to compare with the grandest of the monastic churches erected by the nominal vassals of the Capetians who ruled over the richer and better organized principalities bordering on the Ile-de-France [5].

Far from hindering architectural innovation, the lack of a thriving Romanesque tradition in the Ile-de-France proved to be an advantage once the revival of royal power got under way in the latter part of the reign of Louis VI (1108–37). Not only was there no firmly entrenched notion of how great churches ought to look but, equally importantly, there was very little recent building to stand in the way of a wholesale renewal of the region's ancient and often dilapidated abbeys and cathedrals [191]. The churches which began to fill this vacuum in the late 1130s and 1140s borrowed freely from the highly evolved Romanesque traditions current in the adjoining regions, most notably Normandy and Burgundy. No new architectural types were invented, for the 12th-century great churches of the Ile-de-France fulfilled the same kinds of functions as those built elsewhere in northern France during the preceding period. This confinement of innovation to the formal and technical spheres means that historically there is much to be said for regarding the first Gothic churches in the Ile-de-France as a belated extension of the Romanesque building 'boom'.

6 St-Martin-de-Boscherville, choir looking north-east, *c.* 1120. The proportion of the clearstorey wall voided by windows is much greater in the apse than in the rest of the choir, since Romanesque and Gothic architects realized that apses are inherently more stable than long straight walls and hence less in need of reinforcement to resist lateral thrusts from high vaults.

7 *Opposite:* Rome, S. Paolo fuori le Mura, begun 385 (watercolour by G.P. Pannini, *c.* 1741). Originally all the clearstorey windows were glazed, and a decorative ceiling concealed the roof structure.

Romanesque antecedents
Normandy and England

It was almost inevitable that architects working in the Ile-de-France during the early 12th century would be heavily influenced by the Romanesque architecture of Normandy. Apart from the physical proximity of the duchy and the fact that its rulers, kings of England from 1066, enjoyed power and wealth which the Capetians could only envy, it boasted a more impressive array of great churches than any other north French principality. The destruction wrought by the invading heathen Normans in the 10th century, followed by the extraordinarily lavish ducal and aristocratic patronage of monasticism in the next century, had provided ideal conditions for the formation of a highly innovatory 'school' of architecture. Virtually all the cathedrals and major abbey churches of Normandy were rebuilt grandly in the course of the 11th century, and after the conquest of England this same comprehensive approach was employed across the Channel on an even larger scale and with even more spectacular consequences.

The interiors of 11th-century Norman and Anglo-Norman great churches had attained a remarkable consistency through the use of a distinctively Romanesque device, the bay. Comparison of the nave of St-Etienne at Caen [5] or the choir of St-Martin at Boscherville [6] with one of the Early Christian basilicas, the ultimate ancestors of all Western medieval

great churches, highlights the central role of the bay in articulating architectural structure. The nave of S. Paolo fuori le Mura [7] is a huge rectangular building consisting of a central vessel flanked on each of its longer sides by two aisles. The lateral elevations of the central vessel are divided into three distinct zones or bands: columnar arcades opening into the aisles, flat wall surface decorated with frescoes, and a low clearstorey giving direct lighting. The horizontality of this scheme is mainly a function of the elongated plan but it is enhanced by the detailed handling of the design. The columns are very closely spaced, as in Classical colonnades where they carry flat lintels, so the arches are too small to generate any strong sense of upward movement. The band aspect of the storeys is further secured by the string courses set a short distance above the arcades and by the continuous horizontals of the wall heads, which are uninterrupted by any beams connecting them to the roof. The openings of the clearstorey and the arcade correspond in number and placing, but the height of the intervening stretch of flat wall discourages one from reading them as parts of a single vertical sequence. In fact the artist of the view of S. Paolo has mistakenly shown arcades and clearstorey slightly out of step. The relative smallness of the triumphal arch at the east end of the nave emphasizes the box-like character of the space and also limits our view of the transepts and apse. The elevations of these eastern parts are practically unrelated to those of the nave.

Despite many differences of detail, the interiors of Caen and Boscherville illustrate equally well the transformation of the simple basilican scheme brought about by the introduction of the bay system. Instead of being given over to a multiplicity of narrow arcade openings and small clearstorey windows, the lateral walls are now divided by half columns or shafts into compartments whose length is half the distance separating the lateral walls themselves, a proportion which remained normal throughout the Middle Ages. By linking the supports of the arcades with the transverse arches in the vault over the central vessel, the shafts extend the slow rhythm of the lateral elevations to the interior as a whole. So instead of the rapid but discontinuous rhythms set up by the arcades, clearstorey and roof trusses at S. Paolo, the view along the Boscherville choir reveals an arrangement rather like a series of proscenium arches set one behind the other at wide intervals. At Caen the later vault creates a more complicated effect, but it also exemplifies the homogeneity created by using semicircular arches both across the main space and along its sides. Half shafts were probably first used in Romanesque churches for their primary purpose of receiving the transverse arches of masonry vaults, but both Caen and Boscherville exemplify the mature Romanesque concept of employing shafts in conjunction with rectangular elements to form compound piers. These powerful supports could hardly be more different from the slender self-contained cylinders in the arcades of Early Christian basilicas. Like the use of arches both longitudinally and transversely, the shafted pier brings consistency to the interior. Yet shafts are nowhere introduced purely for decorative effect; they are always linked to arches, except in churches lacking a high vault, where bay-defining shafts run up to the ceiling [145]. The systematic quality of this continuum of shafts and arches encourages one to accept it as representing specific loads and supports, whereas the real loads and supports are the great masses of masonry behind the surface articulation. Gothic architects found ways of dispensing with much of the mass, but the shaft-arch system was to prove capable of almost infinite development.

The elaborate articulation of Norman Romanesque interiors reduced not only the amount of plain walling but also its relative significance. Its role was now essentially negative, a series of intervals between the major components of the elevation. The blank middle storeys of the Early Christian and early medieval basilicas survived only in lesser churches. At Boscherville the middle storey is treated as arcading pierced by small openings into the dark space between the aisle vaults and the roofs over them; in the most ambitious Norman churches, such as St-Etienne at Caen, the middle level is occupied by galleries which rival the aisles in their volume. Deriving at one or more removes from the women's galleries of Byzantine churches, these spaces seem to have had no single clear-cut function in the West. To patrons and architects of the 11th and 12th centuries, galleries were probably status symbols first and foremost.

Considerations of prestige as well as of security against fire must also have played a part in the growing use of that other costly 'extra', stone vaulting over central vessels. The simplest kind of high vault current in the 11th century, the tunnel vault [3], appears to have been less favoured in Normandy than the groin or cross vault, a Roman type formed notionally from two tunnel vaults intersecting at right angles [6]. High groin vaults had the merit of promoting consistency, for aisle vaults were normally of this sort, but their main practical advantage over tunnel vaults was that they did not exert continuous lateral thrusts along the whole length of the clearstorey walls, a force which could all too easily bring about the collapse of the entire upper storey. The lateral thrusts from groin vaults were perceived to be at their greatest on the strongest parts of the clearstorey, the stretches between the windows where external buttresses give additional thickness.

The extensive use of groin vaults in 11th-century Norman churches was a necessary precondition for the acceptance of the rib vault, which can be defined provisionally as vaulting in which groins are replaced by crossed pairs of thin arches or ribs [12]. The origins of the rib are obscure and are likely to remain so because of the loss of the great majority of 11th-century high vaults; the most important point in the present context is that rib vaults were firmly established in Normandy and England by about 1100. Patrons and architects must have found them easy to accept, for their general shape and their relation to the rest of the structure was more or less the same as that of groin vaults. Probably their success had less to do with any supposed technical advantages (about which contemporary written sources reveal nothing) than with their extension of the shaft-arch system to all parts of the vaulting and the consequent increase in the visual homogeneity of the interior. Certainly rib vaults enabled designers to sidestep an aesthetic problem which usually arose when groin vaults whose constituent tunnels were semicircular in section came to be used over bays of rectangular plan, namely the unstable-looking, curvilinear profile of the groins [6].

The substitution of ribs built from carefully shaped ashlar for irregular plaster-coated groins gave the most prominent parts of vaults a much more precise finish. It may also have led to the general early 12th-century improvement of the less prominent masonry of the webs between the ribs. In England the introduction of rib vaults had little or no effect on the design of the walls and piers that supported them. At Durham, for example, the shafts and corbels from which the ribs spring are all set at right angles in the traditional manner [11, 12]. However, when a rib vault was added to the nave at Caen (where previously there had been only a wooden roof), the angled position of the diagonal ribs was acknowledged in the angling of the capitals on the specially inserted supplementary shafts [5]. In the 1120s and 1130s Ile-de-France architects adopted angled shafts and rib vaults as a single 'package', an important instance of the way in which the lack of a strong pre-existing tradition could facilitate the reception of innovatory ideas. Diagonal ribs on angled shafts were probably in use in Lombardy by *c.* 1100, but these are unlikely to have been the source of the Ile-de-France ribs. They are plainer and thicker and belong to vaults whose square plan and pronouncedly dome-like shape are in complete contrast to the rectangular plan and near-horizontal ridges which most high rib vaults in North-Western Europe took over from groin vaults.

The primacy accorded to the bay by Norman and Anglo-Norman architects may partly explain their preference for façades incorporating towers set over the westernmost compartments of the aisles, the scheme which eventually became normal in the Ile-de-France [*23, 49*]. The two-tower façade is ideal from the point of view of bay design as it allows the sides of the towers facing into the central vessel of the nave to be treated almost as if they belonged to a regular bay. In a church like St-Martin at Boscherville, where no ambulatory surrounds the main apse, there is no scope for treating the latter as a series of curved bays similar to the rectangular-plan aisled bays to the west, but in the few Norman and English ambulatoried choirs which retain any evidence for the elevation of the main apse, it is clear that a more or less uniform bay system was employed throughout the choir. Comparison of the choirs of Paray-le-Monial and Sens [*9, 30*] highlights the lack of interest in this kind of consistency in French Romanesque architecture outside Normandy as well as the central place which it was to assume in the Gothic tradition.

Another aspect of the Norman and Anglo-Norman achievement which Gothic architects were to build on and develop was the reinforcement of upper walls against the lateral thrusts exerted by masonry vaults. A device commonly used for this purpose in both traditions was the partial filling of the spaces above the springings of the vaults with masses of rubble set in mortar [*13e*]. These inconspicuous and glamourless lumps of masonry are in fact extremely important, for by supplementing the vertical thrusts which the solid parts of the clearstorey impose on the parts of the high walls near the vault springings they reduce the horizontal component in the lateral thrusts exerted by the vault and thus ensure that the forces acting within the walls are resolved as vertical or near-vertical thrusts aligned close to the centre of the wall mass. Thrust lines and the resolution of forces were concepts unknown to medieval architects, whose grasp of structural matters was essentially intuitive. Children experience the consequences of adding extra top weight when they find that the higher they build a column of toy bricks the harder they have to shove to overturn it.

More conspicuous and hence better known forms of abutment are the quadrant vaults and arches which span the galleries of many Romanesque churches. In the so-called Pilgrimage Churches, for instance, quadrant vaults are an effective means of countering the continuous lateral thrusts coming from the tunnel vault over each main vessel [*3*]. Quadrant arches like those in the nave galleries at Durham [*8a*] can be seen as reduced versions of quadrant

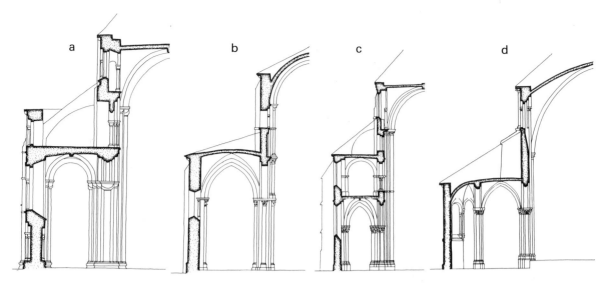

8 Part sections of (a) Durham Cathedral, nave; (b) Paray-le-Monial; (c) St-Germer-de-Fly; (d) St-Martin-des-Champs, Paris, choir.

vaults, providing abutment only where there appear to be the strongest lateral thrusts, that is behind the springings of the high vault. The fact that quadrant arches were used by Norman designers in the galleries of churches which lack any kind of high vault is not necessarily evidence against viewing the examples in vaulted churches as abutments, for most wooden-ceiled Norman and Anglo-Norman central vessels contain wall shafts, another feature which originated as an adjunct to vaulting [145]. Quadrant vaults and arches, and the flying buttresses which later superseded them, were probably conceived as something which leaned inwards so as to generate a counter-thrust neutralizing that coming from a high vault. A pointer in this direction is the etymology of the word 'buttress', which derives not from the medieval French words for the ordinary wall buttress, *arest* (stop) and *pilier* (pier, pillar), but from the term for flying buttress – *boteret* or *arc boteret* (modern *arc boutant*). The sense here and in the German *Strebebogen* is unmistakably that of a halved arch which buts or shoves inwards; and that is after all what quadrant arches and vaults and flying buttresses look as though they do. But many flyers and quadrants are too thin or too steeply pitched to exert much of an inward counter-thrust, so it seems likely that at some stage the word ceased to correspond to the current conception of their structural role. Perhaps already in the Romanesque period quadrant arches were coming to be thought of as a kind of strut for transmitting lateral thrusts to the aisle walls, where massive wall buttresses could be incorporated far more conveniently than on clearstoreys.

Norman and Anglo-Norman designers seldom troubled to introduce quadrants above the aisles of vaulted churches whose middle storeys are lower and more solid than galleries. In buildings such as Boscherville they seem to have assumed that vault thrusts would be contained by means of a distinctive structural trait so far mentioned only in passing, namely the enormous thickness of the main walls. This 'thick wall' structure apparently originated at St-Etienne in Caen, where it may have been intended to absorb thrusts from the high groin vaults which were at one stage to have covered the main vessels. Alternatively, it may owe its existence to the passages which burrow through the length of the clearstorey walls. The functional precursors of these wall passages were access passages formed in the relatively inconspicuous west walls of transepts, but in the nave of St-Etienne their utility is far from obvious and it seems likely that they are there mainly for effect. Towards the end of the 12th century Gervase of Canterbury wrote about wall passages in a way which shows that they were liked for themselves. The thin arcaded screens which run in front of the parts of the passages visible from the central vessel [5, 11] encourage one to see the wall structure as consisting of a succession of perforated sheets or skins, and in that respect they resemble another important feature which grew out of a concern to exploit the aesthetic potentialities of thick walls, namely the multi-layered arrangement of arch orders and shafts in the two lower storeys.

Burgundy

The thick wall, together with the effects of recession and layering that it permitted, was to remain a normal part of great church architecture in England and Normandy during the 11th and 12th centuries [55]. In the Ile-de-France, however, it made no headway at all. Like most of northern France except Normandy, the Ile-de-France remained faithful to the thin walls of the Early Christian and Carolingian traditions. Burgundy also retained the thin wall, and this common background may be part of the explanation why it was that region which contributed most, after Normandy, to the formation of Gothic. However, a more fundamental factor was Burgundy's exceptional contribution to the monastic life of the West. The abbey of Cluny, the monarchic head of a vast international family of Benedictine houses, rebuilt its church from 1088 as the single largest and most lavishly appointed church in Western Europe, a standing challenge to ambitious patrons everywhere. In the early and mid-12th century the ascetic Cistercian monks were to outstrip even Cluny's monastic empire in terms of the number of their houses and the centralization of authority, achievements which worked to transmit elements of Burgundian Romanesque the length and breadth of Europe.

Since the demolition of Cluny in the early 19th century, our best guide to its appearance has been the smaller 'copy' at Paray-le-Monial [9, 10]. Paray does not of course convey the stupendous scale of the original, for its nave has three bays instead of eleven and is 22m high rather than 29.5m. Nevertheless, the design is close enough to enable it to substitute for Cluny in the following discussion. Comparison with Caen and Boscherville [5, 6] highlights the flatter, more planar quality of its design and its greater distance from the dynamic articulation of Gothic interiors. On the other hand, the tall

9, 10 Paray-le-Monial, begun *c.* 1110: interior looking east, and choir from the south-east. The conception of the exterior as the aggregate of easily distinguishable and geometrically simple shapes is typically Romanesque.

proportioning of the central vessel and of the arcades, the sharply pointed arches and the bold projection of the bay-defining members are all anticipations of the verticality which is one of the most memorable characteristics of French Gothic.

The high vaults of Cluny were the culmination of a century's Burgundian determination to raise tunnels over clearstoreys. Their pointed profile – along with that of the main arcade arches the first major appearance of that form in Western medieval architecture – was a crucial ingredient in their stability, for the lateral thrusts exerted by a pointed vault are obviously much more steeply inclined than those from a semicircular vault and can therefore be partly contained within the thickness of clearstorey walls [*13b,c*]. Gothic high vaulting technique was perhaps further anticipated at Cluny by the exposed flying buttresses which pre-demolition drawings show on the nave, although the generally accepted view is that these were later additions. Certainly the high tunnel vaults over the other parts of Cluny and all those at Paray-le-Monial depend for their stability on the extension of the clearstorey wall far above the windows [*10, 13d*], a massive additional load which greatly increases the ability of the walls of the main vessel to withstand lateral thrusts at any level. This simple technique, which has Roman and Early Christian antecedents, was hardly ever used by Gothic designers; large expanses of solid walling were incompatible with their commitment to the concept of structural lightness.

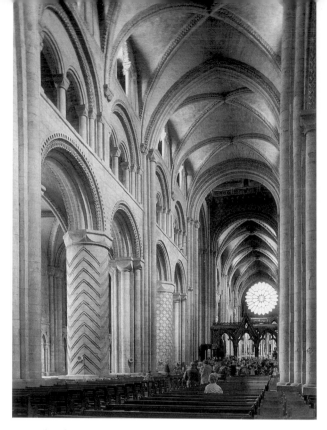

11 Durham Cathedral, nave, c. 1115–30. The 19th-century screen occupies the site of a much more massive medieval structure defining the western limit of the liturgical choir. Under the west arch of the crossing stood another screen surmounted by a large sculptured crucifixion group.

Whether influenced by Cistercian architecture [14] or by the side aisles of Cluny, Ile-de-France designers made extensive use of pointed-arched groin vaults during the 1130s, often in aisles or other subordinate spaces [15, 21]. Pride of place was generally given to a pointed-arched rib vault, the type soon to become standard in Gothic architecture [30]. But the earliest pointed rib vault to have survived is not in the Ile-de-France: that distinction belongs to the high nave vault of Durham [11], begun probably around 1120 and finished by 1133.

The nave vault at Durham was a near-definitive solution to certain aesthetic and technical problems grappled with by Anglo-Norman designers during the previous two or three decades. The earlier rib vaults in the choir aisles at Durham [12] illustrate the compromises which had to be resorted to in order to make arches and ribs of part-circular profile rise to a more or less uniform level. The main arcades, the transverse arches and the diagonal ribs are all of differing widths, and since semicircular arches are automatically half as high as wide, it follows that arches and ribs of uniform height could not be achieved except by using a lower than semicircular profile for the diagonal ribs and a taller than semicircular profile for the transverse arches. Hence the latter are stilted and the former are segments considerably less than a semicircle. The main arcades, as the most important of the three sets of arches, are accorded a regular or very nearly regular semicircular profile. The disadvantages of the Durham choir aisle solution are mainly with the diagonal ribs. Their springings jut out with awkward suddenness from above

12 Durham Cathedral, rib vault in the north choir aisle, 1093–6. The ribs appear to have been built in advance of the webs, as in the nave at Durham [*11*] and in the majority of Gothic vaults [cf. *16, 17*].

13 Diagram showing the oblique lateral thrusts in (a) segmental, (b) semicircular, and (c) pointed-arched vaults, and the conversion of these into vertical thrusts by means of (d) building an upwards extension to the clearstorey and (e) filling the spaces above the springings of the vault with solid masonry.

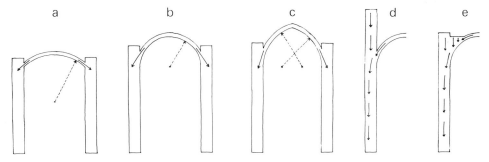

a   b   c   d   e

the shafts, and their shallow segmental curvature, at least when used on a large scale, as in the main vessels of Durham's transepts, is intrinsically weak and generates lateral thrusts at an angle too close to the horizontal to be contained within the walls or within the masonry of any form of abutment then in use [*13a*].

It seems very likely that to the designer of the Durham nave vault pointed transverse arches were mainly a way of avoiding the structural and aesthetic shortcomings of the earlier vaults in the cathedral. Since pointed arches have two radii instead of the single radius of semicircular arches, their width-to-height ratio no longer has to be 2:1. The width of Durham's transverse arches is obviously the same as that of the nave itself, but their height has been adjusted to match that of the diagonal ribs which can now be full semicircles rather than merely segments. The architect of the Durham nave seems to have been the first in Europe to recognize in pointed arches a means of improving rib vaulting. He may have worked out this design entirely on his own, but it is also possible that he drew inspiration from the pointed groin and tunnel vaults at Cluny. The fame of Cluny was such that he would not have needed to see the building for himself.

14 Pontigny, south transept looking south, *c.* 1140. This is the only survivor of the four most senior abbeys of the Cistercian order, all of them in Burgundy. The design of the transepts appears to have been influenced by the church of Cîteaux, the chief house of the order.

So did the nave vault of Durham merely anticipate the pointed rib vaults put up in the Ile-de-France during the 1130s, or did it actually exert a direct influence? No definite answer is possible because intermediate examples may have been lost, but on the evidence available direct influence seems rather unlikely. In the first place, north-eastern England was not the ideal base from which to launch a new architectural idea on the Continent. Secondly, the date of the Durham vault is uncomfortably close to that of the earliest pointed rib vaults in the Ile-de-France. Thirdly, and most importantly, the great majority of the Ile-de-France vaults differ from Durham's in employing pointed profiles for the diagonal ribs as well as for the transverse ribs. Since Burgundian pointed groin vaults [*14*] and their Ile-de-France derivatives incorporate pointed profiles in the equivalent places, the groins, there is a strong probability that Ile-de-France designers arrived at pointed rib vaults not by imitating Durham but by combining Burgundian groins with Norman ribs. A process of creative fusion rather than of wholesale borrowing would certainly be more consistent with the inventiveness exhibited by the other parts of the buildings in which the earliest systematically pointed rib vaults are found.

The beginnings of Gothic

The revival of major church building in the Ile-de-France in the 1130s produced around a dozen buildings, for the most part of relatively modest

15 Paris, St-Pierre-de-Montmartre, north side of the nave, c. 1133–47. The easternmost bay (on the right) was part of a first phase probably finished by 1136. It contained the nuns' choir; hence the curtailing of the high vault responds so as not to interfere with the stalls. The capitals of the responds were removed when the high vaults were renewed c. 1500.

ambition. The Benedictine nunnery church of St-Pierre-de-Montmartre, Paris, built from 1133 on the orders of Louis VI, provides a good starting point for any consideration of the formation of Gothic as it shows very clearly how Ile-de-France architects first attained their paradoxical goal of combining high rib vaults with walls so thin as to be by themselves incapable of supporting such a heavy load [15]. Much of the load is in fact borne by the massive compound responds which jut forward from the walls like internalized buttresses. The enormous difference in thickness between the responds and the walls makes clear that they have been allotted quite distinct structural roles. The responds and the arches they carry form a basic framework or skeleton, whereas the walls have become to some extent non-load-bearing infilling or 'panels'. The structure of the high rib vaults (renewed c. 1500) does not actually behave in this way, but since the ribs were built first and functioned as centering for the construction of the webs [16] it is possible that they were conceived by the architect as an application of the same principle as that embodied in the vault responds. At all events, the skeletal appearance of the vaults complements the wall treatment.

The novelty of 'skeletonized' walls can be appreciated by comparing the nave of St-Pierre with that at Caen [5], whose sides are in essence continuous thick walls with only token reinforcements where the high vaults exert the strongest lateral thrusts. What cannot be seen in the photographs is the difference between the construction of the walls. The smoothly dressed

masonry surfaces of Caen are a skin only one block deep, behind which lies a core of rubble set in mortar. This technique, already very ancient when used at Caen, is a good one provided that the mortar remains hard and strong. If it is poorly mixed or frozen before it has set, the mortar disintegrates and leaves the structure with a potentially unstable core, like a box packed with pebbles. At Montmartre there is far less masonry in the high walls of the nave than at Caen and most of what there is consists of dressed ashlar blocks, in principle if not quite in practice extending through the whole thickness of the walls and supports. It is obvious that a structure made entirely of finely jointed ashlar performs much more reliably than one which is predominantly of mortared rubble. A parallel improvement was made to the masonry of the vault webs, as can be seen in the one surviving original vault, that over the west bay of the choir. The webs here are relatively thin shells formed of coursed masonry blocks, in contrast to the thick rubble-built webs of the vaulting in the nave at Durham [11]. By the next decade coursed ashlar webs had become the rule [27]. It is unknown whether St-Pierre had buttresses resting on the aisle vaults comparable to those which can still be seen at the other major surviving monument of the 1130s in Paris, the choir of St-Martin-des-Champs [8d, 22]. St-Martin's buttresses have a number of features which foreshadow future developments, most importantly their high placing in relation to the vault springings [cf. 31], their combination of narrowness with depth [cf. 25], and their extension up through the ambulatory roof [cf. 42]. The need for these buttresses is not in doubt, since the thin walls of the choir could never have resisted the lateral vault thrusts unaided.

16 *Opposite:* Soissons Cathedral, high vault of the nave during reconstruction after the First World War. Only the ribs rest directly on the centering. From late medieval French documents it is evident that vault webs could be built on earthen mounds raised on platforms, but it is not clear how widespread this technique was or how early it came into use.

17 Lincoln Cathedral, vault of the room adjoining the north-east transept, mid-1190s. The inaccessible location of this vault explains why no-one has ever troubled to remove the thin planking and wattle which supported the webs during building. The webs of the high nave vault at Durham [11] were built by the same method, but there the planking was *c.* 5cm thick.

The masonry at St-Pierre-de-Montmartre is much more carefully cut than in most Norman or Anglo-Norman Romanesque churches, and it appears that Ile-de-France ideas of finish were based on those current in early 12th-century Burgundy. Influence from Burgundy, not necessarily direct, must also account for the pointed groin vaults in the aisles and the pointed arches of the arcades. The aesthetic implications of the pointed arch are already fully apparent here. Their use in the broadly proportioned central vessel contributes a sense not so much of verticality as of dynamic resolution. Pointed arches create a far less serene effect than semicircular arches, for whereas in the latter the eye can follow a single continuous curve up from one springing to the apex and down again, in a pointed arch the sharply angled meeting of more or less steep arcs creates a sense of opposing forces barely held in check. The use of two arcs instead of one generates not merely twice as many elements but elements which are less self-contained; yet, paradoxically, interiors which make systematic use of the pointed arch attain a quality of indissoluble wholeness which goes beyond that created by the use of round arches, for these always remain easy to isolate visually. The creation of overall unity through increasing the number and reducing the autonomy of the constituent elements of the design is in fact one of the basic aesthetic principles of Gothic architecture, although it had been anticipated in the richly shafted walls of Norman and English Romanesque churches. Conscious or unconscious acknowledgment of this principle must account for the eventual acceptance throughout Europe that ambitious Gothic interiors demand to be vaulted throughout.

18 St-Germer-de-Fly, eastern bays of the nave (left) and west wall of the north transept, designed *c.* 1135. The circular openings above the sub-arches of the gallery anticipate the plate tracery of *c.* 1200 [cf. *60*].

The abbey church of St-Germer-de-Fly, about 80km north-west of Paris [*18*], shares many of the advanced traits of St-Pierre-de-Montmartre and St-Martin-des-Champs but, unlike them, conforms to what in most of northern France outside the Ile-de-France would have been recognized as the normal scheme for a great church: a Latin cross plan, a crossing tower (later destroyed), galleries, and a chevet with an ambulatory and radiating chapels. The scale is still relatively small (19m high internally), but the combination of ambitious format and innovatory handling gives us our strongest foretaste yet of the Early Gothic cathedral interior. Many of St-Germer's proto-Gothic features were in fact derived from the (destroyed) abbey church of St-Lucien in nearby Beauvais, begun as early as *c.* 1090. St-Lucien was clearly a building of great importance, anticipating by several decades St-Germer's combination of thin walls, high rib vaults and quadrant arches above groin-vaulted galleries. The source of virtually all its individual elements was Normandy, though no single extant church in the duchy contains exactly the same combination.

19 St-Germer-de-Fly, ambulatory
looking east. The curvilinear profile
of the diagonal ribs is unusual before
the 15th century [but cf. 72] and in
this case is probably a survival from
Romanesque groin vaulting [cf. 6].

Despite its heavy indebtedness to St-Lucien, St-Germer has enough in
common with Parisian churches of the 1130s to show that it was no mere
offshoot of the Norman tradition. As at St-Pierre-de-Montmartre, the vault
ribs and main arcades are all pointed and the shafts receiving the diagonal ribs
are angled. There is even a debt to Burgundian Romanesque architecture
paralleling those of St-Pierre, namely the strange 'shelf' carried on corbels at
the base of the clearstorey. Whereas at Cluny and Paray this feature is part of
the neo-Antique décor of the main elevations [9], here it gives access to an
almost unusably low passage hollowed out behind the high vault springings,
a travesty of a Norman clearstorey passage in a building whose thin-wall
structure made it quite unsuited to contain such a feature. Below the
platform hatch-like oblong openings make a gesture towards enlivening the
high expanse of bare wall and entitle St-Germer to be considered as a possible
source for the four-storey elevation of Notre-Dame in Paris [33].

Although most of the Norman elements at St-Germer appear to have been
appropriated via St-Lucien rather than directly, the design of the radiating

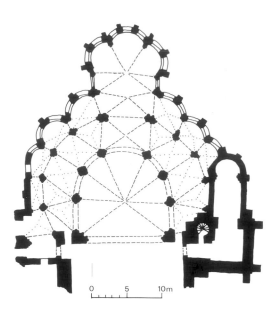

20–22 Paris, St-Martin-des-Champs, choir, begun *c.* 1135: plan, interior looking north-east, and exterior from the south-east. Except for the axial chapel and ambulatory bay, the peripheral spaces are covered by groin vaults.

chapels really does give St-Germer some claim to be a Norman bridgehead into the Ile-de-France [19]. In the vast majority of full-dress Romanesque chevets, radiating chapels open out only from alternate bays of the ambulatory [3, 10]; but here, just as in two early 12th-century Norman ambulatories, those of Avranches Cathedral (destroyed) and Fécamp Abbey, every bay gives into a chapel. Bulky arches at the entrances to the chapels mark the limit of the ambulatory proper, yet the absence of any stretches of wall between the chapels makes it difficult not to regard ambulatory and chapels as a single complex space. At St-Martin-des-Champs this idea is taken an important step further by a process which can be imagined as arising in the course of drawing out the ground plan. If shallow chapels of the St-Germer type are replaced by chapels which are deeper than wide, the result will be a series of solid walls where the sides of adjacent chapels merge [66d]. The darkness and heaviness of this notional scheme can be eliminated by subtracting the solid masonry so as to leave what is visually an outer ambulatory though liturgically still part of the chapels [20]. The formal coherence of St-Martin's double ambulatory is diminished by exceptionally many irregularities of layout and detailing, but the potential of the concept was to be fully realized a year or two later in the far more accomplished choir at St-Denis.

Abbot Suger's work at St-Denis

Over the last hundred and fifty years it has become customary to begin histories of Gothic architecture with the choir added in 1140–44 to the abbey church at St-Denis, 11km north of central Paris. This is appropriate not only because the innovations of the choir were immediately accepted as the basis of a new style of architecture, but also on account of two other interconnected aspects of the building: its splendour and its royalness. Unlike any earlier Parisian church, the remodelled St-Denis was ambitious enough to serve as a pattern for great church architecture; and the abbey's special links with the monarchy meant that the new work enhanced the growing prestige of the French kings.

It is possible that Louis VI established Paris as his centre in preference to Orléans partly because of its associations with earlier royal dynasties. St-Denis was only the most important of several ancient royal burial churches ringing the capital, while at the heart of the city the alliance of church and crown was proclaimed by the nearness of the cathedral and royal palace, both founded in the 6th century by the Merovingian king Childebert. Within his limited means, Louis VI was extremely generous to a number of monasteries in and around Paris, but it was with St-Denis that his relations were the closest. In 1120 he instituted the custom of depositing the crown and other coronation regalia for safekeeping near the relics of St Denis, who was beginning to eclipse St Martin of Tours as protector of the kingdom. That role was put to the test in 1124 when, under St Denis's standard, the *oriflamme*, the king's vassals rallied to repel an invading German army. In gratitude for this unprecedented demonstration of northern French solidarity and resolve, Louis VI granted St-Denis control of an important and profitable fair, the Lendit. Suger, abbot from 1122 and the king's closest adviser from 1127, assumed the mantle of royal propagandist, glorifying the kings together with their patron saint, and his art patronage helped promote the cult of quasi-priestly kingship, for in the decoration of the abbey church the Biblical kings who inspired the cult were allotted a disproportionately prominent place. The myth of sacral kingship was embodied remarkably convincingly in the person of Louis VII who succeeded in 1137. A younger son brought up for a career in the church, sincerely pious, well educated, austere in his personal habits yet with a lofty view of his kingly office, Louis must have seemed the ideal ruler in Suger's eyes.

Almost alone among major art patrons from any period, Suger has left us with writings which purport to explain his intentions. Besides satisfying a well-developed self-esteem, his main motive in writing was probably the need to pre-empt criticism from within the monastery. The main thrust of Suger's tract *De Administratione* was the assertion of the spiritual value of the most gorgeous and costly art works which he had commissioned – gilt bronze doors, stained glass windows, altar plate and reliquaries in precious metals. For Suger the glow of windows and the glitter of goldsmiths' work were not vulgar and impious ostentation but a means of transporting the worshipper beyond earthly beauty towards the divine beauty of Christ, the 'true light'. The most important theological justification for great church building and decoration was referred to by Suger only in passing. This is the concept of the church building as a symbol of the living church, the Heavenly Jerusalem of the Apocalypse and of Ephesians 2:19–22, the latter quoted in Suger's *De Consecratione*. For Suger, the new choir was Sion, and its twelve inner columns (strictly, ten columns and two west responds) resembled the twelve foundation stones of St John's vision in signifying the twelve Apostles.

From the viewpoint of the architectural historian, Suger's discussion of the building is rather disappointing in that it consists mostly of anecdotes about the progress of the work and the author's own part in furthering it. However, the omissions are revealing. There is not the slightest hint that Suger made interventions in the design process comparable to his involvement in the iconography of the glass and metalwork; and the egotism of the man must give some assurance that such a contribution would not have been neglected. There is also no trace of interest in the originality of the architectural means employed by the unnamed designer, although Suger did appreciate what he believed to be an original feature, the transformation of the outer walls of the choir into an almost continuous band of glazing [26]. He was presumably not aware that this effect had been anticipated in the choir of St-Martin-des-Champs [21]. The lack of emphasis in Suger's

23 St-Denis, west front, consecrated 1140. This view shows the façade before the 'restoration' of 1838–40 and the removal of the north tower in 1846. The central portal bore an inscription alluding to the parable of the Good Shepherd (John 10:9): 'I am the door: by me if any man enter in, he shall be saved.' This is the primary meaning of all large portals on Gothic facades whether or not they resemble the central St-Denis portal in being decorated with sculpture depicting the Last Judgment.

writings on the architecture as such was perhaps due to its being a less likely target for criticism than the costly furnishings. St-Denis is certainly less elaborate than the most ambitious 12th-century Romanesque churches, for the austere play of the shaft-arch system is offset only by foliage sculpture, and the few residual wall surfaces are unornamented.

The dilapidated church inherited by Suger was essentially that completed in 775 by Pepin, father of Charlemagne. It was a basilica of deliberately Roman aspect, according St Denis as the Apostle of Gaul architectural honours comparable to those enjoyed by St Peter, Prince of the Apostles [*36a*]. This Roman-ness was to be an important influence on the new choir, but Suger's first work was at the opposite end of the church, where he replaced Pepin's western block with a structure owing nothing to Antiquity [*23*]. The new west block was consecrated with its towers incomplete in 1140, so a start around 1135 seems likely. It is the prototype of a long line of French Gothic façades incorporating two towers, three large sculptured portals and a round window placed high up. This said, it must be admitted that not everything about the St-Denis west block was novel and forward-looking. Pepin's west block had also incorporated two towers, and it is possible that the most surprising feature of the new work, the chapels above the west entrances [*24*], was a further deliberate reminiscence of the abbey's venerable past, for chapels in this position are much more an early medieval than a 12th-century concept. The upper chapels complicate but do not invalidate the generally accepted view of St-Denis as a link between Norman and English Romanesque two-tower façades and those of the French Gothic tradition. A peculiarity which must derive from the most important Norman two-tower façade, that of St-Etienne in Caen, is the discontinuity between the towers and the mighty buttresses on the lower part. Unlike St-Etienne, St-Denis marks the caesura with battlements doubtless intended to invest the front as a whole with military overtones appropriate to a building symbolizing the Kingdom of Heaven. These battlements, together with the borrowings from the ducal burial church in Caen and earlier royal churches including Pepin's at St-Denis, and the prominent place accorded in the sculpture of the west portals to the Old Testament kings who were the inspiration of all Christian kingship cults, leave no doubt that Suger intended the new entrance to embody a multiplicity of regal associations both earthly and celestial.

In many Norman and English Romanesque two-tower façades, and also in most Gothic examples, the towers stand over the western bays of the aisles, and their lower floors are set level with the upper limits of the aisles, galleries and clearstorey. At St-Denis the west block has a total width considerably greater than that of the 8th-century building, but the main divisions of its west face do relate logically to the structure behind it. The buttresses separating the central section from the lower parts of the towers stand in line with the arcades of the 8th-century nave, and the stepped arrangement of the two tiers of windows reveals that the central part of the entrance vestibule rises higher than the parts under and beyond the towers. There is unfortunately no evidence for the form of the original subdivisions within the round window. Suger's texts do not attach any symbolic significance to this feature, so its presence here can probably be attributed to its practicality as a means of lighting the low and broadly proportioned central chapel and also to the suitability of the full circle as a climax to a part of the façade otherwise pierced by semicircular-headed openings.

Suger's claim that he summoned artists from afar to work at St-Denis is borne out by the three large sculptured portals which stand at the beginning of a new era in the history of monumental figure sculpture. The Ile-de-France had no tradition of sculpture to speak of, and the origin of the St-Denis carvers and their ideas is not at all certain. The most epoch-making innovation, the series of over-life-size statues on the colonnettes of the jambs (destroyed in the 18th century), is interesting in relation to Early Gothic architecture in that they are part of an ensemble in which high relief figure sculptures are for the first time incorporated into each major architectural component with a consistency analogous to that of the shaft-arch system of rib-vaulted interiors. Suger wrote nothing about the portal sculptures, perhaps because their didactic value was too obvious to need any defence.

The vestibule within the west block is treated with a massiveness which has often been ascribed to artistic conservatism [24]. In fact, the bulk of the piers and arches was needed in order to support both the upper chapels and

24 St-Denis, vestibule within the western block, south side of the central aisle. The upper openings give into the chapel over the south aisle. In 1806 the floor level was raised by more than a metre and the bases of the piers renewed.

the towers, and the architect has made a virtue of this by transforming the visible surfaces into an exceptionally rich and lively version of the kind of shaft-arch system used at St-Pierre-de-Montmartre and other proto-Gothic buildings of the 1130s [15]. Two important characteristics of the fully-fledged Early Gothic style are also more prominent here than elsewhere at the same date: the extreme elongation of shafts and the tall proportioning of openings. Suger's west block stood farther west than Pepin's, and evidence recovered in excavations has shown that the building with which Suger filled the gap had columnar supports modelled on those of the 8th-century nave. In his *De Administratione* Suger stresses his reverence for the old fabric, believed at St-Denis to have been dedicated by Christ himself.

25 St-Denis, choir from the north-east. The upper storeys date from the 1230s. The central chapels at ambulatory and crypt levels were both dedicated to the Virgin. Their siting at the east end of the main axis enabled them to be lit by the first light of day, a symbol of the Virgin's place at the start of the Christian era. (For some of the many other examples of Lady Chapels in this position see 53, 78.)

26 St-Denis, choir looking north-east, 1140–44. The upper storeys and the piers of the main arcade were replaced after 1231. Under the main arcades were openwork screens, probably of metal, whose doors gave access to St Denis's shrine [see 36a].

27 St-Denis, ambulatory looking north-west. The stilted arches of the vaults over the radiating chapels have been unable wholly to resist the outward thrusts from the wider ambulatory vaults, with the result that the columnar piers have developed a slight outward list.

Immediately after the dedication of the west block and nave extension in 1140, Suger began to rebuild the choir [25–28, 36a]. As we shall see, it is likely that he always intended this project to be only the first stage in a total rebuilding, although his account of the work presents it as an end in itself. If Suger was deliberately concealing his long-term plans, this would illustrate the managerial skills necessary in a community where there were inevitably many who would have preferred to retain the old church, either from religious sentiment or from the desire to avoid the disruption normally entailed in rebuilding within monastic complexes. Obviously, enthusiasm kindled by work successfully concluded helps clear a path for further undertakings, and in fact Suger did embark on a rebuilding or at least a remodelling of the 8th-century transept and nave. However, this was soon abandoned, probably for lack of the huge sums he contributed from abbey funds towards Louis VII's expenses while with the Second Crusade of 1147–9. It was only during the mid-13th century that the old transept and nave were replaced, a campaign which entailed, unfortunately from the point of view of studying the beginnings of Gothic architecture, the destruction of the upper storeys of Suger's choir.

Suger's declared aim in replacing the east end of the 8th-century church was the entirely traditional one of making more space for pilgrims coming to venerate the major relics enshrined behind the altar. The plan of the new chevet follows that of St-Martin-des-Champs [20] in having a continuous circuit of radiating chapels housed partly in very shallow apses and partly in what looks like an outer ambulatory [36a]. Such visual blurring of liturgical distinctions was often to result from Gothic architects' concern to develop the repetitive and systematic nature of their designs, but this particular manifestation found few imitators. A possible reason for the resistance may have been dislike of the undisguisable clash between the spatial openness of the architecture [27] and the compartmentalization produced by the chapel-defining screens which formerly stood between each column and the outer wall.

Before examining the credentials of the St-Denis choir as one of the most innovatory of medieval buildings, it may be useful to consider a major element of the design which must have seemed archaic at the time, that is before it became a commonplace of Early Gothic architecture. The columns between the ambulatory arcade and chapels and the slightly thicker columns which carried the main arcade (replaced in the 13th century) have a Roman air about them curiously at odds with the modernity of the rest of the interior. Moreover, columns are the simplest and most self-contained kind of support, the very antithesis of the elaborately articulated compound piers which Ile-de-France architects had been developing hitherto. The presence of these 'anomalous' columns has to be explained in terms of the concern of Suger and his architect that the choir should preserve a measure of continuity with the ancient columnar basilica onto which it was built [36a]. It is very likely that when Suger finally decided to remodel Pepin's nave, he planned to retain its columns.

Columnar piers were a regular feature of Romanesque chevets [3, 9], but their use in the straight-sided part of an eastern arm was very rare; the two major north French examples – St-Benoît-sur-Loire and Mont-St-Michel – were both in different ways the outcome of Roman or at least Italian influence. In neither church are the supports so close to the slim proportions of Classical columns as the piers between the ambulatory and radiating chapels at St-Denis.

The use of columns affects profoundly the aesthetic character of the ambulatory and chapels. The linearity of the interior as well as its vertical emphasis are much less than if the ribs sprang from the shafts of compound piers, and because the column shafts are not bulky enough to generate strong plastic effects one tends to look beyond them to the almost unbroken circuit of large stained glass windows lighting the radiating chapels. As a result of placing the emphasis on the outer bounding wall and its windows the ambulatory and chapels register as a single space even more clearly than their precursors at St-Martin-des-Champs. The character of this space is less determined by vaulting than are the St-Denis west vestibule and the other Parisian interiors of the 1130s in which supports reflect the compound nature of the rib vaults they carry; yet the vault does make an important contribution to spatial unity, for the unvarying height of its arches and ribs and the consistent centering of its rib intersections both have the effect of playing down the considerable variations in the shapes of its constituent compart-

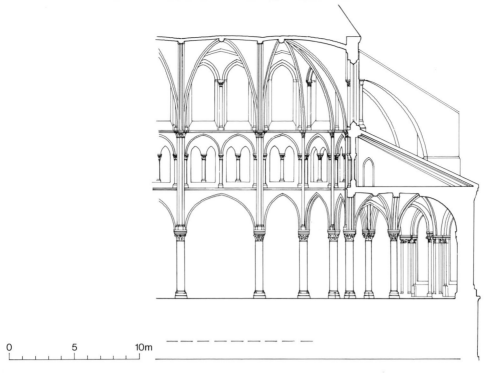

0 5 10m

28 St-Denis, reconstruction of the east part of the choir (upper storeys conjectural). The broken line indicates the nave floor level, the solid line the crypt floor level.

ments. As at St-Martin-des-Champs, the 'frame-and-infill' concept embodied in rib vaulting is applied to the walls of the radiating chapels, the window glass equating to vault webs and the residual strips of masonry to ribs [21, 26]. The openings extend down almost to the floor, but otherwise the glass-to-masonry ratio and the visibility of the windows from the central vessel of the choir are not significantly greater than at St-Martin. The clearstorey of the main apse at St-Martin follows an Early Christian and Romanesque tradition of generous lighting in apses [6, 10], and it seems likely that the continuous glazing of the radiating chapels there was conceived as an extension of that tradition. The indebtedness of the St-Denis chapels to those of St-Martin suggests that the clearstorey of Suger's church also incorporated a continuous band of windows.

Further informed guesses as to the appearance of the destroyed upper storeys of the St-Denis choir are necessary if one is to reach an assessment of the significance of the surviving parts in the development of Early Gothic [28]. Suger's writings reveal only that the central vessel was rib-vaulted, and that the ribs were built independently and in advance of the webs [cf. 16]. However, additional evidence on which to base a hypothetical reconstruction is available from three sources: the west block, the surviving lower parts of the choir, and later 12th-century Gothic choirs whose designs were specially strongly influenced by St-Denis. The west block is particularly suggestive as regards the levels and general character of the lost upper storeys of the choir because, as recent research has shown, its upper parts were completed by the architect of the choir. The use of the same springing level in the main arcades of the choir and the west block proves that correlating the renewed extremities of the church was a real concern, and it is a reasonable assumption that when the choir was being designed at the end of the 1130s Suger and his second architect were already anticipating that it would eventually be linked to the west block by a remodelling or rebuilding of the 8th-century nave. In the reconstruction drawing of the choir [28], the high vault is shown at the same level as the vault over the east bay of the central upper chapel in the west block, and the middle storey is based on the upper story of the central east bay of the vestibule [24, upper left]. The paired windows of the clearstorey are based on those in the slightly later choirs at St-Germain-des-Prés and Sens [31], both of which have unvaulted false galleries like that shown here.

Corroborative evidence for false galleries in Suger's choir is their presence at Avila in Castile and Vézelay in Burgundy [29], the only 12th-century Gothic choirs where the St-Denis ambulatory and radiating chapels were imitated. At Avila the ambulatory and chapels are separated by columns comparable to those at St-Denis in their slenderness and in carrying nothing except the vaults. At Vézelay the compound piers in the same position have a stoutness appropriate to their role as supports to the outer wall of a gallery. Only the double ambulatory of Notre-Dame in Paris has columnar piers carrying a gallery wall, but their girth is proportionately greater than that of the piers in the St-Denis ambulatory, and the weight of the gallery wall is in any case minimized by the large openings which pierce it [35, 41b]. Further evidence against proper galleries at St-Denis is that the upper surfaces of the vaults of the ambulatory and chapels bear no traces of either flooring or an outer wall. What can be seen above the vaults is the lowest parts of thin walls on top of the radial ribs. Since it is not known how high these radial walls rose originally, their function cannot be ascertained. If they were no higher than the crowns of the vaults, they are likely to have been conceived as a means of countering outward thrusts from the ambulatory vault on the narrow, stilted vaults over the chapels. If they rose above the vault crowns it seems probable that they filled the triangular space under the roof and that, like the abutting walls in this position at Laon and Chartres [41c, 73a], they were intended to stiffen the walls of the main vessel against the lateral thrusts exerted by the high vault. Abutting walls are included in the reconstruction drawing [28].

One of the few things that can be said with confidence about the upper parts of the St-Denis choir is that the responds to the high vault must have been far less massive than those at St-Germer [18] and St-Pierre-de-Montmartre. In fact the columns in the main arcade have room on the abaci of their capitals only for slim high vault responds such as occur in the later choir of Notre-Dame in Paris [33]. Without massive responds the upper walls would have lacked the most obvious means of reinforcement. The analogy with other 12th-century Gothic churches suggests that the absence of bulky responds was compensated for by making the upper walls thicker than the

29 Vézelay, south side of the choir, c. 1160–80. The inconsistencies in the main arcades and the high vault responds are the result of revising the design in the course of execution.

main arcades, with the extra thickness of masonry resting on the adjacent parts of the aisle and ambulatory vaults. This 'false bearing' technique, so called from the fact that the arcade piers are not centred under those of the gallery, is most easily studied in cross sections [41a,c], but in the nave of St-Pierre-de-Montmartre [15] it is just possible to see through the openings of the middle storey that the wall at this level is thicker than the main arcades. The latter could perfectly well have been given the same thickness as the upper walls, but the result would have been to impair the quality of structural lightness that was to remain for centuries the hallmark of French Gothic. False bearing is only one of several technical sleights-of-hand which Gothic architects were to deploy in the interests of preserving the illusion of lightness. The best known and most important of these devices is the flying buttress.

Until quite recently it was an almost universally accepted axiom that flying buttresses were unknown in the West before c. 1175. However, within the last few years numbers of specialists have begun to admit that at least some of the flyers on first-generation Gothic churches may be original features rather than later additions as had usually been assumed. At St-Denis nothing survives in the fabric of the choir which can be construed as the remains of flyers, but there are a few pieces of circumstantial evidence which seem to point to their former existence. There is also the distinct possibility that the architect was aware of the 9th- or 10th-century flyers on the vestibule of Hagia Sophia in Constantinople, for that church was famed in the West as the most splendid in Christendom, and Suger confessed to hoping that its treasures did not surpass those he had commissioned himself. Nevertheless, it is unlikely that the St-Denis master would have contemplated using flyers if older colleagues in the Ile-de-France had not already experimented with such closely related forms of abutment as quadrant arches and partly exposed abutting walls [8c,d]. The thinning of the high vault responds which St-Denis's columnar main arcades must have entailed could probably not have been compensated for completely by the use of false bearing, since the thickness of the upper walls was limited by the extreme slenderness of the main arcades. Some form of abutment to the high vault would have been essential.

The only features of the extant fabric which can be interpreted as evidence for flyers are the thin but deep buttresses which project from between the apses of the radiating chapels [25]. They can hardly have been intended to absorb lateral thrusts from the vaults over the chapels and ambulatory; those thrusts would have been adequately met by the walls built above the radial ribs of the vaults as well as by the very substantial masses of walling which occur at each junction of adjacent apses [28, 36a]. At St-Martin-des-Champs [22] the analogous wall masses do not need to be augmented by inter-apsidal buttresses, either to resist the thrusts from the ambulatory and chapel vaults or to provide stiffening for the much-windowed outer wall, which is at least as thin as that at St-Denis. The stability of the ambulatory walls at both churches is in any case assured independently of their buttresses by their curved and indented form, for this works rather like the concertina pleats by which a piece of paper can be made to stand on edge and resist a certain amount of lateral pressure. Admittedly, the axial chapel at St-Martin does have shallow inter-apsidal buttresses, but they are justified by the smaller indentations between its apses and by the very wide span of its vault. That the deep inter-apsidal buttresses at St-Denis served as bases for flying buttresses is suggested not only by their depth but by the height to which they rise. Normal practice in Early Gothic architecture, exemplified by the transepts at Noyon [48], was that deep buttresses which did not carry flyers were tapered back to the wall, starting from the level at which their abutment value was thought to cease. It follows that the uppermost parts of the St-Denis buttresses were redundant unless they carried flyers.

If flyers of typical Early Gothic depth rose from the inter-apsidal buttresses, their inner parts would have had to be set over the radial ribs of the ambulatory and chapel vaults. This is the arrangement followed in the lower flyers on the choir of St-Remi at Reims, begun c. 1170 [42]. A building probably started very soon after the completion of Suger's choir in 1144, and certainly conceived as a simplified version of it, is the choir of St-Germain-des-Prés in Paris, where flyers sit entirely on solid chapel-separating walls. It has been suggested that these walls were included specifically in order to provide a more secure base for deep flyers. The same explanation does not work so well for the similar walls at Noyon Cathedral, which are accompanied by very massive inter-apsidal buttresses impossible to explain logically except as supports for flyers essentially like the late medieval ones now occupying this position [*41a*, *48*]. The only surviving flyers which closely resemble the reconstruction of St-Denis's flyers proposed here [*28*], both in their form and in their relation to the structure below, are those on the choir of Vézelay. Like virtually all flyers on 12th-century Gothic churches, they have often been regarded as additions to the original fabric. However, it is difficult to see how the high, generously windowed clearstorey which Vézelay seems to owe to St-Denis could ever have withstood unaided the thrusts exerted by the high vault [*29*]. Apart from a Cluny-type upwards extension of the clearstorey wall – a solution totally at odds with Gothic aesthetics – flying buttresses were effectively the only means of stabilizing a clearstorey of such fragile ossature.

In the reconstruction drawing of the St-Denis choir [*28*], the flyers are shown conforming to the general Early Gothic usage according to which the undersides of their upper ends are at the level where the lateral vault webs begin to curve inwards over the clearstorey windows. One can only guess at the intention behind this correspondence but it seems likely that flyers were perceived as a device for countering thrusts transmitted directly from the curved parts of lateral webs and indirectly from the upper parts of longitudinal webs. The thrusts exerted by and through the vertical parts of the lateral webs were met by the columnar buttresses directly below the heads of the flyers. In many 12th-century and later Gothic buildings the problem of how to bring narrow flyers into contact with thrusts exerted along the full length of the clearstorey walls was met by the well-tried method of introducing masses of mortared rubble into the lower parts of the spaces between the walls and the haunches of the vault [*13e*].

Even without its destroyed upper storeys, the St-Denis choir remains recognizable as an extraordinarily precocious design. Indeed, if the dating evidence were not so secure, it is unlikely that any responsible scholar would ever have assigned it to the early 1140s on the basis of its style. The fact that the choir remained a modern building throughout the late 12th century makes it difficult to accept the widely held view of the development of Early Gothic architecture as a process of gradual and continuous evolution giving rise to new concepts at a roughly uniform rate. The picture is rather of two successive phases entirely different in their nature and duration. First, the creation at St-Denis of a radically new version of the 'skeletal' structure of the 1130s, mainly in response to the problems generated by substituting thin neo-Antique columns for compound piers. Second, the diffusion of the new manner throughout the Ile-de-France and northern France generally, in the course of which the implications of St-Denis were explored at a fairly leisurely pace and with comparatively few surprising consequences. A similar pattern recurs often in the history of art, and in Gothic architecture other important examples are the French Rayonnant and English Perpendicular styles.

The first Gothic cathedrals

The instantaneous acceptance of the style of the second St-Denis master should not be seen simply as the inevitable consequence of exposure to artistic genius. The uniquely ambitious character of St-Denis's choir and the royal associations of the abbey have already been identified as aspects of the work likely to have commended it as a model to intending patrons in northern France, but in the eyes of the bishops its royalness would have seemed specially important, for their king was their patron, their protector and, by virtue of his anointing at his coronation, almost their colleague. The list of thirteen bishops invited to dedicate the new choir in 1144 reads like a roll-call of the cathedrals which would be rebuilt during the next hundred years. Within a decade the most senior French prelate taking part, Samson, archbishop of Reims, had replaced the east and west parts of his 9th-century cathedral with extensions unmistakably modelled on St-Denis. Since Reims Cathedral was the coronation church, its refashioning must have reinforced the regal associations of the new architecture.

Although Early Gothic architecture was primarily a movement to replace obsolete churches in the Ile-de-France rather than an art movement as such, the fact is that no great church was built in the region using any other style. The main influence here must have been the growing sense of political cohesion due to the increasingly effective exercise of royal power. Early Gothic was not a centrally directed movement, for Louis VII was in no position to give significant material support for great church building, but the moral authority deriving from his office and from his own character must not be underestimated. If the uncritical royalism of Suger was exceptional, there was certainly a growing acceptance among the higher clergy that France was potentially a nation united under the leadership of its king rather than an agglomeration of warring principalities.

A new kind of architecture originating in northern France during the mid-12th century could hardly have failed to be touched in some way by the revivalist fervour which the Cistercians and other reformed monastic orders injected into the religious life of the country. The scope for direct borrowing from the severely simple buildings regularly erected by the Cistercians was obviously very limited, although Laon, one of the most splendid of the Early Gothic cathedrals, includes a few important elements drawn from this source. Yet the possibility exists that Early Gothic was conceived right from the start as a reformed style, for the wall surfaces of the St-Denis choir are unornamented and its carved capitals are free of all trace of the grotesquery so despised by St Bernard. The splendour of St-Denis is of a chaste and cerebral kind which is unlikely to have raised any Cistercian hackles, and although its ambition exceeded the narrow limits the Cistercians had laid down for themselves, this would have been acceptable by virtue of the function of the choir as the setting for a saint's shrine. Even the Cistercians had to see their traditions of austerity yield to the need to honour a saint, for immediately

30 Sens Cathedral, main vessel, begun late 1140s(?). The clearstorey was enlarged and the adjacent vault webs rebuilt in the late 13th century [cf. *31*].

after St Bernard died in 1153 the east end of the church at his abbey of Clairvaux was rebuilt grandly as his shrine chapel.

An even closer conjunction in time and place links Gothic architecture and Scholastic philosophy, for when work began on the choir of St-Denis Paris was already well on the way to becoming the intellectual capital of Europe. Parallels of various kinds have been drawn between Scholasticism and what was unquestionably the most intellectually refined architecture yet seen in the medieval West, but short of invoking the theory developed by the *Annales* school of cultural historians, that the unity discernible in the attitudes and artifacts of a single era is to be explained by reference to deep and hardly recoverable patterns or 'habits' of thought, it is difficult to see how the supposed correspondences can be accounted for historically. There is absolutely no evidence from this period that any cleric ever became deeply involved in the designing of a major church, though this is not to say that such a thing could not have happened. Certainly Suger was no Scholastic, and the choir of St-Denis includes nothing which cannot be explained as the architect's response to a fairly basic brief. The discourse of 12th-century Parisian architects is irretrievably lost, but that of one of their late 14th-century successors, Jean Mignot, survives in the records of the disputes over the design of Milan Cathedral, and it is notable that Mignot's statements reveal familiarity with the terminology and debating procedure still current in the Paris Schools in his day. Although this does not prove that Mignot and his predecessors were intellectuals, it indicates that at some stage there had been contacts between practitioners of the two kinds of cultural activity for which Paris was most renowned in the mid-12th century. While discounting any suggestion that Gothic originated as a species of petrified philosophy, one must readily admit that the spread of the new architecture beyond Paris would have been aided by its origin in the same milieu as Scholasticism. To the growing numbers of French and foreign higher clergy who had spent some of their formative years studying in Paris the Parisian associations of Gothic would have seemed an almost automatic commendation. All the same it is important to emphasize that the consequences of such links are not predictable. The English bishop Roger of Worcester was Paris-educated, yet his patronage resulted in a building far less French than that commissioned around the same time by the Benedictine monks of Canterbury Cathedral, on whose horizons Paris would not have loomed nearly so large [52, 57].

At the mother church of the ecclesiastical province covering the southern part of the Ile-de-France, the authority of St-Denis's architecture is revealed in a remarkable way. Sens Cathedral had been started some time before 1142 in a plain Romanesque style, but when only the outer walls of the choir had been finished, perhaps in the late 1140s, the original designs were scrapped and a much more wholeheartedly Gothic main vessel was begun [30]. There is no way of knowing for certain whether the main vessel was a completely new design or a reworking of the original scheme, but the latter seems more likely since the second campaign incorporates elements derived from the same sources as the first. The aisle-high chapels which substitute for transepts derive either from the early 11th-century cathedral of Chartres or from the half-dozen or so comparatively small churches in the area between Chartres and Paris which made use of this plan during the 1130s [36b]. Traces still visible on the outer wall of the choir aisles and ambulatory show that the main arcade arches were to have been semicircular and that the aisles and ambulatory were to have been covered by groin vaults as purely Romanesque as the semidome in the surviving transeptal chapel. The most striking feature of the outer wall is the enormous size of its windows [31], a reminder that stained glass was already a major art form before the emergence of Gothic architecture.

The most important elements of the existing central vessel at Sens which appear to be borrowings from the Paris–Chartres 'group' of churches carried over from the original designs are the broad proportions and the alternation between massive compound piers and far slighter columnar supports. St-Pierre-de-Montmartre [15] parallels the breadth and the bulky piers, and the destroyed churches of St-Magloire in Paris and St-Etienne at Dreux both incorporated alternating supports, though their 'weak' piers were single columns rather than the pairs used at Sens. The central vessels at St-Magloire and Dreux were vaulted in square compartments each flanked by two aisle bays, and there is a possibility that a similar arrangement was part of the original design for Sens. What seems certain is that the central vessel as it exists today was the first Gothic building to combine alternating supports with vaults whose ribs are alternately single and in groups of three. How the

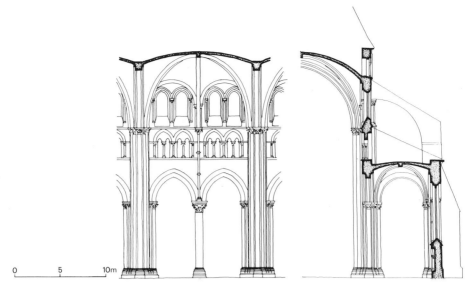

0   5   10m

31 Sens Cathedral, elevation and section showing the clearstorey and high vault in their original state.

second architect of Sens came to adopt these six-cell or 'sexpartite' vaults must remain an open question as the only earlier examples still surviving are those added around 1120 to the nave of St-Etienne at Caen [5]. It is possible, as some writers have suggested, that the three deep western bays of the St-Denis choir resembled the westernmost choir bay at Vézelay [29] in carrying a compartment of sexpartite vaulting. Influence on Sens from the lost upper storeys of Suger's choir is more certain in the case of the paired units of the false gallery and clearstorey.

The high vault at Sens is now more like the Caen vault than it was originally. Until the late 13th century its lateral ridges were not horizontal but steeply sloping [31]. What the merits of this common feature of Early Gothic high vaults were thought to be is not clear, as it causes a slight increase in lateral thrust at exactly those places where the clearstorey wall cannot be reinforced by buttressing. The thrusts coming from the parts of the vault webs next to the trios of ribs are several times stronger than those from the webs above the single ribs, a disparity echoed in the rather dramatic alternation between bulwark-like compound responds and puny single shafts, the latter made up of attached monoliths and hence of no value as reinforcement to the walls. As at St-Pierre-de-Montmartre [15], the compound responds make a major contribution towards keeping the thin walls of the central vessel upright, but here they are supplemented by a Cluny-type extension above the clearstorey. These two well-tried devices would probably not have been sufficient to contain the powerful lateral thrusts exerted by a high vault of such exceptional span, and there is a good chance that the flyers of a simple pre-1200 pattern which survived into the 19th century were contemporary with the main vessel [31]. It is unlikely that flyers were intended in the first campaign because the buttresses on the outer walls are tapered back below the wall head, with the result that the flyers have

32 Senlis Cathedral, south side of the choir, begun *c.* 1151–6. The original clearstorey and sexpartite high vault were replaced *c.* 1510.

33 *Opposite:* Paris, Notre-Dame, transepts and choir looking north-east; choir begun *c.* 1160, complete except for the high vault in 1179, clearstorey windows enlarged from *c.* 1220. The transept bays and the western bays of the choir were returned to their original state in the 19th century, except that glazing was introduced behind the oculi.

to stand entirely on the transverse arches of the aisle and ambulatory vaults.

The broad central vessel and bulky compound piers of Sens did not pass into the repertory of northern French Gothic architecture. No doubt they were regarded as having been superseded by St-Denis's narrow central vessel and slight high vault responds. Sexpartite vaulting, on the other hand, became a standard feature of late 12th-century Gothic, perhaps because of the rhythmic interest it gives to long central vessels or perhaps because it promoted consistency by echoing the square or nearly square compartments of quadripartite vaulting habitually employed in aisles and galleries. The colleagues of the Sens master were apparently not much impressed by the visual and structural consistency created by his combination of sexpartite vaulting with alternating supports. Most later 12th-century architects used these vaults over continuous ranges of columnar piers, and only the earliest known imitation of the Sens vaults, those formerly at Senlis Cathedral, were set above alternately compound and cylindrical piers [*32*], the latter single rather than double as at Sens.

The Early Gothic cathedrals are in general no higher than the largest Norman and Anglo-Norman churches. The one surviving exception is Notre-Dame in Paris [*33, 34, 36c, 41b*] whose 33m-high main vessel outdid the 32m of the destroyed nave at Cambrai Cathedral (begun *c.* 1150), the 29.5m of Cluny, and the 31m of Speyer and St Paul's London, the two highest Romanesque cathedrals in Germany and England. This gigantism must have been intended as an assertion of the pre-eminence of Paris among the cities of the kingdom and also as a demonstration of the status of the mother church of

a city where many churches had been rebuilt recently. The choir of Notre-Dame is about a third as high again as the nave and transepts projected at St-Denis, although the width-to-height proportion of the central vessel is almost exactly the same, 1:2.5. In common with many other Early Gothic architects, the Notre-Dame master adopted the short columnar piers used in the St-Denis choir. He must have liked them for their own sake and he may or may not have been aware that they owed their existence to a concern to match the arcade piers in the 8th-century nave retained by Suger. The history of medieval architecture includes many such instances of specialized forms later attaining a currency which would have surprised their originators. We have become accustomed to seeing plain cylindrical supports in the main arcades of Early Gothic cathedrals [32, 39, 41], but something of their original strangeness can be retrieved by looking at them through the eyes of the German Romantic writer and philosopher Friedrich Schlegel, who in 1805 found Notre-Dame's stocky piers disconcertingly out of character with the verticality and compound form of the high vault responds. Schlegel felt impelled to explain them away as replacements for compound piers, made during the 18th century in order to bring the interior into partial conformity with Neo-Classical taste. He might have added that they and the uniformly triple responds which they receive are hardly a logical complement to the alternately triple and single ribs of the high vault. The wide diffusion of this combination of columnar piers and sexpartite vaulting, notwithstanding the dictates of strict logic, may reflect a general desire to perpetuate something of the character of the ancient columnar basilicas which the 12th-century Gothic cathedrals were succeeding. Although there is every reason to think that Early Gothic was perceived at the time primarily as a modern style, it had not yet developed to the point where it lost the capacity to incorporate allusions to earlier architectures.

Whether or not the columns of Notre-Dame were intended to evoke the ambitious 6th-century cathedral built by St Germain and King Childebert, the walls which they carry are as thin relative to their height as those of any early medieval basilica. At most levels they are somewhat less than 1m thick, a prodigious technical feat inconceivable without earlier Parisian experiments in thin-wall structure such as St-Pierre-de-Montmartre and the St-Denis choir. The mouldings around the gallery openings acquire a reedy slenderness that complements the high vault responds and also gives to the walls an almost paper-thin aspect. This effect is also promoted by the completely unmoulded clearstorey windows glazed only a few centimetres behind the main wall plane. The wheel-like oculi which originally relieved the expanses of bare wall between gallery and clearstorey opened into

34 Paris, Notre-Dame, interior looking north-east: nave, begun late 1170s. Among many departures from the choir design [33] are the greater width of the main vessel, the triple arches in the gallery, the horizontal ridges of the high vault and the construction of the gallery piers from large coursed blocks fronted by edge-bedded shafts [cf. 43].

otherwise unlit roof spaces whose darkness would have emphasized to the full the metallic quality of their 'spokes' and faceted rims. Around 1220–30 the clearstorey windows and the oculi were destroyed to make way for longer windows, but in the 19th century the original design was recreated in some bays [33]. The inserted clearstorey windows alter radically the balance of the elevation as well as the light level, yet it would be difficult to deny that they are even more consonant with the brittle linearity of the gallery than what they replaced. The string course below them echoes that under the gallery and so generates, in conjunction with the vault responds, a rectilinear grid which was not there before. But the main change produced by the enlargement of the windows is a drastic reduction in the role of plain wall surface as a positive element in the design. Notre-Dame's development of the Parisian and Ile-de-France tradition of small openings in upper storeys was to exert only local influence; as the subsequent history of the choir illustrates, the future lay with designers who developed the shaft-arch system at the expense of wall surfaces.

The soaring central space of the choir culminates in a sexpartite vault whose fine-gauged ribs and smooth ashlar-built webs match closely the character of the main elevations. The three-dimensional geometry of the high vaults reveals the Parisian background of the designer, for just as in the original quadripartite choir vault at St-Pierre-de-Montmartre (and formerly in the nave vaults there), the diagonal rib intersections come well above the apexes of the wall ribs and transverse ribs and create a markedly domical effect. These vaults and those in the galleries were probably abutted by two sets of flyers arranged essentially as at Noyon [41a], but only parts of the high and deep buttress piers rising from the outer walls survived the remodelling of the original buttressing in the 13th and 14th centuries. The need for flyers to counter the effects of vault thrusts on Notre-Dame's exceptionally thin walls can hardly be doubted, for the wall buttresses at clearstorey and triforium level are mere tokens, far too shallow to have any value as abutments. Admittedly, there is the possibility that the transverse ribs of the gallery vaults carried quadrant arches like those at St-Germer [8c] or triangular walls of the type proposed for St-Denis and still existing at Laon [28, 41c], but any kind of structure confined within the gallery roof space would have risen too low to abut the high vault. The points at which the undersides of flyers would have joined the wall buttresses are marked by mouldings continuous with the abaci of the capitals on the clearstorey windows. Similar mouldings occur below the still-existing flyers of c. 1180 on the comparatively small-scale nave at Champeaux (c. 45km south-east of Paris), a church showing many other similarities to Notre-Dame and connected to the bishop and chapter by very strong ties of patronage.

Abutment of vaults over high and steeply proportioned naves has sometimes been identified as the main purpose behind the Early Gothic use of vaulted galleries, particularly by those historians unable to accept that flying

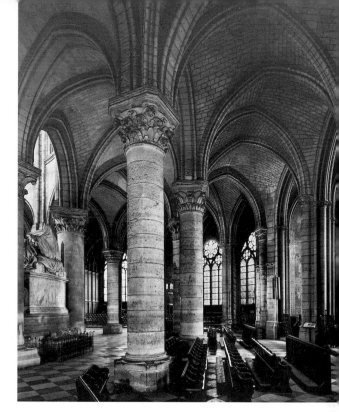

35 Paris, Notre-Dame, ambulatory looking north, begun c. 1160. The columnar piers are much larger than their counterparts at St-Denis [27] and are made of shallow drums rather than monoliths. Around 1300 the original outer wall was removed to make way for chapels and some of the vault shafts were replaced by curious diagonal buttresses which anticipate those in the nave of St-Ouen at Rouen [187].

buttresses existed before c. 1175. However, there is no obvious reason why the high aisles, unvaulted false galleries and tall central vessel of the projected nave at St-Denis could not have been executed on a larger scale had the occasion arisen. At Notre-Dame, and also at Senlis, Noyon, Laon and St-Remi in Reims, vaulted galleries were surely adopted for themselves rather than for their value as abutments, since their generous windows and their rib vaults endowed interiors with a spaciousness and a visual consistency that must have been regarded by many people as improvements on the St-Denis scheme [39, 43]. Galleries had been normal adjuncts to northern French great churches throughout the 11th and early 12th centuries, and this was probably still a recommendation in the Early Gothic period.

The ravine-like sheerness of Notre-Dame's central vessel is accentuated by the shallowness of the transepts (even in their present lengthened form) and by the lack of any upward extension of space into a lantern tower over the crossing [33]. The sense of confinement is in fact eased progressively, beginning with the shadowy spaces behind the oculi, continuing with the limited views into the galleries and culminating in the spacious vistas which open out beyond the minimal barrier formed by the widely spaced columns of the arcades. Whereas the galleries are only a single 'aisle' deep, the aisles proper are double. In the 13th century they were made into gloomy, rather amorphous spaces by the addition of chapels between the buttresses, but originally they would have resembled the clearstorey in being dominated by the thin enveloping wall. The ambulatory of Notre-Dame married the two-aisle format of St-Denis with the continuously windowed walls of the chapel-less chevet at Sens; and here again the later addition of chapels prevents us from experiencing fully the intended effect [35]. The influence of Sens practically guarantees that the outer windows were very large, at least twice the size of those in the clearstorey.

The grand simplicity of Notre-Dame's three-tiered exterior massing disappeared under a welter of buttresses, pinnacles and gables in the late 13th and early 14th centuries, but it can be visualized by mentally stripping away the small projecting chapels from the choir of Bourges and thinning out by half its dense scaffold of flyers [64]. Much better than a view of Notre-Dame surrounded by the grandiose townscape of present-day Paris, the aerial photograph of Bourges Cathedral in its closely packed and still essentially medieval setting conveys how domineering this huge and beautifully ordered structure must have seemed to those who saw it rising in the later 12th and early 13th centuries. The reaction of contemporaries to the first generation of Gothic cathedrals can hardly be imagined by us, for whom big buildings are associated primarily with mundane functions, but their response was perhaps not too different from the exhilarated pride with which most Victorians greeted the unveiling of the Crystal Palace.

The other outstanding Gothic cathedral of the first generation is at Laon, 97km north-east of Paris [37]. Laon borders on Flanders and Champagne, regions which could boast limited numbers of Romanesque great churches, and it was the creative exploration of these local antecedents which gave Laon much of its distinctive character. Whereas Notre-Dame outdid all other churches in and around Paris mainly by dint of sheer scale, Laon gives the impression that the patron and architect wished to incorporate all the most imposing features of the grandest churches within the ecclesiastical province of Reims. That Laon was conceived in so frankly competitive a spirit is by no means unlikely, for the prime mover behind the new building seems to have been Bishop Gautier de Mortagne, whose formidable administrative and financial skills were deployed with the aim of giving substance to his ducal status and his prestigious title of second peer of France. As a former dean, Gautier was unusually well placed to mobilize the chapter, the body normally responsible at any cathedral for raising funds and directing operations. Despite renovation after a fire started by rioting townsmen in 1112, the 8th-century cathedral of Laon must have seemed conspicuously inferior to virtually every other cathedral in the Reims province, where ambitious schemes of partial or total replacement were either complete or under way. Even the reformed monastic orders so liberally patronized by Bishop Barthélemy, Gautier's predecessor, had built themselves churches in the immediate vicinity of Laon which must have put the much repaired cathedral to shame.

The contrasting approaches of the architects of Notre-Dame and Laon are revealed in everything from the basic shapes of the buildings to the smallest details of their design. The dissimilarity of these two great churches,

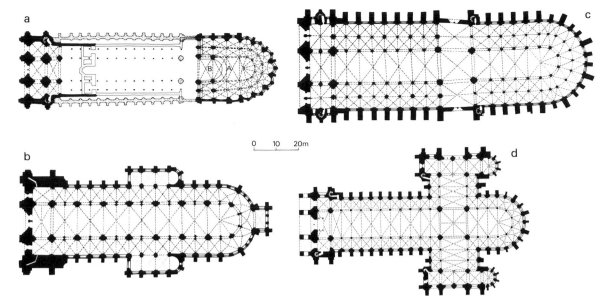

36 Plans of (a) St-Denis; (b) Sens Cathedral; (c) Notre-Dame in Paris; and (d) Laon Cathedral, omitting post-12th-century alterations. The plan of St-Denis shows the 8th-century church (open) with the additions finished by 1144 (solid), and the scheme for total rebuilding, abandoned in 1151 (stippled). The shrine of St Denis stood at A, the high altar at B. The plan of the west choir bays is largely conjectural.

probably both designed shortly before 1160, bears witness to the creative vitality of Gothic architecture from its inception and gives promise of its infinite capacity for diversification in later periods. At Notre-Dame the emphasis was firmly on the staggered and tiered spaces extending, with only minimal interruption by the transepts, between the east end and the huge twin west towers apparently envisaged from the outset though mostly built in the early 13th century. At Laon the east-west vessels are not just lower and narrower, both individually and in aggregate, but shorter internally by about a fifth (before the later extension of the choir). These inequalities are more than made up for by the huge wingspan of the transepts, by the lantern tower illuminating the crossing and by the towers planted at the four corners of the transepts, although these and the two-storey eastern chapels were afterthoughts of c. 1170–80. Internally, the effect of all this is to create a complex of broadly proportioned spaces radiating out from a crossing whose pivotal role is established by its great height and brilliant lighting [38]. Externally the picture is again of outward expansiveness, but contained by the prodigious verticals of the towers [37].

The Romanesque sources of this splendid scheme are fairly clear. The long transepts with two tiers of eastern chapels and bridge-like galleries across the ends seem to derive from St-Remi at Reims (c. 1007–49), the largest Romanesque church in Champagne. St-Remi was possibly also the model for Laon's rather short choir. Lantern towers illuminating the crossing were known in northern France from Carolingian times, but the immediate

37, 38 Laon Cathedral. *Left:* reconstruction of the late 12th-century scheme (the details of the transept towers shown as partly built in the 13th century). Only the western transept towers were completed and only the south tower of the west front ever received its spire. *Below:* transepts looking north-east, *c.* 1165–75.

source for Laon's great tower may well be the same as that for the transept corner towers, namely the enormous and barely completed transepts of Tournai Cathedral in Flanders [*40*]. The Tournai transepts also have what appears to be the only earlier example of a four-storey elevation with an arcaded triforium incorporating a wall passage, though admittedly the heavy paired arches fronting the passage are less striking anticipations of Laon's band-like arcading [*39*] than the passageless arcaded triforium of the nave at Tournai or its derivative in the Gothic choir at Noyon [*41a*].

The string courses above and below the band triforium at Laon combine with the vault responds to form a tiered grid whose small-scale, rather busy character is compounded by the shortness of the bays, about two-fifths of the width of the main vessel rather than the usual half. The introduction of the band triforium has important implications for the structure of the high walls

39 Laon Cathedral, south side of the nave looking east, *c.* 1175–90. Pressure from the high vault has caused the upper storeys to tilt outwards. The simple and repetitive crocket capitals remained standard in France well into the early 13th century [cf. *61, 65*].

40 Tournai Cathedral, from the north. From right to left: nave and transepts, early and mid-12th-century; choir, 1243–55. The towers at the corners of the transepts were apparently modelled on those of St-Trond in eastern Belgium (1055–82). The gables and pinnacles on the choir clearstorey are a device for increasing vertical emphasis [cf. *111*].

as well as for their surface articulation. Its total thickness is about 1.5m, as against the 1m of most of the rest of the high walls, and consequently the back wall of the passage has to stand on the near parts of the gallery vaults [*41c*]. This is essentially a variant of the false bearing technique already discussed in relation to the choir of St-Denis. The thickness of the other three storeys at Laon is close to that adopted as the normal wall thickness at Notre-Dame, but proportionately it is much greater, for the walls of the Laon choir were, until their slight raising when the high vault was rebuilt in the early 13th century, around 23m high as against the 33m of the Notre-Dame choir. Paradoxically, the greater thickness of the walls at Laon is exploited to promote an impression of structural lightness more consistent than at Notre-Dame [*33*]: bare walling is eliminated from the upper storeys by the open triforium arcades and by an extension of the shaft-arch system framing the windows which successfully distracts attention from the smallness of the actual openings. A further important difference between the Laon and Paris masters' use of shafts is apparent in the responds to the high vault. At Paris these are uniform despite their association with a sexpartite vault; at Laon they enact much more wholeheartedly the illusion that shafts function as supports for specific arches, since their number and placing correspond exactly to the alternation of ribs in the high vault.

Compared to Notre-Dame, the earlier phases of Laon are conservative in their building technique. Whereas at Paris the walls consist almost entirely of large ashlar blocks, the relatively thick walls at Laon include extensive rubble cores and their facing masonry is made up of smaller blocks. The high walls at Laon were in fact thick enough to enable the master to dispense with what had been a significant reinforcement in the choir at Notre-Dame. The responds to the high vault at Notre-Dame are mostly coursed with the walls and consequently form an integral part of their structure. At Laon, however, the responds contribute nothing to the rigidity of the walls as they consist of lathe-turned cylinders attached at regular intervals by stone rings. Since the stratification planes of the stone as it lay in the quarry are set on edge relative to the horizontal beds of mortar at the ends of each cylinder, the shafts are described as 'edge-bedded'. In the load-bearing shafts carrying the arches of the triforium and the twin-arched 'screens' of the gallery, on the other hand, the stratification planes are, or ought to be, horizontal. Edge-bedded shafts were a well-established though generally minor element in Romanesque architecture, where their main value, as here, was the elimination of the labour of shaping cylindrical components from the same blocks as the courses of the wall behind. Their relatively inconspicuous Gothic début was at St-Denis, in the upper chapels of the west block and the radiating chapels of the choir [27]. In the Laon master's detailing of these shafts he showed himself a proponent of 'structural honesty', marking each join by a prominent ring. By using short lengths of coursed shaft in lieu of rings [60], or longer shafts [34], or even invisible metal cramps, most other Early Gothic architects were able to exploit the advantages of the technique without making quite such a parade of its limitations. Others again saw its aesthetic potential [57].

When the east bays of the nave were reached around 1170 a second architect introduced several modifications to the original scheme, of which the only important one was to make alternate piers compound [39]. Probably because the shafts attached to these piers failed to relate convincingly to the high vault responds, the experiment was discontinued and the western bays were built with only discreetly alternating bases and abaci. Although not themselves influential, Laon's compound piers are important as crude precursors of the far more complete integration of vertical accents attained towards the end of the century at Chartres [60]. As in most French great churches built over a long period, experimentation with detailing is not conspicuous enough to impair the unified effect achieved through close adherence to original designs.

The sexpartite high vaults of the late 12th-century choir at Laon [41c] were originally as domical as those in the Notre-Dame choir, but in the early 13th century they were replaced so as to match the nearly horizontal lateral ridges of the nave vaults. The flying buttresses constructed at this time have often been regarded as a complete innovation, but the presence of flyers on the 12th-century choir is attested by the fact that the buttresses on the

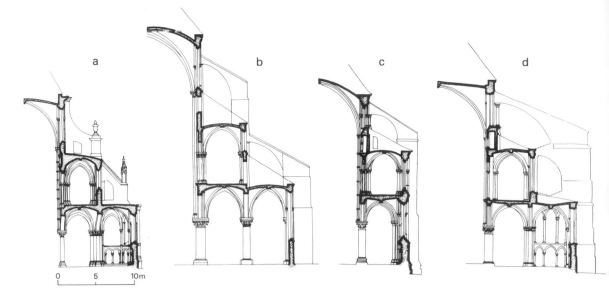

41 Part sections of (a) Noyon Cathedral, chevet; (b) Notre-Dame, Paris, choir; (c) Laon Cathedral, choir; (d) St-Remi, Reims, choir. The detail of the flyers at Notre-Dame and Laon is partly speculative as the originals were replaced in the early 13th century.

gallery walls, like those between St-Denis's radiating chapels, rise higher than was necessary if they were there simply to abut the vaults at the same level. The same feature recurs in the gallery buttresses of several other major Early Gothic churches (including Senlis Cathedral) whose clearstoreys have been subjected to a later remodelling. Confirmation that flyers were part of the original design at Laon is the almost playful echo of them on the clearstorey-level stage of the chapels which open out of the towers at the east corners of the transepts [37]. The general appearance of the 12th-century flyers is probably perpetuated in those on the simplified 'copy' of Laon begun c. 1190–1200 at Limburg-an-der-Lahn [103]. Reluctance to rely wholly on flying buttresses is evident from the inclusion under the gallery roofs of abutting walls pierced by only the narrowest of quadrant arches [41c].

Late twelfth-century variations

One of the very few 12th-century flying buttress systems to have survived is that of the choir of St-Remi at Reims, begun around 1170 [41d, 42]. Like Notre-Dame in Paris, this is a double-aisled and galleried structure, yet its buttresses are based on those of the ungalleried choirs of St-Denis and St-Germain-des-Prés. Hence the huge main flyers clearing in one jump both aisles and the gallery and springing from buttress piers whose inner parts rest on the vaults of the outer aisles. The St-Remi master's own contribution was simply to heighten and deepen the buttress piers and to add very short lower flyers abutting the gallery. The prodigious depth of St-Remi's buttress piers chops up the smoothly contoured exterior into a series of discrete segments, but this was the price that had to be paid for the realization of two unique internal effects, the extremely shallow curvature of the high vault and the brilliant illumination of the gallery [43].

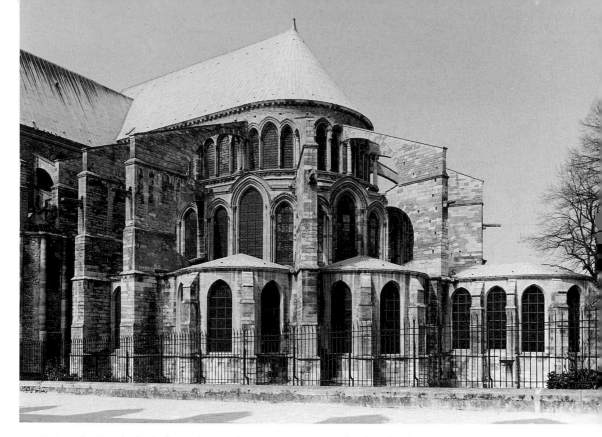

42 Reims, St-Remi, choir from the south-east, *c.* 1170–80. The fluted columns under the upper flying buttresses were modelled on those of a Roman gateway in Reims. Compare the parapet-less treatment of the eaves with the Canterbury choir [56]. The perfunctory detailing of the flying buttresses illustrates the general tendency in Gothic architecture to think of the exterior as a by-product of the interior.

From the point of view of vault design, the advantages of the deep buttress piers are that they minimize the span of the upper flyers while providing the securest possible base from which the flyers can fulfil their task of countering the powerful horizontal component in the lateral thrust exerted by a shallow high vault [13a]. The value of these buttress piers for the gallery lighting is that they relieve the outer wall of all except token buttresses and so enable the windows to expand to maximum width and be less shaded than usual. The exceptionally high level at which the flyers meet the clearstorey wall is explicable as a function of the high vault design, for, as in the Laon choir and other major Early Gothic buildings, the undersides of the heads of the flyers are set level with the points at which the lateral vault webs begin curving inwards over the windows. However, at St-Remi this curvature starts little more than 2m below the lateral ridges, and therefore the heads of the flyers are much too high to receive the thrust from the vault directly. This may have been a mistake, but it is more likely that St-Remi's designer understood a characteristic of flyers not mentioned so far, namely their capacity to function as parts of a rigid framework which locks the whole clearstorey into its correct upright position – much as one side of a box is kept in place by the edges of the adjoining sides. The other components of this framework are the buttress piers, the buttresses and residual walling between the clearstorey windows, and the horizontal bands of masonry below and above the windows. The masonry over the windows is given a certain longitudinal, beam-like rigidity, which it would otherwise lack, by the considerable load imposed by the timber roof and its heavy lead covering. The lower flyers at St-Remi are even higher in relation to the gallery vault than the main flyers are to the high vault, but no doubt they too were thought of primarily as a means of giving rigidity to the window wall as a whole.

The interior of the choir of St-Remi [43] ranks as one of the most accomplished of Early Gothic interiors, although its breadth, the consequence of being built onto a Romanesque transept and nave, makes it seem less a paradigm of the style than Laon or Notre-Dame. The proportions of the main vessel are saved from squatness by the high vault, whose shallowness maximizes the verticals of the side walls. Exceptionally, the height of the vault is little more than half its span, but by using unconventional four-centred curvatures for the ribs it became possible to avoid transverse ribs with obtusely pointed profiles and awkwardly sudden springings such as occur in the high nave vault at Durham [11]. The main aim behind this unique design was surely to minimize the obstruction caused to the clearstorey. The same readiness to put windows before vaults is evident also in the gallery of the apse, where in order to allow the central window in each group of three to rise as high as possible the outer webs of the vaults are made to slope steeply upwards. The no less remarkable downward extension of all the gallery windows involves pitching the roofs of the radiating chapels and outer aisles as low as is consistent with their rain-shedding function. Free passage of light from the gallery into the main vessel of the choir is assured by keeping the piers narrow in elevation and by concentrating all their shafts at the front of deep rectangular masses ignorable if not quite invisible from the main vessel. The concern to promote luminosity and structural slightness at the expense of mass also accounts for the elimination of solid walling above the apexes of the main arcades.

The triple lancets in the clearstorey at St-Remi [44] are the first in Gothic architecture, although the concept was not new [10]. The almost rectangular configuration of the clearstorey lancets determines that in the quadripartite vaults over the rectangular bays the upper parts of the lateral webs are virtually horizontal and the lower parts are bent back behind the diagonal ribs so as to form vertical planes set at an acute angle with the window wall. Structurally, this arrangement has the advantage of concentrating almost all the outward thrusts from the vault on the narrow strips of

43 Reims, St-Remi, choir. The main aim in replacing the short eastern arm of the 11th-century church was to create a grander and more spacious setting for the shrine of St Remigius, which was detached from the high altar and moved further east. The present shrine is 17th- and 19th-century.

the clearstorey wall which are reinforced externally by columnar buttresses and flyers. The clearstorey windows were obviously intended to be the main light source in the central vessel, and it is unfortunate that they are now outshone by the flood of daylight pouring in from the aisles and radiating chapels, the only parts of the choir to have lost their 12th-century stained glass [43]. Originally this would have been the darkest level of the central vessel, for the windows lighting it are placed unusually far from the main arcades on account of the double aisles and extremely deep radiating chapels.

All the lighting effects and structural devices considered so far are deployed in the service of one central concept stemming from the designer's frank acceptance of the inherited breadth of the choir, namely his treatment of the elevation as a series of horizontal bands. The uniquely close match in length between the apse bays and the straight-sided bays is the main means of establishing the consistency of these bands, but the important contribution made by the vault and upper storeys can be gauged by comparison with the far less emphatically layered elevation of Laon [39]. St-Remi's continuous belt of lancets is in fact so little interrupted by the vault shafts that one hardly notices the latter, at least in the apse. Yet the two upper storeys also reveal the limits of the St-Remi master's enthusiasm for horizontals. Evidently he felt that the band effect was adequately conveyed by the arrangement of the openings, so in the surface articulation of the clearstorey and triforium he gave priority to verticals. This was accomplished partly by omitting the usual storey-separating string course, but mainly by making the shafts between the clearstorey openings descend into the triforium so as to break up its row of six small arches into three pairs [44].

The rich surface articulation and the height of the combined upper storeys enable them to function as an impressive climax to the elevations in a way which complements and reinforces the role of the clearstorey as the brightest level of the central vessel. Their tripartite form also completes the simple numerical progression which begins with the single arches of the main arcade and continues with the paired openings of the gallery. Less obviously perhaps, the bay-softening horizontality of the clearstorey and triforium is reconciled to the vertical, bay-emphasizing format of the arcade by the gallery, whose elevation contains elements of both storeys. From the point of view of the overall development of Gothic architecture, the upper storeys at St-Remi represent a significant step towards the 13th-century concept of the clearstorey as the dominant feature of the interior [60].

The sequence of openings in the elevation and the linkage between triforium and clearstorey may not have been due entirely to the artistic vision of the St-Remi master. Like most churchmen of his day, the patron, Abbot Pierre de Celle, would have been familiar with the passages in St Augustine's writings which deal with the symbolism of numbers. For Augustine, six was the perfect number because the works of Creation were completed (*perfecta*)

44 Reims, St-Remi, clearstorey and triforium at the junction of the north choir wall with the apse.

in six days. It also expresses the perfection of the Creation itself since it is the first number comprising the sum of its parts, that is its fractions: one, two and three – a sixth, a third and a half. The succession of arches in the arcade, gallery and clearstorey of each bay at St-Remi embodies this equation exactly, with the most elevated position allotted to the highest number. Three is of course the number of the Trinity and by fusing the triforium with the clearstorey the St-Remi master was able to achieve a close approximation to the traditional kind of three-storey elevation used in the Romanesque nave and transepts at St-Remi. The early 12th-century writer Rupert of Deutz specifically mentions the three-storey elevation as a symbol of the Trinity, and there seems little doubt that both he and Suger, who wrote of the tripartite west front of St-Denis in similar terms, were only articulating formally what most medieval clergy would have taken for granted. Today number symbolism may seem esoteric, not to say pointless, but in the 12th century no patron would have forgotten that the Creator had disposed 'all things in measure, number and weight' (Wisdom 11:21) or would have quibbled with St Augustine's assertion that all things in Creation teach us about their author, that they are traces or signs (*vestigia*) of the Trinity. In fact, the choir of St-Remi is among the most perfect Trinitarian symbols in Gothic architecture, for the play on the number three encompasses the triple windows lighting each of the three levels of the main apse and even the number obtained by multiplying the number of bays in the choir elevations –

eleven – by the number of storeys, that is thirty-three. This figure is not fortuitous, as one might suspect from the fact that the number of bays has no obvious symbolic value on its own, for thirty-three is the number of years Christ lived on earth. By making the curved apse bays and the straight-sided bays more nearly equal in length than at any other Early Gothic church the designer was deliberately emphasizing the integrity of the thirty-three-unit sequence enveloping the central vessel. Other examples of Trinitarian symbolism in choirs are the dimensions of the eastern arm of Beverley Minster (see p. 173) and the building time of the St-Denis chevet as reported by Suger (three years and three months). The nave of the earliest of all cathedrals, St John Lateran in Rome (begun 312), is $333\frac{1}{3}$ Roman feet long.

The peripheral spaces of the choir present a further variation on the themes of triplication and horizontal continuity [45]. Inevitably treated differently from the double aisles, the radiating chapels and single ambulatory are nevertheless assimilated quite closely by screening each chapel entrance with three arches on columns carefully matched in height and detailing to the stouter columns between the aisles. The walls separating the outer aisles from the western radiating chapels are fronted by compound responds, but

45, 46 Reims, St-Remi. *Below left:* south choir aisle and ambulatory. The capitals are decorated with rich and varied versions of Classical acanthus foliage. *Below right:* south wall of the axial chapel.

47 Noyon Cathedral, apse of the south transept, begun *c.* 1160. The translucency and double-layer construction of the second level visible anticipate triforia of the Rayonnant period [*80, 84*]. The wall passage below links the galleries of choir and nave.

between the chapels, where one would expect similar responds, the walls are tapered to fit behind coursed engaged columns as slim as the intervening monolithic columns. Beyond their triple arcaded screens, the radiating chapels are very deep [*42*], like those of the choir added to Reims Cathedral from *c.* 1150. The axial chapel is singled out from the others by its even greater depth and also by the internal passage running through the thickness of the window wall |*46*|. Like many of the most innovatory details of the St-Remi choir, this passage was to prove influential only after 1200, but viewed in the context of the 1170s it falls into place as part of a quite widespread taste for hollowing out the window walls of subordinate parts of major churches. The gallery-level chapels under the towers at the east corners of the transepts at Laon make use of the motif, but the most spectacular and probably the earliest example is in the apsidal transepts at Noyon [*47*].

The wall passages of the Noyon transepts, like the apsidal plan, were inspired by Tournai Cathedral, the grandest Romanesque church in Flanders [*40*]. Until 1146 the bishoprics of Tournai and Noyon had been held in plurality, and the adoption of Tournai features at Noyon is an unusually clear-cut instance of architectural rivalry. Norman and Anglo-Norman apses such as those at Cérisy-la-Forêt or Peterborough may be the ultimate origin of Noyon's tiers of windows combined with superposed wall passages, but the Tournai transepts have the only earlier example of the

48 Noyon Cathedral, from the south-east: choir, probably complete by 1160; transepts, begun *c.* 1160; bishop's chapel (on the left), *c.* 1190–1200. The lower flyers on the choir are 15th-century, the upper ones 18th-century. The gallery and radiating chapel roofs originally fitted directly under the sills of the clearstorey and gallery windows.

Noyon arrangement, that is clearstorey-level passages placed outside the window apertures [48] and on top of passages that open towards the interior [47]. Tournai's passages are also covered by short transverse tunnel vaults whose voussoirs act as ties linking the much-pierced 'skins' of masonry between which the passages run. The only fundamental difference is that the lower passages at Tournai are backed by solid walling rather than glass. Yet for all its debts to earlier designs, the voiding and layering of the Noyon transepts surpasses even the radiating chapel walls of St-Denis and the clearstorey of St-Remi as an exercise in transforming walls into luminous and seemingly weightless frameworks.

Façades *c.* 1150–90

Few major façades were built during the second half of the 12th century because the naves of most of the Early Gothic cathedrals remained unfinished until well after 1200. The earliest Gothic west fronts, those at St-Denis [23] and Chartres, were not the final stages of new buildings but replacements for earlier and simpler façades. Chartres takes from St-Denis its twin towers whose breadth exceeds that of the aisles behind them [*62*], and the basic concept of the triple sculptured portal. However, because the 11th-century nave at Chartres was far wider than that to which Suger added his west front, there was space between the towers for all three portals and for three huge windows. The Chartres front lacked a round window (that there now was added *c.* 1200), presumably because its designer saw the oculus at St-Denis as nothing more than the solution to a problem he himself did not face, that of lighting a broad but low upper chapel. Whether Chartres also took a lead from St-Denis in the matter of spires is not clear, as there is no evidence for the form of the wooden terminations originally planned for Suger's west front. The north tower at Chartres, begun in the late 1130s before the façade in its present form was conceived, had a wooden spire which was probably similar in shape to the stone structure of *c.* 1160–70 which still crowns the south tower. No other spires of this date or earlier have survived, but the chances are that it was due to the influence of Chartres that tall needle-like spires of stone or timber came to be regarded as indispensable adjuncts to major Gothic towers. Of all features of Gothic great churches, spired steeples were the most obviously non-functional and hence the most open to attack by critics of clerical ostentation. In a manual of church symbolism written around 1250 William Durand, bishop of Mende, says that spires signify the striving of men's minds towards heaven. For once a guidebook cliché turns out to correspond with medieval perceptions.

The west front of Senlis (*c.* 1170) is a small-scale, 'rationalized' version of St-Denis. Its towers conform to the width of the aisles and incorporate vertically continuous buttresses, and its openings are distributed strictly in accordance with the cross-section of the nave. By comparison with that in Suger's façade, the oculus at Senlis is both small and unimportant in its function, being used to light the space between the high vault and the roof. The only evidence of willingness to give oculi a major role at this period is the large wheel window built incongruously into the east wall of the sacristy at Noyon, and perhaps intended originally for the west front [*48*]. Curiously, it seems to have been the Cistercians who revitalized the tradition. During the middle decades of the 12th century many of their churches were being built with façades incorporating ever larger cusped oculi derived from the small oculi with cusped surrounds used at Cluny and its Burgundian derivatives [*10, 14*]; and the earliest known examples of circular windows extending the full width of a central vessel appear to be the now fragmentary roses at the Cistercian abbeys of Trois-Fontaines in northern Champagne and Kirkstall in Yorkshire, both of *c.* 1150–60. The oldest full-width rose window on a cathedral façade is at Laon [*38*], a city ringed around with houses of the Cistercians and their spiritual and architectural fellow-travellers, the Premonstratensians. Confirmation of the Cistercian parentage of the north transept rose at Laon is the cusping of its constituent circles. Its date is *c.* 1175.

Apart from the rose and the later upper storeys of the right-hand tower, the north transept façade at Laon [37] is as plainly treated as the Senlis west front. The four-storey structure of the regular bays in the transept is denied in the three-tier disposition of the openings, and a triforium-like arcaded screen masks the main roof more effectively than the St-Denis battlements. In complete contrast to this matter-of-fact termination is the slightly later west front, the grandest Gothic façade begun during the 12th century [49]. Most of what distinguishes it from the transept front can be seen as the third Laon master's response to the tricky aesthetic problem of how to combine three large sculptured portals with a façade which has towers hardly wider than the nave aisles. Very wide towers of the St-Denis kind were rejected, perhaps on grounds of cost or perhaps because they would have been out of scale with the transept fronts. The Senlis west front had shown that side portals fitted between the buttresses of aisle-width towers were too small to carry important programmes of monumental sculpture. The problem disappeared in the High Gothic period when major churches became much larger, but the master of the Laon west front was obliged to work within the constraints imposed by a scheme decided on twenty-five to thirty years earlier.

His solution was to allocate as much as possible of the total width to the side portals, whose inner jambs are set in front of the high walls of the nave, the position ordinarily taken by the buttresses separating the side and middle portals. At Laon these buttresses take up a good part of the clear width of the central vessel and so prevent the middle portal from dwarfing the side portals. Accepting the fact that the vertical divisions in the portal and window zones would not tally, he used sleight-of-hand to disguise the disparity. Strong verticals were eliminated from the window zone by converting what on the north front had been simply buttresses into supports for deep tunnel-like embrasures framing the rose and the two large openings beside it. The masonry still functions as buttressing, but now one is encouraged to see it less as a feature in its own right than as intervals between the embrasures. The most important device for distracting attention from the disparate vertical divisions is the setting of the portals into porches which project so far forward that the front edges of their jambs appear, when viewed from the square before the cathedral, to be directly below the jambs of the three large window embrasures. The process of linking the two sets of verticals is completed by setting gargantuan pinnacles over the porch piers. To bring pinnacles and piers close together and thus give maximum value to the verticals in the portal zone, the porches are each endowed with a gable. The central gable also cuts the strong horizontal below the rose. Several of the innovations of these mighty porches were to be widely adopted in the next century, notably the three gables [cf. 62] and the pinnacles, among the first examples not forming part of a spire.

49 Laon Cathedral, west front, begun c. 1190–95. The oxen in the towers commemorate the beasts which appeared miraculously to haul stone for early 12th-century repairs to the previous cathedral.

The parts of the façade discussed so far give the impression of a single huge block tunnelled into by six cavernous recesses. Almost the only relief from the prevailing massiveness is provided by the rose, an ingenious amalgam of elements from the triforium oculi at Notre-Dame in Paris with a large cusped circle like those in the north rose at Laon [33, 38]. Above the rose a bold stepped string course marks the boundary between that part of the façade which functions as a plinth and that which is treated as a virtuoso exercise in structural openwork. The inspiration behind this dramatic contrast was undoubtedly St-Denis [23], but the south-west tower at Chartres [62] must be the source for the arrangement of openings in the main body of the towers and for the angled aedicules. The octagonal structures at the top of each angle seem to be based on the west tower of Notre-Dame at Etampes (c. 1160?), but no earlier example equals either the openness of the Laon towers or their diagonal emphasis, the latter a clear acknowledgment of the conditions under which towers are actually seen, and as such an interesting sequel to the exploitation of recession in the design of the portals. Laon Cathedral was intended to have no fewer than seven towers [37], but even with only five it evokes Sion, among whose towers the Psalmist enjoined his people to seek their God. To the precariously constituted town commune of Laon, and to the heavily taxed peasants working the bishop's rich lands, the towers probably spoke most eloquently of the temporal power and pride of the institutional church.

Early Gothic in England

Cultural affinity with northern France was the key factor in England's very early receptiveness to Gothic architecture. The language of the upper classes was French, from 1135 the country had been ruled by kings who wielded greater power in France than the French kings, and many of the higher clergy were either recruited from France or had very strong links there. The sources of the renewal of English architecture in the third quarter of the 12th century were the Ile-de-France, Picardy and French Flanders, the lands through which travellers from England normally approached Paris. Henry II's Continental dominions appear to have contributed nothing. In the case of Normandy this is perhaps rather surprising, for the duchy, like England, was receptive to Ile-de-France influences from the 1150s onwards. In Aquitaine Gothic was still unknown, while in Poitou, Anjou and Maine Gothic influences had not dislodged regional preferences for churches of simple format.

The introduction of the Gothic style into England was neither a single event nor a concerted and continuous process. It was rather a series of more or less disconnected episodes, only some of which had important consequences. Probably because no great church building was erected in the south-east until the mid-1170s – around two decades after the arrival of the first north French influences – the architecturally more productive north and south-west were enabled to develop autonomous traditions of Gothic great church design. Since these traditions remained vigorous until *c.* 1200, the discussion of late 12th-century England is divided into sections on each of the three regions. These are arranged in order of the dates at which the several versions of great church Gothic came into being.

Besides cultural openness towards France, the main circumstance which helped make the English receptive towards Gothic architectural ideas was the mid-12th-century lull following the post-Conquest 'boom' in great church building. Most of the comparatively few major projects undertaken between 1150 and 1190 owed their origin to accidental fires (Canterbury, Glastonbury) or to an increase in the importance of their patrons (Wells, Waltham). One rebuilding can be attributed to the inadequacy of the Romanesque church (York), a situation which recurred beyond England's borders in areas of Britain lacking a tradition of Romanesque great church building (St David's, St Andrews). Many wholly new churches were put up in the late 12th century by the reformed monastic orders, chiefly the Augustinians and Cistercians, but with very few exceptions their simplicity disqualifies them from consideration in this book. However, at least some of the churches which the Cistercians built in the north of England from about 1155 were Gothic, and these rank as the earliest examples of the style in the region.

The north

The Cistercians have long been hailed as 'missionaries of Gothic' on the strength of their having disseminated an elementary version of Gothic from the Burgundian homeland of the order to many areas of Europe previously unacquainted with the style. The relative uniformity of these simplified Gothic churches, as of their purely Romanesque predecessors, was due to the order's uniquely centralized structure, a structure designed to enforce adherence to its traditions of simplicity in all aspects of monastic observance, including architecture. However, the northern English Cistercians do not fit the general pattern, for they made use of a more evolved strain of Gothic than was known in the mother houses in Burgundy. Unfortunately it is not at all clear which of the many mid-12th-century Cistercian churches in the north of England served as the channel through which Gothic influences reached the region, since these buildings are fairly consistent in style and the documentary evidence for their dating is poor. What can be affirmed is that at least one northern Cistercian church must have been built in the Gothic style by the late 1150s, when the second phase of the now mostly destroyed choir of York Minster was begun in a hybrid northern French Gothic-cum-Burgundian Cistercian Romanesque manner. The presence of the Burgundian elements at York virtually proves that the northern English Cistercians were the medium by which both the architect and the Gothic elements of his design were transmitted, for if Archbishop Roger had summoned a French architect direct from France, he would surely have turned to one of the cathedral workshops, where such heavy Cistercian influence was inconceivable. On the other hand, it was all but inevitable that a French master recruited locally would have worked in a Cistercianized style, for the Cistercians were from c. 1150 by far the most important patrons of large-scale church building in the north. A parallel to York is provided by Avila Cathedral in Castile. Begun c. 1160 by an architect whose previous work must have been at Cistercian abbeys farther north, Avila's detailing is also a mixture of Burgundian Cistercian Romanesque and French Gothic. The parallel is not an exact one, however, for whereas the overall format of York followed English Romanesque precedent, that of Avila's east end derives from St-Denis. Further discussion of the style whose central monument was the York choir is best focused on its surviving near-copy, the choir of Ripon Minster [50]. Ripon served as a kind of subsidiary cathedral within the huge York diocese, and its main patron was also Archbishop Roger.

Comparison of the choir of Ripon with the nave of Durham [11] points up its very limited indebtedness to the Anglo-Norman tradition. The similarities which do exist are confined to the general scheme of the elevation and cause no serious dilution of the Gothic character of the design as a whole: the tallness of the main arcades, the thick walls of the upper storeys, the clearstorey passage which the thickness permits, and the triple arcades in front of the clearstorey passage. The only important element which places Ripon further than York from Durham is its false gallery with low and narrow openings. Ripon was to have resembled Durham in having rib vaults over every vessel, but only those over the aisles were actually built. In fact the latter owe nothing to the pointed-arched high vaults in the Durham nave, and their carefully coursed webs and consistently pointed ribs conform to French usage.

A comparison of Ripon with Laon [39] shows many detailed differences but also an essential kinship. They share the slenderness and wide spacing of the arcade piers, the resultant sense of openness between aisles and main vessel, the boldness of the high vault responds, the thinness of the main arcade arches and, above all, the fine-gauged tubular aspect of the arch mouldings as well as the shafts. The shallow transverse tunnel vaults linking the window wall of the clearstorey to its arcades find no place in the main elevations of Laon, but they had passed from Tournai into French Gothic architecture by c. 1160 (the likely starting date of the Noyon transepts) if not earlier. To accommodate the clearstorey passage both upper storeys at Ripon are given a thickness which is matched at Laon only by the triforium, but the thinness of the main arcade arches is preserved by means of the false bearing technique employed at Laon and many other 12th-century Gothic churches [41c]. The use of coursed masonry for the high vault responds instead of Laon's and Noyon's attached edge-bedded shafts enhances the ability of the thick upper walls to resist lateral thrusts from a stone vault without the aid of flying buttresses. The survival of thick-wall construction must provide most of the

50 Ripon Minster, north side of the choir, c. 1160–70 (glazing of the middle storey and other alterations to the right-hand bay, c. 1300; crossing arch, c. 1500). The stone high vault intended to spring from the unusually massive responds was omitted when work reached the clearstorey level, and a flat wooden ceiling was built instead. That was replaced c. 1300 by a wooden vault, of which the present vault is a 19th-century copy.

explanation for the general rarity of flyers in late 12th-century England.

Another feature of Ripon which looks like a French designer's concession to local usage is the profiling of the main arcades, similar in their general disposition to those in the west block at St-Denis [125a,g] and of a richness rarely found in France later than the St-Denis choir. Even more eccentric from the point of view of a French cathedral architect of c. 1160 are the simple block capitals and the piers. The latter are clusters of eight shafts with only the stepped arrangement of their abaci to recall the compound piers of the Norman and Anglo-Norman past [5, 11], a resemblance which may have commended them to English patrons. What is certain is that they represent a decisive rejection of the French Gothic columnar pier in favour of something more visually consonant with the rest of the elevations. Block capitals are legion in Cistercian buildings, but clustered piers are rare in northern France, and most of the few known examples occur in ancillary buildings rather than in churches. On the evidence available, which may well have been seriously distorted by the destruction of most northern French Cistercian abbeys, it seems that the clustered pier was first introduced into churches at two Premonstratensian abbeys in Picardy, Selincourt and Dommartin, the latter begun in 1153. Relations between the Premonstratensians and the Cistercians were extremely close in all matters, and their Picard houses were probably visited by English Cistercian abbots travelling to and from the annual General Chapters held at the order's chief house of Cîteaux near Dijon. Clustered piers were to remain for two hundred years the standard type of support in the northern English great church.

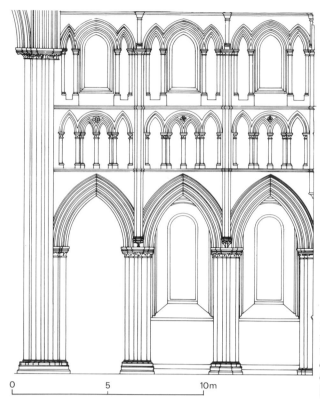

51 Byland Abbey, reconstruction of the south transept east elevation, *c.* 1170–80. The clearstorey carried a wooden tunnel vault [cf. *128*].

Around 1170 work began at Byland Abbey near York on the most ambitious 12th-century Cistercian church in Europe [*51*]. Why it did not cause a scandal within the order is as mysterious as the motivation behind such un-Cistercian magnificence. The importance of Byland in the stylistic development of northern English Gothic is that it represents an anglicizing of Ripon. After the substitution of a wooden ceiling for the intended high vaults, Ripon was already far closer to English Romanesque norms than had been intended originally, but at Byland, which was begun without any intention of vaulting in stone, the implications of this departure from French usage could be followed through. All the openings of the clearstorey now rise to the wall head, and the vault shafts have become mere wall shafts, demarcaters of the bays. The triple shafts between the bays are all thinner than the single ones in the corners of the main vessels, whereas the shafts in the bulky clusters at Ripon correspond exactly to the number, arrangement and sizes of the ribs of the intended vault. The reduction of the shafts in gauge and number shifts the emphasis away from the vertical succession of arches within each bay and onto the horizontal band-like character of the storeys. A further instance of backtracking on the French scheme of Ripon, and one which enhances the longitudinal integrity of each storey, is the thickening and enriching of the main arcades to the point where they rival the effects of depth and layering in the clearstorey and false gallery.

Probably because it acclimatized Ripon's French innovations, Byland became the fountainhead of a whole 'school' of Gothic in northern England

and Scotland during the last quarter of the 12th century. Its deep arcades, banded upper storeys and token bay divisions were reproduced almost line for line in the choir at Tynemouth and the nave of Old Malton (both *c.* 1190), and its influence in the early 13th century can be traced in the eastern parts of Hexham, Whitby, Beverley [*129*] and Glasgow [*128*] and in the transepts at York and Rievaulx, although in some of these buildings the false galleries incorporate the large single arches which the choir of York had taken over from the Anglo-Norman tradition.

The south-west

The contribution made unintentionally by the Cistercians to northern great church architecture was one of the long-term effects of the devastation of the region wrought by William the Conqueror in 1069–70, the so-called 'harrying of the north'; for when recovery finally came in the early and mid-12th century, it was the reformed orders and not the Benedictines who were finding favour with patrons. In south-west England, to a much greater extent than in the north, the Cistercians had to rub shoulders with other monastic orders. Unfortunately, the total destruction of their mid-12th-century churches makes it impossible to know whether they resembled their northern brethren in being pioneers of a regional Gothic manner. Some evidence that they did play such a role survives in the ruins of the earliest known example of south-western Gothic, the church of the abbey of Keynsham near Bristol, probably begun in 1166. Keynsham had as its co-founder Roger, bishop of Worcester, a circumstance which must explain the use of identical detailing in the rebuilding of the west end of Worcester Cathedral, apparently after the collapse of one of its Romanesque towers in 1175 [*52*]. This is one of the earliest of the many Gothic additions to English Romanesque churches whose dimensions, structure and proportions derived from the old bays to which they were joined [cf. *145*]. Given the opportunity to build a complete new cathedral, it is more than likely that the architect of Worcester's west bays would have built higher and with a less prominent middle storey. But this was probably the first large-scale Gothic work in the south-west, and its failure to dislodge the traditional premises of great church design seems to have encouraged later exponents of the style to devise their own compromises between traditional and innovatory formats. Where Worcester did give a clear lead was in the realm of surface articulation and decoration.

It is far from obvious what kind of French Gothic the Worcester master knew, for his sources are completely reworked in the service of a highly personal vision. The triple openings of the triforium recall the choir galleries at St-Germer-de-Fly, the full-length vault shafts are reminiscent of Parisian work of the 1130s and 1140s, and the extreme attenuation of shafts and arch mouldings suggests direct or indirect knowledge of Notre-Dame in Paris. Yet this wirily linear scheme encompasses many details drawn from recent and not so recent Romanesque architecture in the vicinity of Worcester. The arches formed of continuous roll mouldings uninterrupted by capitals can be seen in the early 12th-century chapter house at Worcester; arches enclosed within higher arches of the same width like those on the Worcester triforium occur at Gloucester Cathedral (begun 1089) and Malmesbury Abbey (begun c. 1145–55); and at Malmesbury and Keynsham there are even parallels for the extraordinary icing-like wall bosses on the tympana of the triforium. Like the neo-Antique columns of St-Denis or the Anglo-Norman galleries in the York choir, Worcester's Romanesque elements show how old ideas re-presented alongside new ones could unexpectedly acquire a new lease of life. In most of the south-western and Welsh churches influenced by Worcester, notably St David's Cathedral (begun 1181) and Glastonbury Abbey (begun soon after 1184), the Romanesque element is increased. The great exception to this is Wells Cathedral.

There can be little doubt that the rebuilding of St Andrew's, Wells from c. 1180 was part of a plan to make it the centre of the diocese of Somerset in place of Bath Abbey. Full cathedral status came only in the early 13th century, a development which the existence of a partly completed cathedral-like church would have aided. The dating evidence for the new building is poor, but it seems clear that the revised design implemented in the nave was drawn up some time during the 1190s. As at Worcester, a thick wall structure is overlaid by fine-drawn tubular arch mouldings and shafts so elongated as to lose their columnar plasticity [55]. A distinctive trait of Wells is the triplication of all shafts, even in contexts where single shafts would be normal. The clustered piers substituted at York, Ripon and Byland for the French columnar pier are attributable to the same quest for purely formal coherence, but the Wells master was prepared to take his eschewal of columns to the point of completely eliminating shafts from the clearstorey and triforium. With him it seems to have been an article of faith that shafts, even in attenuated guise, were properly used only in conjunction with major supporting elements. He relented a little in the end elevations of the transepts [54], though it is possible that the shafts between the lower windows were introduced for the sake of making this level match the arcades opening through the east wall of the choir, for the present 14th-century east arcade shows a similarly sparing use of shafts [151]. The Wells master's aversion to columns was probably in part a reaction against south-western Romanesque, whose hallmark was the columnar pier in a particularly massive form.

As was noted above, Wells is almost completely devoid of Romanesque ornaments. There are no chevron-decorated arches and no scallop capitals, and the only important elements of local Romanesque origin, the continuously moulded arches on the upper storeys, are those least incompatible with Gothic aesthetics. What inspired this purge of Romanesque motifs? Clearly the Wells master must have known that they were of much earlier origin than the Gothic ornaments, and it is likely that he was old

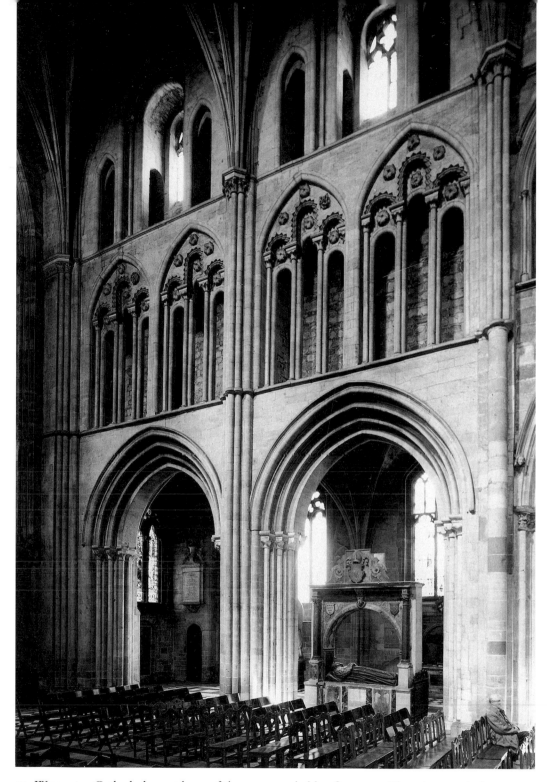

52 Worcester Cathedral, west bays of the nave, probably after 1175. The minor capitals have Romanesque scallop designs whereas the vault respond capitals have Early Gothic foliage carving. The use of coursed rather than attached shafts is characteristic of late 12th-century south-western English Gothic.

enough to remember the advent of the new style in the south-west. Whether or not it was the destroyed south-western Cistercian churches which were his introduction to Gothic, the possibility cannot be excluded that his purism owed something to the Cistercians. Another possible incentive to banish Romanesque survivals was the desire not to be outdone by the French-designed choir of Canterbury (below, pp. 84–90). The prime mover behind the rebuilding of Wells, Bishop Reginald FitzJocelin, had personally witnessed the burning of the old choir at Canterbury in 1174, and was too familiar with northern France not to be aware that chevron and scallop capitals were passé. Specific debts to Canterbury are difficult to pinpoint, and the only more or less obvious examples are the large depressed arch framing the upper lancets of the transept end walls [54], which looks like a non-columnar version of the analogous parts of the eastern transepts at Canterbury, and the general arrangement of openings in the upper storeys of the lateral elevations, which recalls nothing in 12th-century English

53 Wells Cathedral, from the north: Lady Chapel, ambulatory and east part of the choir c. 1320–40; west part of the choir, c. 1180–90; crossing tower, early 14th-century and mid-15th-century; transepts and nave, c. 1180–1240; upper parts of the west towers, late 14th-century and early 15th-century. In the foreground are the chapter house, completed c. 1304, and the hall and houses of the vicars choral (priests who fulfilled the choir duties of absent canons); in the background is the bishop's palace. The spacious precincts of many English cathedrals were established during the early Middle Ages when population pressure was generally much less intense than in Continental towns.

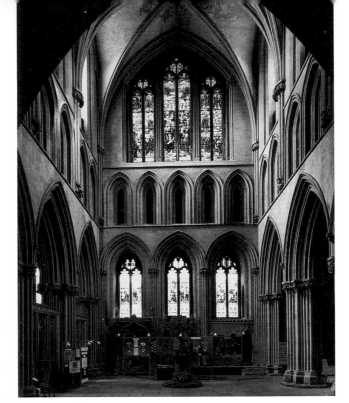

54 Wells Cathedral, south
transept, c. 1180–90
(tracery 15th-century).
The piers are cruciform in
plan with triple shafts on
the ends and in the angles.

architecture so much as the narrow eastern bay of the liturgical choir at
Canterbury [59]. Of course neither of these borrowings makes Wells look
remotely like Canterbury. If the Wells master had inspected for himself the
work of William of Sens he either disliked most of what he saw or decided it
was too alien to be assimilated.

Although the interior of Wells must have been impressively unified before
the shoring arches were inserted into the crossing in the 14th century, one
major adjustment was made to the original designs as carried out in the choir
and transepts. The latter |54| achieve an easy balance not only between
verticals and horizontals but also between the upper and lower registers: the
clearstorey is practically as high as the arcade and the high vault responds are
as tall as the arcade piers. In the nave [55], the vault responds are virtually
eliminated from the triforium in order to make way for extra arches which
line up with the others to form continuous bands running unbroken from the
crossing to the west wall. Their rapid rhythm is as even as, and still more
insistent than, the slower stride of the main arcades. Transverse divisions in
the structure of the nave are acknowledged only by the dwarf responds to the
high vault, barely a third as long as their counterparts in the transepts.
Presumably the intention behind this unique stressing of the triforium at the
expense of bay divisions was to dramatize the tunnel-like vistas traditional in
the long naves of English great churches. The change can also be viewed as a
reversion to the Romanesque banded elevation comparable to that already
encountered at Byland [51]. The actual source of the continuous arcading

with short vault shafts sprouting from its spandrels was almost certainly the mid-12th-century chapter house at St Augustine's, Bristol, where the curtailing of the shafts is justified by the function of the arcading as seats. There are also precedents for very short vault responds in the main vessels of great churches, among them the choir of Durham. From a French standpoint it is no doubt an egregious solecism that the shortest shafts in the nave receive the largest arches, the ribs of the high vault.

In recent years Wells Cathedral has attracted two rival and seemingly irreconcilable interpretations. According to one, it is merely a Romanesque thick-wall structure converted by the application of ornament into a superficial semblance of a Gothic design. The other holds that it is the earliest building in Europe to shed completely all Roman or Romanesque survivals. There is some truth in both views. Precedents for almost all aspects of the structure can indeed be found in Anglo-Norman Romanesque architecture, but since thick walls continued in use in England throughout the Middle Ages, the French thin wall technique can hardly be regarded as a satisfactory touchstone for Gothic on the English side of the Channel. The aesthetic gulf that separates Wells from the Anglo-Norman tradition can be gauged by comparing *11* and *55*. That the differences are almost all to do with the modelling of surfaces does not make them less significant than if they concerned the structural design. Regarding the suggestion that Wells is more Gothic than contemporary French churches, it must be acknowledged that Ile-de-France Gothic did not become so consistently linear and non-columnar until the 1230s [*80*]. However, since many of the innovations of Wells were to make way during the early 13th century for French ideas emanating from Canterbury, over-emphasis of the precocity of Wells could easily lead to the bizarre conclusion that English architecture of the next generation became less Gothic as a result of exposure to renewed influence from France.

The south-east

Compared to the south-west and the north, south-eastern England saw almost no major church building in the third quarter of the 12th century. There were neither the wide open spaces for the Cistercians to colonize nor major institutions whose churches did not adequately reflect their pretensions. The oldest Gothic survivals in the region are not great churches, although the elevations of both could readily have been adapted for large-scale use had the occasion arisen. In fact neither the circular nave of the Temple Church in London (in use by 1161) nor the far less purely French choir of the hospital of St Cross in Winchester (begun *c.* 1161) was well placed to exert important influences, for both were essentially private

55 Wells Cathedral, nave, begun *c.* 1190 (shoring arches inserted under the crossing *c.* 1338). The extension of the clearstorey openings below the springing level of the vault is extremely rare in the 12th century [cf. *29*].

churches away from the public gaze. Nevertheless, both are interesting in the present context as evidence of the region's early receptiveness to French ideas, in particular to an idea not mentioned so far, the use of dark polished marble shafts.

When the choir of the cathedral priory of Christ Church, Canterbury was gutted by fire in September 1174, it did not take the monks long to realize that this disaster presented them with an extraordinary opportunity. The murder in the cathedral of Archbishop Thomas Becket in 1170 made Christ Church the centre of a spectacularly successful relic cult, even before Becket's formal canonization in 1173. In his lifetime the archbishop had not been well disposed towards the priory, but the martyred Becket brought the monks enormous benefits, not only great wealth but a sense of having recovered what they believed to be their rightful place at the centre of English religious affairs. Around 1188, when their pre-eminence was under threat from Archbishop Baldwin, they commissioned one of their number, Gervase, to write a history of the monastery whose most remarkable passages are the descriptions of the Romanesque churches and the year-by-year account of the rebuilding which he himself had witnessed. Although he was writing ostensibly to promote the greater glory of his house, Gervase was clearly deeply interested in the building for its own sake. For us his text has supreme rarity value as the only detailed contemporary account of a major medieval building project, but his work is impressive by the standards of any period. Gervase's powers of observation were highly developed, and though laconic he is almost invariably accurate and precise; no modern investigator of the building has been able to prove him wrong on any important point, although by his own admission his explanations are not comprehensive. Perhaps the most remarkable and reassuringly 'modern' attitudes displayed by Gervase are his admiration of the technical, artistic and diplomatic skills of the French architect, William of Sens, and his enthusiasm for the innovatory aspects of the building, which he tellingly contrasts with the old work damaged in the fire. Such unreserved celebration of human advance is very rare in a medieval writer and contrasts strikingly with the hostility to innovation normally displayed by medieval clerical authors. No doubt this aspect of Gervase's work is attributable mainly to the absence of ancient 'authorities' for architecture comparable to those presiding over subjects more regularly written about in the Middle Ages. There is no need to stress how different are the emphases of Suger's and Gervase's texts, but it is worth noting that the Englishman wrote not a word on the symbolism of the building.

According to Gervase the monks hoped at first to reinstate the choir as it had been before the fire. Their reaction was understandable, as this was a very lavishly decorated building and also fairly new, having been begun in the time of Prior Ernulf (1096–1113) and consecrated in 1130. Although a purely Romanesque design, Ernulf's choir possesses great significance for English

Gothic architecture as it was the earliest example of what became a common solution to the problem of the inadequate size of the eastern arms of most great churches built immediately after the Norman Conquest. The transepts and nave of the cathedral begun in 1069 were left intact, but its short choir was replaced by a far longer one providing ample space both for the choir stalls of the growing community of monks and for the shrines of the great throng of sainted but only recently rehabilitated pre-Conquest archbishops. Previously the monks' stalls had stood under the central tower, the usual place in the 11th century, and their removal into the new addition had the aesthetic merit of disencumbering the crossing. Although the new east arm was three times longer than the old one, the walls and roof of its main vessel were kept exactly level with those of the old transepts and nave to which they were joined. Hereafter it was quickly accepted as normal in England that major Romanesque churches would acquire eastern extensions more modern in style than their western parts but equal or nearly equal in height [145]. No-one would have failed to grasp the symbolism underlying the juxtaposition of modern, richly finished choirs reserved to the clergy and older simpler western parts accessible to the laity. Of course naves and transepts were often rebuilt later, as at Canterbury, but such campaigns were generally self-contained, for heterogeneity had become the established

56 Canterbury Cathedral from the south-east. From right to left: east part of the Trinity Chapel (the Corona), 1180–84; west part of the Trinity Chapel (St Thomas's Chapel), 1179–84 (note the 'squeezing' due to the retention of the Romanesque radiating chapels); presbytery, reconstructed 1179–84; eastern transepts, remodelled 1177–9; liturgical choir, remodelled 1175–7 (note the abutting walls protruding through the gallery roof); western transepts, 15th-century; crossing tower, c. 1433–1503; nave, begun by 1378; south-west tower, early 15th-century; north-west tower, early 19th-century.

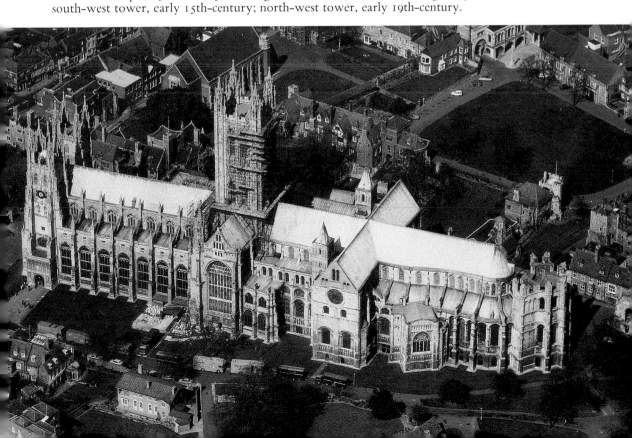

English norm. Complete rebuilding schemes were undertaken only very rarely.

William of Sens eventually succeeded in persuading the monks of Christ Church that the high walls of the main east-west vessel were too badly damaged to be repaired. The new central vessel would be built within the old aisle walls and over the crypt, which had survived the fire unscathed. The unaisled eastern transepts were to be kept, but refaced internally and raised. It was apparently foreseen that Becket's relics were to be enshrined in the place of honour behind the high altar in a specially built eastern extension, but since the relics were safe on their original site in the axial chapel of the crypt, it was decided to begin at the west with the liturgical choir [59]. Here William of Sens's resourcefulness was tested under conditions without parallel in France. Not only was the spacing of the piers dictated by that of the crypt supports, but the height was severely limited by the retention of the Romanesque crossing tower to the west. The small increase in height gained, which is represented by the clearstorey of the new work, brought the total internal height to 21m, the same as that of the Romanesque nave. This is respectable by English standards but lower than any of the French buildings discussed in this chapter except Senlis and the choir of St-Denis. In combination with the prodigious length of the choir, which at 92m was almost as long externally as the whole central vessel of Sens Cathedral is internally, the restricted height perpetuated the English tradition of long low vistas.

William's use of the height available to him is odd. On top of the old aisle walls he added an extra tier of windows which brings the height of the main arcades to around sixty per cent of the elevation. A four-storey design was clearly out of the question, and even the two upper storeys as built look distinctly hunched above the leggy arcades. Comparably distended arcades and compacted upper storeys were planned for the nave of St-Denis and actually built from c. 1170 at the now destroyed northern French cathedral of Arras. Arras and St-Remi in Reims [43] parallel the springing of the high vault from below the base of the clearstorey. This and the short vault responds, which are not found at Arras or Reims, are abnormal in French terms but, as was mentioned in relation to Wells, they conform to Anglo-Norman usage. Even more clear-cut cases of concessions to local taste are two features reproduced from the old choir, the alternately circular and octagonal piers in the liturgical choir and the clearstorey incorporating a wall passage and open arcades [cf. 11]. The clearstorey was William's single greatest deviation from French convention, and it would be interesting to know how willingly he adopted what Gervase indicates was an admired feature. The robustly eclectic attitude to precedent apparent in the rest of the design suggests that it did not cause him too much heartache.

57 Canterbury Cathedral, choir, 1175–84. This is the most important of the very few major Gothic buildings not conceived as a series of uniform bays. Its character changes in accordance with a west-east progression from less to more prestigious functions: liturgical choir, presbytery, shrine chapel. The piers become first more complex, then of richer materials, the floor level rises, and the lighting increases.

58 Canterbury Cathedral, Trinity Chapel. Until its destruction in 1538, the shrine of St Thomas Becket occupied much of the floor area of the central vessel. The French-made foliage capitals are among the finest of their period.

The paired units in the middle storey of the liturgical choir [59] recall the false galleries postulated for St-Denis and their probable derivatives at Sens [31], St-Germain-des-Prés and Vézelay [29]. The north side of the choir has a false gallery, but this was a departure from the original scheme, which envisaged a proper windowed gallery like that actually completed on the south side. Despite the unique shallowness of the arches to the gallery openings, William managed to fit them in front of obtusely pointed transverse tunnel vaults carried across the galleries on shallow segmental arches. This distinctly archaic form of abutment was otherwise used in the Early Gothic period only at Mantes, west of Paris (c. 1175). The south gallery at Canterbury has of necessity an extremely low-pitched roof which, to a less determined pragmatist than William, would have ruled out steep triangular abutting walls like those at Laon [41c]. Nevertheless such walls are included between the transverse tunnel vaults, with only their uppermost parts visible above the gallery roof [56]. At Arras too flyers were rejected in favour of high abutting walls, but there at least their whole depth was visible externally and the contrast with the pitch of the gallery roofs was less extreme.

Arras and two other lost great churches of the French far north, Notre-Dame in Valenciennes and Cambrai Cathedral, were formative influences on William. They shared a trait not now represented in a major French Gothic church, namely the use of shafts of dark limestone polished to look like marble. Well before Gothic had penetrated this region, Tournai was a centre for the manufacture of architectural components and church fittings in a hard blue-black limestone named after the city. As was mentioned earlier, the taste for dark shiny shafts reached English shores at least twenty years before William of Sens. At Canterbury Cathedral itself, the cloister and other buildings had been rebuilt using differently coloured polished stones during

59 Canterbury Cathedral,
liturgical choir looking north-west.

the 1160s. The stones used in the Gothic choir do not include Tournai. Most shafts appear to be fossiliferous limestone from Purbeck on the south coast of England. The vogue for 'marble' before 1174 seems to have been fairly limited, and it was undoubtedly the Canterbury choir which established dark polished shafts among the indispensable trappings of the great church in 13th-century England. The success which this and other atypical French features were to enjoy would probably have surprised William had he remained in England after his crippling fall from the scaffolding in 1179.

At the time of William's accident, the liturgical choir, the eastern transepts and the presbytery (the four bays east of the crossing) stood complete except for the high vaults over the presbytery and the outer transept bays. East of the liturgical choir William was experimenting, especially in the piers of the presbytery, which present a whole series of variations on the theme of freestone piers and attached marble shafts [57]. The carousel of shafts round the crossing piers may have been based on such recent designs as the piers in the nave aisles at Notre-Dame in Paris (c. 1175), but the presbytery piers were almost certainly inventions of William's, for he twice revised them during construction. The other chief innovation of the presbytery is the introduction of fully exposed flying buttresses, the début of the form in England [56]. Compared to the roughly contemporary flyers at St-Remi [42] these are cautious affairs, for they hug the slope of the aisle roofs and are built only one stone deep. It is hard to believe that either they or the segmental arches traversing the aisle roof spaces are as important for the abutment of the high vault as the thick upper walls and their conventional buttresses. The lateral thrusts from the high vaults at Canterbury are in any case far less than usual because the vault webs are built of tufa, an open-textured volcanic stone much lighter than most building stones.

William of Sens was succeeded by William the Englishman, who built Becket's shrine chapel, the Trinity Chapel [58]. Since this part of the church owes nothing to earlier English buildings and virtually everything to the same kind of French sources as those used in the choir and eastern transepts, there must be a very good chance that the Englishman was working largely from designs formulated by the first William before his return to France. Some of the main differences are not stylistic but symbolic. Such are the raised floor level and the doubling of the clearstorey windows, both of which can be proved to be departures from William of Sens's designs [56]. The height of the floor clearly signified Becket's elevation to the company of holy martyrs, and the brilliant light shed by these double windows and their far larger counterparts in the aisles was a reflection of the spiritual effulgence of the relics which gave the Trinity Chapel its *raison d'être*. An almost theatrical playing up of the contrast with the more restricted lighting of the presbytery is evident in the extension of the window openings to within about a metre of the floor, although St-Denis as it stood in the 1170s paralleled the low window sills and the contrast in light levels and floor levels between the shrine area and the presbytery. The desire to enhance the general visibility of these veritable window-walls from the shrine area would account for the elimination of solid jambs in favour of a high wall passage and also for the selection of narrow but deep twin-column piers on the Sens pattern. The presence of the shrine determines not only the subject matter of the glass in the windows – the posthumous miracles wrought by Becket's intervention – but also the materials of the inner columns, rare cream and pink stones symbolizing Becket's virginity and martyrdom and also the brains and blood spilt at his death. The one major feature of this scintillating ensemble that can be seen as embodying a purely stylistic progression from William of Sens's work is the triforium, an enriched version of the third storey at Laon [39] and perhaps the earliest example in a great church of the banded passage triforium soon to be adopted in France as the normal kind of middle storey [60, 68].

The Canterbury choir was England's first encounter with full-dress French cathedral Gothic, and its magnificence as well as its association with Becket virtually ensured that the response among English patrons would be favourable. But Canterbury was an end as well as a beginning, for William of Sens was apparently the last of the handful of French architects who found employment across the Channel in the later 12th century, and the completion of work under his successor brought to a close the relatively short period of English receptiveness to French Gothic ideas. Moreover, Canterbury did not become the fountainhead of a new Gothic movement in quite the same way as St-Denis had been. Its bewildering profusion of ideas immediately underwent a filtering process at the hands of its English admirers, and it was out of their work that the main streams of early 13th-century English Gothic arose.

CHAPTER II

Thirteenth-century Gothic

THE INFLUENCE of northern French architecture abroad was already considerable by 1200, as we have seen in the preceding chapter, but starting in the second and third decades of the 13th century its international prestige began to grow in proportion to that of the kingdom of France itself. A prerequisite for the emergence of the French crown as the foremost power in the West was the extension of the king's rule to almost the whole of the area of modern France. The unexpected death of Richard I of England in 1199 opened the way to Philip II's conquest of Normandy and Anjou from 1204, and within a decade these successes were followed by the launching of the crusade against the Albigensian heretics in the south, a pretext for the intrusion of royal power into a region where it had not been felt for centuries. Old cultural allegiances were not displaced overnight in these newly acquired lands, as their contrasting responses to Gothic architecture testify, but the foundations of France as one nation had been effectively laid.

France's 13th-century kings were on the whole circumspect in their relations with other major powers. However, after the death of Louis IX in 1272, expansionist tactics on the northern and eastern borders were accompanied by increasing pressure on the papacy, culminating in the removal of the papal court to Avignon in 1306. Although the French kings benefited from this association, so blatant a suborning of the highest spiritual office had already begun by *c*. 1300 to erode Western Christendom's sense of common purpose, something which the greatest 12th- and 13th-century popes had successfully fostered. Fear of French imperialism may well have contributed to France's loss of leadership in architecture after *c*. 1270. Even by the early 13th century there was a widespread perception of the typical northern Frenchman as a chauvinist, unshakeable in his certainty of the superiority of all things French. No doubt the international currency of French Gothic architecture had contributed to the formation of this self-image.

Another point of pride with the French in the 13th century was their wealth. The imposition of direct royal rule on most of France proved very beneficial to the economy, for it facilitated both internal and external trading and enabled the kings to intervene in various ways to promote the development of the towns. Military considerations were probably paramount in Philip II's improvements to the road between Amiens and Paris but they had the effect of opening up the capital to Amiens-made cloth and

Picard corn, and no doubt helped make Paris seem the obvious place to recruit an architect for the rebuilding of the cathedral from 1220. The cathedral chapter at Amiens enjoyed good relations with the rich burgesses of the town, and it appears to have been the support of the latter that enabled the first phase of work on the new church to proceed very rapidly. Certainly the lack of such support at Reims, where chapter-town relations were extremely bad, was a great hindrance to the building of the cathedral there. However, the central element in the financing of a cathedral was normally the chapter's own income from its lands. By around 1180 the agrarian economy of northern France was burgeoning, with more land under cultivation than ever before, and in the period c. 1190–1230 schemes of rebuilding were inaugurated by every cathedral chapter in the region which had not already committed itself during the late 12th century. Confidence generated by economic boom conditions must provide much of the explanation for the most obvious characteristic of the 13th-century French cathedrals, their gigantic size.

In the chronology of Gothic architecture the 13th century is not an arbitrary division but a real and distinct period. From c. 1200 northern French cathedral design underwent a renewal which culminated in the 1230s with the creation of the Rayonnant style, a version of Gothic more long-lived than any of its predecessors and also far more often used for major new projects outside northern France. By 1300 the era of French leadership was drawing to a close, at least in the areas of Europe most productive of great churches, and Rayonnant was beginning to be supplanted by a series of more or less autonomous national and regional Late Gothic styles. A further justification for treating the 13th century as an entity is the fact that a pan-European subdivision into shorter periods is impossible to achieve without doing violence to the diversity and richness of Gothic outside its place of origin. To categorize as High Gothic the styles of great church architecture current during the early 13th century in England, Normandy or Burgundy simply because they came into being around the same time as northern French High Gothic would imply a degree of indebtedness which did not actually exist and would also tend to encourage dismissal of their later phases, which overlapped with the early Rayonnant period, as 'provincial' or 'retardataire'. Similarly, later 13th-century architecture in Western Europe as a whole can only be called Rayonnant if one is prepared to play down the regional influences which coloured and in some cases transformed what had begun as a Parisian style. Brief and incomplete though it was, the European ascendancy of Rayonnant nevertheless ranks as the pivotal epoch in the history of Gothic.

French High Gothic

The term 'High Gothic' as used in English and French writing on medieval architecture embodies a construct of at best doubtful merit. The adjective 'high' is part of a value judgment which places the very different cathedrals of Chartres, Reims, Amiens and Bourges at the peak of French Gothic, and which sees the greater homogeneity of the Rayonnant phase as a symptom of decline. Thus High Gothic is acclaimed as an architecture of individuality and pioneering vigour whereas Rayonnant is stigmatized as repetitive and over-refined. This interpretation, a product of the modernist privileging of 'primitive' over 'classic' phases of art, has to be set aside if one is to reach an understanding of 13th-century architecture which is rooted in history. It is obvious that the diversity of the High Gothic cathedrals was due not to exploratory striving for its own sake but to the fact that none of the solutions thrown up before *c.* 1230 was found sufficiently impressive to be accorded the status of a model for general imitation. By the same token, the much greater uniformity and longevity of Rayonnant within northern France suggest not creative stagnation so much as unanimous approbation from patrons and their architects. Taking into account the view presented in the last chapter that Early Gothic is a comparatively unchanging style, the High Gothic period can be recognized as one of unresolved experimentation, a brief transition between two much longer and more productive eras.

It is not difficult to see why art historians have tended to overrate High Gothic. Chartres, Reims, Amiens and Bourges each present better than any other 13th-century French church a coherent and comprehensive image of the Gothic cathedral, for they were carried out more or less in accordance with their original architects' intentions, and they received a full complement of sculpture and stained glass. By the time they were nearing completion, opportunities to build new cathedrals from scratch were rapidly drying up in northern France, and most of the region's outstanding examples of great church architecture in the Rayonnant style were partial rebuildings or completions of schemes begun in the High Gothic period. Another factor working in favour of High Gothic and against Rayonnant is the nature of history writing itself. Chartres, Reims and Amiens make a good story because together they form an exceptionally clear and satisfying developmental sequence. The formal development of Rayonnant, on the other hand, is not nearly so dramatic, being less a linear evolution than a rather subtle process of diversification which is difficult to summarize. This puts Rayonnant at a disadvantage, for all too easily the historian's narration of stylistic change entails the presumption that constant radical innovation is the hallmark of a healthy artistic tradition. In brisk surveys such as this, a preoccupation with large-scale evolutionary patterns is almost unavoidable, but it tends to foster the impression that an artist's main business is formal invention as an end in itself rather than problem solving or responding to the needs of the patron. Despite these reservations, and in order to discuss early 13th-century French Gothic outside the Ile-de-France before broaching the Rayonnant style, Chartres and its immediate successors will be discussed in the traditional way as part of a distinct period, rather than as a transition towards the near-definitive solution represented by the reconstruction of St-Denis from 1231.

It seems providential that the only 13th-century cathedral to have preserved virtually all its original stained glass is Chartres, where this medium first achieved unchallenged dominance in the central vessels of a great church [60]. The prime examples of Early Gothic churches retaining most of their glass point up the originality of Chartres in this respect: St-Remi in Reims, where the glazing of the long windows lighting the gallery can hardly be seen at all from the central vessel [43]; and Canterbury, where the recessing of the clearstorey openings makes the glass invisible from most diagonal viewpoints [57]. Even more fundamental to the achievement of visibility for the glass at Chartres than its setting close to the front plane of the elevation is the height of the clearstorey, the tallest of any built hitherto. The Chartres master could simply have grafted his enormous upper windows onto one of the established Early Gothic formats, but he chose instead to make them the starting point for a complete rethinking of the premises of Gothic cathedral design. The gallery is omitted, and the notional space thus vacated is shared out between the clearstorey and arcade, with the result that the tiered effect of 12th-century Gothic elevations is abolished [cf. 39]. The band triforium and its wall passage are retained but now function formally as an intermediary between the depth of the aisles and the flatness of the clearstorey. The loss of complexity is a gain in consistency, for the two main storeys of the lateral elevations are made up of arched units as tall in their proportions as the main vessel itself. The clearstorey has become the clear storey *par excellence*, the unchallenged climax of the interior. Our attention is irresistibly drawn to it, partly because the cusped oculi it contains are the only significant decoration in the elevations, but mainly because it is the most important source of lighting. The symbolic value of this illumination from on high is underscored by the arrangement of the stained glass: huge haloed figures of the saints gathered into the company of heaven in the clearstorey; detailed narrations of saints' earthly lives in the lower and smaller windows of the aisles. From the 14th century, if not earlier, churches which adopted the immense windows invented at Chartres were being called 'lanterns', an image surely intended to evoke not only the light emitted from between the bars of a lantern but also the role of the saints as spiritual beacons.

There are several late 12th-century designs which might have inspired the high clearstorey and three-storey elevation of Chartres, but none of them is so similar as to reduce the Chartres master's creative leap to an easy step. Most of the few earlier examples of three-storey elevations incorporating a band triforium are monastic churches in the vicinity of Laon: St-Yved at Braine, St-Vincent in Laon (destroyed) and St-Michel-en-Thiérache. Some or all of these buildings would have been known to the Chartres master since the Laonnois was evidently his training ground, but it is important to remember that the same scheme had already been made acceptable as a basis for great

60 Chartres Cathedral, nave looking north-west, *c.* 1194–1220. The central shaft on the crossing pier, which lacks a proper capital, was originally intended to rise into one of the corners of a lantern tower like that at Laon [*38*].

church architecture by its use in the later parts of the eastern arm at Canterbury [58], a building which the Chartres master knew either personally or through drawings. Yet none of these churches anticipates the elongated proportions of Chartres or the extension of its clearstorey windows below the springing level of the high vault. One of the very few Early Gothic examples of such an extension is in the choir at Vézelay [29], which may in this as in many other things reflect the choir of St-Denis. But even if the lost clearstorey of St-Denis did not extend below the vault springings, it must have played a far greater role than the clearstoreys of galleried churches such as Laon, a fact which suggests that the clearstorey-dominated interior of Chartres was to some extent conceived as a return to the original principles of Gothic. Nevertheless, Laon may have made an important contribution, for the arrangement of openings in the transept and nave façades there [37, 49] contradicts the four-storey structure of the body of the church and implies a high clearstorey and three-level elevation. The rose in the north transept façade at Laon is surely the actual prototype for the oculi of the Chartres clearstorey, and possibly also for the concept of oculus and twin lancets grouped to form a single composition, though in this respect it is less compelling than the windows of the bishop's chapel at Noyon [48]. The largest oculi seen hitherto in the lateral elevations of a Gothic church, those in the 'triforium' of Notre-Dame in Paris, seem in comparison mere adventitious ornaments, over-emphasizing an unimportant part of the elevation [33]; it is not surprising that the influence of Chartres led to their replacement in the early 13th century by windows which enhance rather than impede the verticality of the rest of the design. By allotting such a central role to the clearstorey the Chartres master had virtually ensured that further inventiveness would be focused on this area.

A lesser mind than the Chartres master might have been content to assemble elevations out of enlarged and elongated versions of the equivalent parts of Early Gothic designs. This process accounts for only the triforium; everything else is reworked so as to emphasize the tallness of the proportions and the dominance of the clearstorey. The supports are no longer obstinately self-contained classicizing columns but adaptations of the piers flanking the high altar at Canterbury [57], in which the attached marble shafts of the originals are replaced by shafts forming part of the same courses as the core. The main aesthetic value of the Chartres pier design consists in its greater verticality, especially in relation to the high vault responds. The omission of a capital from each of the shafts below the high vault responds is a perfunctory though effective way of securing the floor-to-vault continuity which had eluded the designer of the eastern nave bays at Laon [39]. The use of quadripartite vaults is also explicable in terms of the Chartres master's preoccupation with verticality, for their thick transverse ribs link every opposite pair of responds and so form heavily stressed transverse divisions which articulate the central vessels as a series of short upright compartments.

61 Chartres Cathedral, interior looking east. The decision to omit galleries may have been influenced by the lack of them in the 11th-century cathedral burned in 1194. The alternately circular- and octagonal-sectioned elements in the piers are a last vestige of Early Gothic pier alternation [cf. 32, 39].

The novelty of the effect within the context of French Gothic can be appreciated by comparison with the naves of Laon or Paris [34], where the diagonal ribs of the sexpartite vaults generate longitudinal rhythms complementing the strong horizontal element in the lateral elevations. Quadripartite vaults have the important advantage over the sexpartite form that they exert far less powerful thrusts along the length of clearstorey walls. At Bourges the need to ensure the longitudinal stability of sexpartite vaults precluded a tall clearstorey on the Chartres pattern [71].

The vision of structural lightness created by the screen-like clearstorey walls is an illusion. The tremendous lateral thrusts from the high vault are met not by any internally visible feature but by an unprecedented array of flying buttresses, three tiers instead of the single tier which was the Early Gothic maximum [62, 73a]. The most important flyers at Chartres are the middle tier. They abut close to the level where modern commentators consider high vaults most likely to break if they lack adequate abutment, that is where the radii of the transverse ribs form an angle of thirty degrees to the horizontal. None of the tiers conforms to the Early Gothic usage of abutting at the springing level of the wall ribs [41d]. The extremely high placing of the upper tier recalls the main flyers at St-Remi in Reims [42], and their function was presumably the same, that is to form an open framework locking the wall head into its proper vertical position. It is possible that they were also intended to counter the additional lateral thrusts generated when high winds blow against the steeply pitched outer roofs. Awareness of St-Remi is

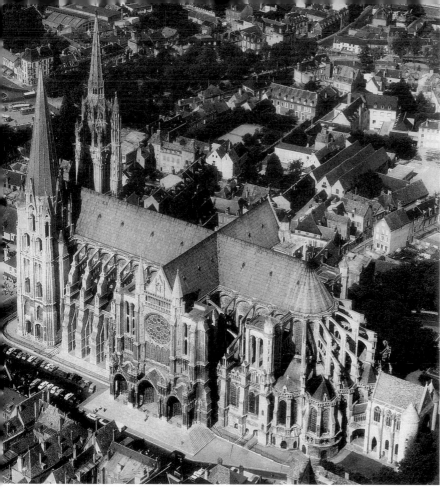

62 Chartres Cathedral, from the south-east. The west towers are mid-12th-century; the timber spire of the north-west tower was replaced in stone in 1506–13. None of the seven further towers begun or planned in the post-1194 rebuilding was completed.

63 Reims Cathedral, from the south-east, begun 1211: choir, transepts and four eastern bays of the nave, completed by 1241; west bays and west front, begun 1255; west towers, probably designed c. 1255, begun 1435 and completed (except for their spires) c. 1475. The shortness of the transepts is due to the need to fit them between the archbishop's palace (in the foreground) and the canons' cloister to the north (destroyed).

suggested by the narrow span of the flyers and the large proportion of the buttress piers which stands above the aisle vaults.

The heftily detailed arcade which links the two lower tiers of the Chartres flyers shows an incipient awareness of the decorative potential of buttressing, although ornamental refinements were not the forte of the architect, and indeed they could not be, given the open texture of the stone most readily available: Admittedly, the slightly later buttresses of the transepts and choir show a progressive thinning of the excessively bulky nave design [62], but it was left to the Chartres master's successors at Reims and elsewhere to refine and develop his work in this sphere (see pp. 111–12). However, flying buttresses were only one among a whole battery of techniques used to keep the high walls of Chartres upright. At the top of the clearstorey, enormous corbelled-out masses of masonry increase the vertical thrust, and hidden under the aisle roofs is the distinctly archaic device of abutting walls [73a]. Most retrograde of all is the extreme thickness of the high walls, which registers outside in the residual walling between the clearstorey windows and inside in the stockiness of the piers. Anxiety about the stability of the

64 Bourges Cathedral, from the south-east: crypt under the choir, after 1195; choir, c. 1200–1214; nave, c. 1225–55; buttress-cum-tower south of the west front, after 1313; north-west-tower, 1506–42. Bourges was the church of the primate of Aquitaine, hence its size, greater than that of any other French cathedral south of the Loire. Externally, there is nothing to show that this is not a galleried church like Notre-Dame in Paris. The strange 'limpet' chapels of the chevet apparently derive from those on the early 11th-century eastern rotunda of St-Bénigne in Dijon.

65 Soissons Cathedral, choir looking north-east from the south transept, dedicated 1212.

clearstorey and the central vessels generally must account for the rejection of the Early Gothic combination of thin piers with thick upper walls oversailing the aisle vaults.

One might think it would have been an obstacle to the influence of Chartres that it is marooned among the rich cornfields of the Beauce, a region lacking an important current tradition of Gothic. But two things besides ambition and artistic quality placed Chartres in the limelight: its standing as France's premier shrine of the Virgin and the origin of its architect in the Laon-Soissons area, one of the major centres of Early Gothic. The repercussions from Chartres began there as early as *c.* 1200 with the start of work on the choir of Soissons Cathedral [*65, 66c*]. Soissons is often excluded from the canon of High Gothic masterpieces, no doubt because of its lesser scale (30m high internally, 7m lower than Chartres). Nevertheless, it is of great interest as a critique of Chartres by someone with the kind of detailed knowledge that could probably only have been acquired by working there. After Chartres what is immediately striking is the thinness of the supports and walls of the main vessels. The architect of Soissons realized that his colleague had, through over-faithful adherence to Laon precedent, failed to exploit a source of reinforcement which would have obviated massive walls, namely the high vault responds. Although the responds at Soissons look quite like those at Chartres, they differ in being built not from attached edge-

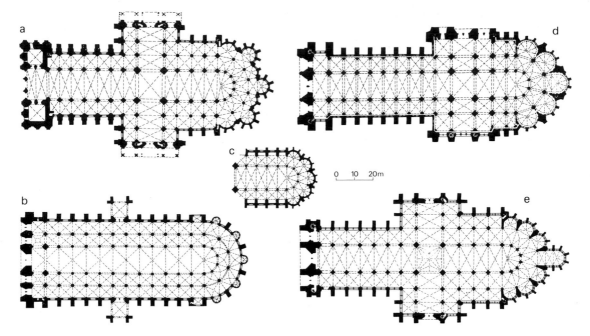

66 Plans of (a) Chartres; (b) Bourges; (c) Soissons, choir; (d) Reims; (e) Amiens. At Chartres the irregular arrangement of the radial ribs in the apse and ambulatory results from the retention of the crypt of the Romanesque choir. The other four plans show different ways of avoiding the stark contrast at Chartres between the long rectangular-plan bays and the narrow intervals between the apse piers. The proportion of floor area occupied by supports is higher at Reims than in any other French 13th-century cathedral.

bedded shafts but from coursed masonry which forms part of the main walls and therefore provides a very significant strengthening to them.

The piers at Soissons appear positively willowy compared to the regular pier type at Chartres [cf. 61]. They are basically columnar, but in order to establish continuity with the high vault responds there is a single very thin coursed shaft. The whole design comes from the narrow apse bays at Chartres and was to be used again in that position at Reims [68]. The Soissons clearstorey shows the same process of selecting Chartres variants, for its tall lancets and small oculi are closer to the choir aisle windows at Chartres than to the clearstorey. However, the elongation of the lancets and the reduction of the oculi enable the lateral webs of the vault to assume the normal pointed profile instead of the rounded form used at Chartres. A third modification of Chartres which can be seen as both a simplification and a refinement is the vaulting of the ambulatory. Each compartment is an eight-part vault uniting the shallow radiating chapels with the ambulatory proper [66c]. A six-part version of this scheme occurs at Chartres, but only in the west bays of the outer ambulatory [66a]. The Soissons design, with various numbers of ribs, proved popular, especially in the Low Countries and the Baltic [83, 114]. More fundamentally, Chartres and Soissons established the polygon as the normal plan form for both radiating chapels and main apses, although the traditional semicircular form did not disappear immediately.

67 Reims Cathedral, north side of the choir. The stained glass in the clearstorey windows conveys a grandiose vision of the pastoral primacy of the archbishop of Reims, with Christ, the Virgin Mary (the spiritual church, Christ's bride) and the Apostles in the upper parts of the lancets, and the archbishop, his suffragan bishops and their cathedrals in the corresponding positions below.

In May of 1210 fire damaged the cathedral of Reims, a church partly 9th-century and partly Early Gothic. The decision to scrap everything and begin a new building modelled on Chartres may well have been prompted by the existence of the newly completed choir at Soissons, whose bishop was the most senior suffragan of the archbishop of Reims. However, instead of simplifying Chartres, Reims sets out to excel it, and does so largely in ornamental terms. The masonry of Reims is in fact the most richly sculptured at any French cathedral, and its high cost was probably a major factor in the unusually prolonged building time, eighty years as against the twenty-five of Chartres.

The key position of Reims in the history of Gothic architecture is due to the design of its windows [67, 68], a reworking of the Chartres clearstorey design [60]. At Chartres the lancets and the oculi above them were placed so close together that one naturally reads them as a single composition, though they were in fact conceived and built as three distinct apertures. From the thin, plate-like character of the residual walling left round the openings comes the term 'plate tracery' normally applied to this kind of design. At Reims the windows are thought of as single openings voiding the whole area between vault, responds and triforium, into which are built bar-like mullions, arches and oculi. Hence the name 'bar tracery'. Every interstice is glazed and flat wall surface is eliminated completely. This technique was already used in 12th-century rose windows, where the basic round aperture is subdivided by thin stone bars treated as a radiating arcade [48]. No doubt the stimulus to develop the constructional technique of rose windows came from the inclusion in the Chartres clearstorey of what were obviously miniaturized roses, albeit of a different species. The local origin of the first architect of Reims, Jean d'Orbais, must explain his borrowing from the clearstorey of St-Remi in Reims the motif of thin tubular shafts and arch mouldings incorporated into the front of the mullions and curved tracery bars [44]. Their role is crucial in persuading one that the bars are not merely residual walling but a virtually autonomous arched structure within the window apertures [74a]. The full achievement of this effect required that each oculus be separated from the adjacent web of the vault, as at Soissons. Yet the frail-looking tracery of Reims is quite out of character with its surroundings. The walls and piers of the central vessels retain the thickness of Chartres and in fact the walls are more overbuilt than at Chartres, since they derive significant reinforcement from the coursed construction used for the greater part of the massive vault responds [73a,c]. Ponderousness prevails even in the high vault, whose transverse ribs are given a bulk matching that of their responds, and whose low, steeply pitched springings obscure the traceried heads of the clearstorey windows in any but frontal views [68].

Other architects lost no time in devising more hospitable environments for the tracery window. First and foremost among these was Robert de

68 Reims Cathedral, choir looking east. As at Westminster [133], the stalls of the liturgical choir were placed in the nave, in order to keep the crossing clear for coronation ritual. Unique to the Reims choir is the carefully managed transition from the widely spaced and massive piers at the west end to the closely spaced and slender apse piers.

69, 70 Amiens Cathedral, nave, begun 1220. *Above left:* looking north-east from the south aisle. *Above right:* nave bay design. The nave was put up before the transepts and choir because part of the east end of the site was occupied by buildings which could not be demolished immediately.

Luzarches (see p. 120), architect of the rebuilding of Amiens Cathedral from 1220. Robert's piers are of similar thickness to those at Chartres and Reims, but their effect is far less oppressive because they are more widely spaced and also far taller in their proportions, approximately twice as high relative to their girth. The tremendous vertical impetus generated by the piers is part of a larger pattern of extreme verticality, for the main vessels here are more steeply proportioned than in any earlier church. At 43m the internal height of Amiens is also unprecedented.

Yet Amiens is no mere prodigy. Its author's artistic and intellectual finesse are well exemplified by his treatment of the shaft-arch system in the main vessels. The piers of the main arcades fulfil completely the promise of the Chartres piers in that their shafts towards the main vessels are wholly continuous with the central shafts of the vault responds. The latter consist of only three shafts because the high vaults at Amiens are without wall ribs, a simplification which acknowledges that the arches forming the outermost parts of the clearstorey tracery are well able to double as ribs. Probably the idea of omitting wall ribs came from the main apse at Reims, since this was certainly the inspiration for linking the triforium to the clearstorey by means of shafts extended down from the mullions of the latter [67]. But whereas the Reims system involves making the storey-linking shafts at the centre of each bay perch awkwardly on brackets jutting out from the main wall plane, at Amiens all the equivalent shafts start from the sill of the triforium. A similarly compelling visual logic governs the high vault responds, whose constituent shafts increase in number and fineness from the floor upwards and thus partake of the character of the levels where they occur: bold single shafts on the still relatively robust piers, triple shafts between the fine-gauged roll mouldings of the arcade arches, and five-shaft groups in the upper storeys, where the delicate linearity of tracery has full rein.

Beginning with the nave of Amiens, French great church interiors became centred around window tracery. The absence of any contemporary comment on the change means that we can only speculate whether the enthusiastic reception accorded to tracery was tinged with pride that this novel form was as purely Christian and Western in origin as the metalwork-inspired decoration being developed on great church exteriors at around the same time (see pp. 130–31). Unfortunately the contribution of tracery to the aisles at Amiens can no longer be appreciated except in drawings [70 and p. 292], since the two-light Reims-derived windows were mostly removed in the 14th century to allow the addition of lateral chapels. Robert de Luzarches concurred with the Chartres master that aisle windows should be smaller and simpler than clearstorey windows, so for the latter he elaborated the Reims pattern by substituting for each of its two lights a scaled-down version of the whole window. The result is the first four-light tracery in Gothic architecture. The greater richness of the triforium compared to those at Chartres and Reims was achieved mainly by exploiting Early Gothic sources; Sens [30] or St-Germain-des-Prés in Paris for the general arrangement, the nave of Notre-Dame in Paris for the triple arches [34], and the nave of Noyon for the trefoils. In using plate tracery rather than bar tracery Robert de Luzarches was perpetuating the hierarchical distinction made at Chartres and Reims between simple arched triforium and traceried clearstorey. Robert was determined to give maximum prominence to his unprecedented enrichment of the upper storeys, for he rejected the steep, low-springing vaults of Chartres, Soissons and Reims in favour of much

shallower vaults which from most viewpoints cause little obstruction to the tracery in the arched heads of the clearstorey windows. These light-looking vaults, in conjunction with the apparent fragility of the clearstorey and the consistent elongation of the proportions, enabled Robert de Luzarches to restore to French Gothic the visionary quality threatened by the structural massiveness of Chartres and Reims.

From the vantage point afforded by Amiens, the success of the Chartres type of elevation appears inevitable. It had been adopted for the three most ambitious cathedrals built in northern France during the early 13th century, and it was soon to become the basis of the next phase of French Gothic, the Rayonnant style. But to a well-informed observer of the late 1220s the triumph of the Chartres succession would have seemed far from assured, for the cathedral at Beauvais, the see between Amiens and Paris, had just been begun according to designs heavily influenced by a building which may well have been seen at the time as a serious rival to Chartres. This is Bourges Cathedral, which like Chartres was begun in the mid-1190s [*64, 66b, 71–73b*]. Bourges lies well to the south of the Gothic heartlands, and the same is true of its earliest imitations, the choirs of St-Martin at Tours (begun *c.* 1210, destroyed) and Le Mans Cathedral (begun 1218). In 1227 a francophil archbishop of Toledo, who was probably aware of the diversity of recent French Gothic, accepted Bourges as the model for his new cathedral, by far the most ambitious church of its century in Spain [*115, 116*]. It is easy to see why Bourges had admirers, for, though quite different from Chartres, it is in some ways even more impressive.

In each of the four arms of Chartres the aisles are firmly subordinated to a towering central vessel [*61*], but at Bourges the pre-eminence of the central space is secured not so much through greater height as through the sense of hugeness generated by the inclusion of only a few exceptionally long compartments of sexpartite vaulting. Nothing could be further from the closely spaced and heavily stressed bay divisions which slow one's visual progress along the central vessels at Chartres. Yet the length of the bays at Bourges also mitigates the dominance of the central vessel in that it increases the visibility of the aisles. These are more impressive than the aisles of any earlier Gothic church, being not merely double, as at Notre-Dame in Paris, but staggered in height, with the inner aisles attaining about three-fifths of the height of the main vessel. The walls of the inner aisles include clearstoreys and triforia which are even more closely matched in height to their equivalents in the main vessel. Perhaps the most remarkable thing about Bourges is that the spatial effect which its five parallel vessels create is not diffuse but unified and concentrated. The concern to give these qualities their full value is probably sufficient explanation for the omission of transepts.

71 Bourges Cathedral, interior looking north-east. The piers of the main arcade are almost uniform in design but their thickness alternates according to their position relative to the sexpartite vault.

The inspiration for the five-vessel scheme of Bourges may have come from Cluny, where, perhaps not coincidentally, the uncle of Henri de Sully, the founding archbishop, had been abbot in the 1170s. Cluny was the only earlier French church to combine five staggered vessels with very tall arcades. The Bourges architect probably also knew the three-vessel choir and transepts of Arras Cathedral, where comparably high arcades incorporated piers far more slender than Cluny's and hence far less obstructive of diagonal views into the aisles. In fact the Bourges master seems to have been acquainted with almost all the greatest Early Gothic churches. As was noted in the last chapter, Notre-Dame in Paris influenced the plan and exterior massing of the east end [*36c, 41b, 64, 66b*], and here again Archbishop Henri's connections could be significant, for his brother Eudes was bishop of Paris when Bourges was begun. Notre-Dame may also have inspired the unique design of the piers; certainly the only surviving precursors of their shallow capitals and fine shafts surrounding a cylindrical core are the piers in the nave aisles there. The shafts at Paris are edge-bedded, as were those on the related piers in the destroyed northern French church of Notre-Dame in Valenciennes. The chief interest of the latter piers is that they anticipated in a modest way one of the most striking features of the three inner vessels at Bourges, the impression that the piers split at capital level into large segments carrying the main arcade arches and aisles vaults and smaller segments extending upwards as responds to the upper vaults. Such a reading is facilitated by the clear visibility of the cores of the piers between their shafts, and also by the extreme thinness of the arcade arches. The latter are actually very similar to the ribs in the adjoining aisle vaults, a resemblance which, like the great length of the bays, serves to draw attention to the lateral vistas. A further effect unique to Bourges is generated by the perfect vertical continuity between pier shafts and vault responds, by the even spacing of the shafts and by their almost consistently fine gauge: this is the sense that the interior consists of a series of gigantic but wire-thin arches soaring upwards from the floor against a neutral background of pier cores and vault webs. That such a reading is to some extent inconsistent with that which emphasizes the cylindrical cores of piers and responds is not a criticism of the coherence of the design, only an indication of its exceptional subtlety and richness.

The walls of the main vessel and inner aisles at Bourges derive their distinctively membranous aspect from the extreme shallowness of all openings, whether arcade arches, clearstorey windows or triforium arcades. A similar effect is created by the abnormal size of the vault webs relative to the ribs. The thin, squat and obtusely pitched arches enclosing the triforium arcades are a puzzling feature until one realizes that they are actually only the front edges of arches extending through the full thickness of the triforia [*72, 73b*]. Similar but more felicitously detailed arches occur in the gallery level of the transepts at Noyon [*47*], where they provide longitudinal rigidity. This

72　Bourges Cathedral, inner and outer ambulatories. The capitals differ from those at Chartres [61] in that the depth of their central parts is not related to the diameter of the pier cores. The windows are graduated in complexity in accordance with the height and importance of the spaces which they light: single lancets in the outer aisles, paired lancets and small oculi in the inner aisles, and triple lancets and large oculi in the central vessel [cf. 64, 71].

must also be their intended role at Bourges, at least in the main vessel, where the sexpartite vaults exert powerful thrusts along the thin walls they rest on. Without these arches roughly half way between arcades and vaults, the upper walls might indeed have buckled, for the extreme length of the bays increases both the strength of the longitudinal thrusts and the proportion of void to solid in the clearstorey. At the end of the 13th century, sexpartite vaults were successfully raised over the choir at Beauvais without recourse to such arches, but there the bays are exceptionally short.

Whereas most large medieval churches were built in an essentially longitudinal east-to-west sequence in order to complete the liturgically most important parts as soon as possible, at Bourges various circumstances made it expedient to erect the choir in a vertical sequence, as a series of horizontal 'layers'. The choir was completed only around 1214, so it would have been possible at many points to modify the design without impairing its homogeneity or leaving tell-tale traces like those in the presbytery at Canterbury. How far the design actually was modified is a matter of dispute. Some scholars think the unique radiating chapels which perch over every third buttress on the outer wall of the crypt must have been an afterthought, decided on only when work had moved from the crypt to the main level of the choir [64]. Others note that since the crypt exists only to level up and extend the site of the Romanesque cathedral it had no liturgical function and hence no need of chapels. It is theoretically possible that even so fundamental an aspect of Bourges as the staggered cross-section was only adopted around 1205, when work began on the wall between the outer and inner ambulatories. What is at stake here is not merely Bourges's building chronology but its independence from Chartres, where the bay design must have been settled before 1200. Historians who admire Bourges more than Chartres have tended to discount or ignore the possibility of any link. However, it strains credibility more than a little to suppose that the Bourges and Chartres masters simultaneously yet independently lighted on cylindrical-cored piers with coursed shafts linked to high vault responds, high three-storey elevations incorporating band triforia, and clearstoreys with lancets under large oculi. Like the Wells master's borrowings from Canterbury, the debts of Bourges to Chartres are completely integrated into a design that could never be branded as derivative.

Since Bourges is a fusion of Early and High Gothic elements, one might imagine it would have been attractive to conservative patrons and designers. In fact very few of the Early Gothic features of Bourges are reproduced in the churches which adopted the staggered five-aisle format. None of these has high sexpartite vaults and none, presumably as a result, copies the triforium-enclosing arches of Bourges. Toledo and the early parts of Beauvais have triforia whose more basic band format must be due ultimately to the influence of Chartres, like their comparatively thick walls [*115, 116*]. Le Mans, near the southern border of Normandy, is coloured by regional influences, but embodies a broadly similar response. The conclusion is inescapable that what people most admired at Bourges was its spatial organization. The five-aisle scheme was perceived as an alternative to the conventional three-aisle basilica and not, like the Chartres system, as a catalyst to formal innovation. The only exception to this generalization seems to be the Amiens piers [*69*], whose extreme tallness is anticipated only at Bourges. The triforia and lower clearstorey at Bourges, largely on account of the squat proportions of the arches bounding them, fail to incorporate openings of maximum size and thus violate one of the fundamental principles of French Gothic; if the elevations had been more conventionally coherent, perhaps the Bourges system as a whole might have been more widely accepted. Another peculiarity not repeated was the omission of transepts. In symbolic terms the discarding of the cruciform plan was obviously an impoverishment, but practical considerations also favoured transepts, since their eastern aisles normally functioned as chapels. The transepts at Toledo compromise the spatial cohesion of the longitudinal vessels and thus illustrate further the limitations of Bourges as a model for great churches.

Bourges has the least elaborate buttressing of all the High Gothic cathedrals, thanks to its low clearstorey and the smaller lateral thrusts which

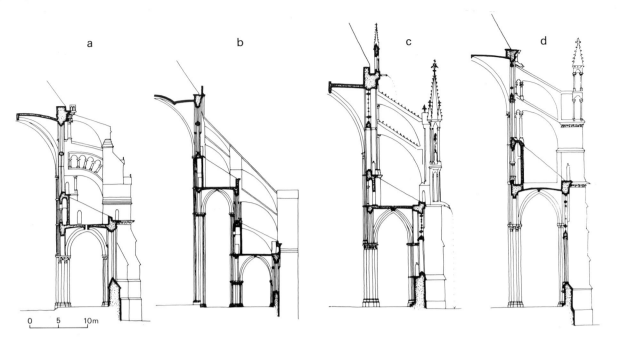

a   b   c   d

0   5   10m

73 Part sections of (a) Chartres, nave; (b) Bourges, choir; (c) Reims, nave; (d) Amiens, nave.

its sexpartite vault exerts compared to quadripartite vaults [*64*, *73b*]. Because they look both daring and calculated and because they are functional in purpose, 13th-century flying buttresses have often been thought of during the last hundred years as anticipations of modern civil engineering techniques. The case of Bourges serves to dispel this misconception, for the flyers here are of uniform design despite the fact that those aligned with the intermediate single ribs of the high vault are receiving lateral thrusts between two and three times less than those taken by the other flyers. At Beauvais a century later it was decided that intermediate flyers could be dispensed with altogether [*191*]. Bourges and Beauvais fail to conform even to the very rough and ready rules embodied in the earliest known computations of vault thrusts, those in the notebook of the mid-16th-century Spanish architect Rodrigo Gil de Hontañón. Rodrigo Gil made no use of the fairly highly evolved medieval science of statics, and in fact his formulae were nothing more than correlations of the area of the buttresses with the span of the vault to be abutted. The Gothic architect's approach to structural design was not theoretical but empirical, being based on intuition, common sense and observation of the performance of earlier structures. Modern analytical techniques have enabled civil engineers to reach reasoned assessments of the respective merits of the several High Gothic designs, but unfortunately their work cannot help us with the central historical problem, namely what sort of notions 13th-century architects had of the nature of the forces which buttresses were intended to neutralize.

Comparison of the cross-sections of Chartres, Reims and Amiens [*73a,c,d*] shows that the buttressing of Chartres, like its internal elevations, became accepted as the normative type for early 13th-century Frence great churches. At Reims, the ultra-cautious Chartres scheme was revised by eliminating the abutting walls under the aisle roofs and by reducing the number and bulk of the flyers. Reims's two tiers of thin, agile-looking flyers abut the clearstorey at levels corresponding to the intervals between the three tiers at Chartres. Their resemblance to timber struts or shores is reinforced by the coursing of their masonry, most of which forms an inclined band running parallel to the straight upper edge. About half a century after Reims was begun, the same principle had been taken to its limits at St-Urbain at Troyes, where a particularly audacious designer reduced his flyers to copings carried on the thinnest arches [86]. The Reims abutment system bears witness to growing technical confidence, not just in its thinner flyers but also in its much shallower buttress piers. Perhaps the aim was to reduce the shadows cast across the clearstorey glazing by the flyers [146, 167]. A more influential innovation of the Reims buttress piers is their tall pinnacles [63]. These are the earliest in Gothic architecture, although the idea of a continuation of the buttress piers above the coping of the flyers had already been reached at Canterbury [56] and Soissons. The ornamental aspects of pinnacles are discussed below (p. 130), but considered structurally they are only an extension of the concept of placing additional loads at the top of clearstorey walls to counter lateral thrusts exerted by high vaults [13].

The upper walls of Amiens [73d] have shed all the external massiveness of Chartres and Reims, and what at the two earlier churches were low passages cut through deep jambs are now high, narrow arches carried on slender shafts. Yet even at Amiens the lightness is partly illusory, for concealed behind the spandrels of the clearstorey walls (and therefore visible only from the roof-space above the high vaults) are arches analogous to those which form a deep external frame to the heads of the clearstorey windows at Chartres and Reims. The value of a massive extra load on the wall head as an aid to reducing the eccentricity of vault thrusts was clearly appreciated here and at the many later 13th-century churches where the Amiens arrangement was imitated. Another cautious feature of Amiens, also widely copied, is the reversion to the Chartres type of deep buttress piers partly set on top of the transverse ribs of the aisle vaults. The fact that the Amiens flyers join the central vessel at similar levels to those at Reims in spite of the great disparity between the height and pitch of vaults in the two churches is one of many indications that early 13th-century French architects had not reached any general agreement about the levels at which flyers should abut.

The stability of the vaults at Amiens depends partly on the use of the novel *tas-de-charge* technique. This involves substituting massive, horizontally coursed springer blocks for what one readily accepts as a series of independent and radially constructed ribs [75]. A tentative move towards the *tas-de-charge* can be seen in the springings of the 'screens' to the radiating chapels at St-Remi in Reims [45], but the earliest instances of its fully

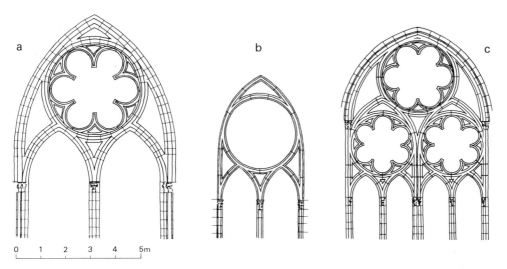

74 The jointing of window tracery in the choir clearstoreys of (a) Reims; (b) Notre-Dame, Paris; (c) St-Denis.

developed form seem to be at Chartres, where it links the springings to the similarly large and horizontally coursed blocks in the lowest flyers. The main advantage of making vault springings from blocks far bigger than the stones used elsewhere in the building was the strengthening of those parts of the structure most subject to lateral thrusts.

Another technical refinement related to the use of larger blocks, and which appears to have been importantly developed at Amiens, is the use of components of standardized size and shape. From its first appearance, bar tracery was largely built with systematically jointed blocks, so that equivalent components destined for windows of the same size would have been interchangeable by the setting masons who put up the stonework [74]. The incised cylindrical piers at Durham [11], one of the rare Romanesque examples of the use of standardized components, confirm that the main aim in applying this technique to window tracery was to facilitate the uniform manufacture of a series of unusually large and complex units of geometrical patterning. The Amiens choir piers of c. 1235 may be the earliest of the few instances in Gothic architecture of the extension of standardization to elements other than tracery, but whether the purpose was aesthetic or economic is not clear. An aspect of the choir piers which surely did have economic implications is the use of only two stones for each of the courses between the bases and capitals. Obviously, the amount of mason's time needed here was less than at Chartres, where the similarly sectioned piers (which are built of courses of irregular height) contain six to eight stones per course. A form of standardization less developed than in the Amiens choir piers occurs in the piers and responds in the earlier nave and transept at Amiens, which are made from courses whose height is neither exactly uniform nor very varied. Because the responds are coursed independently of the intervening stretches of wall, their components, like those of the piers, could be made in the masons' lodge throughout the year including winter when they would be stockpiled to await installation during the building season. The only 'tailor-made' components cut immediately in advance of installation are the uppermost courses, where the height had to be adjusted to enable the capitals to be set at a uniform level. This quasi-standardization, like the pure form used in the Amiens choir piers, recurs at a few French Rayonnant cathedrals, but by the end of the 13th century both forms had fallen out of use except in tracery. Individual joints are carefully portrayed in several German late medieval architectural drawings, and it is possible that at some stage such drawings became the normal means of determining the dimensions of every ashlar block used in a building.

Early thirteenth-century regional styles in northern France: Burgundy and Normandy

During the early 13th century the Ile-de-France built far more churches than any other part of northern France, but there was also a great deal of activity in the three principalities adjoining to the north and east. Flanders, Champagne and Burgundy were the lands through which passed many of Europe's main north-south trade routes, and it is clear that by the 1190s they were beginning to function as a corridor for the transmission of architectural ideas as well as more basic commodities. One of the best illustrations of the process is Lausanne Cathedral, not far from the eastern borders of Burgundy, where the clearstorey follows the Anglo-Norman scheme adopted barely a decade earlier at that other outpost of French Gothic, the choir of Canterbury Cathedral. Lausanne and the Trinity Chapel at Canterbury [58] also exemplify the low three-storey elevation incorporating a band triforium, a pattern which became the norm in Burgundy, Champagne and Flanders during the early 13th century. As was noted in the discussion of Chartres, the oldest examples of this type were in the vicinity of Laon. Its continued appeal in the early 13th century was probably based at least partly on the fact that it incorporated the same essential reform as Chartres, namely the abolition of the gallery. When Chartres finally began to exert direct influences on the northern and eastern 'schools' in the late 1220s it did so alongside much older sources like Noyon, Laon and St-Remi at Reims.

The single most ambitious and accomplished example of this alternative to High Gothic illustrates how certain Early Gothic ideas continued to develop in the early 13th century despite their rejection at Chartres. The choir of Auxerre Cathedral, in Burgundy, has in its aisle walls a continuous passage [76] clearly intended to emulate that in the same position at Reims Cathedral but whose detailed treatment comes closer to the passage in the axial chapel at St-Remi [46]. Whereas both Reims passages are combined with arched window embrasures, at Auxerre the jambs continue straight up behind the vaults to meet ceilings formed of large slabs set slightly above the apexes of the wall ribs. Window heads and vaults are thus separated by shallow, shadowy voids. The source of this arrangement was either the windowless

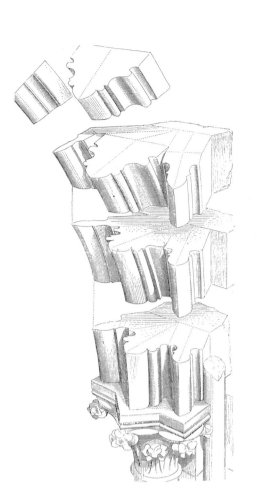

75 The *tas-de-charge* technique (see pp. 112–13).

76 Auxerre Cathedral, ambulatory and axial chapel looking north-east, begun 1215.

west bays of the axial chapel at St-Remi or the west wall of the nave there, both with voids ceiled by almost flat segmental arches. The ribs descending between the windows are as obviously modelled on the outer wall of the gallery at St-Remi as the triple 'screen' of the axial chapel is on the arcade which carries that wall and screens the radiating chapels [45]. The stability of the columns in the screen – the thinnest load-bearing shafts of the period – is assured by the use of the *tas-de-charge* technique [75] for all the masonry of the vault between the capitals and the springings of the three arches linking the columns. In other words, this part of the vault is structurally an upward extension of the columns. The sense of fragility conveyed by the slenderness of the axial chapel screen and by the omission of solid masonry from between vaults and windows is extended to the interior as a whole by giving all shafts and ribs elongated proportions strongly reminiscent of Bourges.

77 Dijon, Notre-Dame, north side of the nave, *c.* 1220–30.

The main elevations at Auxerre were modified during construction so as to make them more like Chartres, and the effect originally intended can best be studied in the very closely related nave of the exceptionally grand parish church of Notre-Dame at Dijon [77]. Here, as in the ambulatory at Auxerre, influence from St-Remi is very strong. The near-equality of the lancets in the St-Remi clearstorey has become complete equality, thanks to the use of the flat-ceiled Auxerre-type passage, and their close spacing and lack of shafts is borrowed from St-Remi's aisles [42, 44]. The clash between the horizontal rectangles formed by the clearstorey openings and the pointed profile of the wall ribs and vault webs is a very sophisticated effect in itself, but it is also a unique way of combining forms that echo both the banded arcading of the triforium and the single arches of the main arcades. An even more mannered contrast between rectilinear and arched elements is generated by the widely spaced shafts of the vault responds which overlap and yet leave visible the springings of the main arcade arches. The source of this detail appears to be that belated work of Early Gothic, the extension of the choir at Laon, begun *c.* 1205. In the hands of the Dijon master it acquires greater prominence on account of its detailing as well as greater significance from being part of a larger pattern.

Common dependence on late 12th-century sources rather than direct influence accounts for the correspondences between Dijon and Auxerre and a considerable group of early 13th-century churches in Flanders, whose outstanding members are Oudenaarde, Our Lady at Bruges and St Martin at Ypres. The influence of Tournai [40], reinforced by the transepts at Noyon [48] and Cambrai (destroyed), lies behind their most distinctive feature, the clearstorey with an external passage screened by arcading. Interesting though these buildings are as a regional group, perhaps the most remarkable thing about them is their modest ambition and quality in relation to the Flemish economy, the most developed in Northern Europe.

Whereas Burgundy's regional Romanesque traditions were quickly effaced after the advent of Gothic architecture, in Normandy the situation was entirely different. Even the earliest surviving Gothic great church in the duchy, to all appearances the design of an architect newly arrived from Laon, has to be classed as a Franco-Norman hybrid. Lisieux Cathedral (begun c. 1160) is French only in its detailing, for the Laon scheme has been drastically edited to bring it into conformity with Norman notions of great church design. There is no triforium, the middle storey is a vaultless and windowless false gallery, and in order to sustain a high vault without recourse to flying buttresses the upper walls are considerably thickened. The next major Norman church, Fécamp Abbey (begun in 1168), is still more strongly coloured by local preferences than Lisieux, with compound piers taking the place of columns and high walls thickened to the point where they can contain a clearstorey passage. In the choir added to St-Etienne at Caen c. 1190–1200, the proportions of the main vessel and individual storeys follow quite closely those of the Romanesque church [5], whereas the detailing includes motifs drawn from a wide range of Early Gothic sources including Noyon and Canterbury. It might have been expected that the French conquest of Normandy in 1204 would have been followed by a curtailing of the independence of Norman Gothic but, as the choir begun c. 1230 at Bayeux Cathedral shows [78, 79], this did not happen.

Onto a bay design which takes from St-Etienne not only its Romanesque structure and proportioning but some of its ornaments, the designer of Bayeux grafted a heterogeneous collection of borrowings from early 13th-century Ile-de-France and English Gothic. Pinpointing the individual sources is no simple matter, since the motifs of French origin are almost completely transformed and many of what look like English motifs are as likely to be parallels evolved from similar Romanesque premises as direct importations from across the Channel. Thus the alternately polygonal and right-angled capitals and the continuously undulating profile of the deep arcade arches are strongly reminiscent of Wells and Lincoln respectively [55, 122], yet both have local antecedents which can be seen as the earlier stages of a development internal to Norman Gothic. The deep enclosing arch in each bay of the triforium is clearly a modernized version of the standard Norman Romanesque type of gallery, but the plate tracery within these arches could derive either from the nave triforium at Bourges [71] or from early 13th-

78 Bayeux Cathedral, choir from the south-east, begun *c.* 1230. The rainwater disposal system is unusually elaborate for the date. From the high roofs it passes down vertical drains behind the image niches on the clearstorey, along channels on the upper surfaces of the flyers, down vertical drains in the buttress piers, and finally out through gargoyles on the lower parapets.

79 Bayeux Cathedral, north side of the choir.

century English false galleries like those at Salisbury [*131*]. Perhaps the only motif at Bayeux which can definitely be ascribed to English influence, even if at several removes, is the series of small sculptured roundels sunk into the wall in the manner of Wells [*55*]. Bayeux typifies the strength of Norman traditions as a filter of outside influences, as well as the strength of the design sense which enabled Norman architects to assimilate diverse influences so successfully.

The chevet at Bayeux is French in its general conception, like all the major Norman Gothic chevets of the late 12th and early 13th centuries. Nevertheless, the detailed handling, particularly of the exterior [*78*], is characterized by the same firmly controlled eclecticism as the internal elevations of the main vessel. An important consideration was evidently the preservation of as much as possible of the smooth contouring of Romanesque and proto-Gothic chevets, for the indentations between the radiating chapels are bridged by arches derived ultimately from the early 12th-century choir at Fécamp or from St-Martin-des-Champs in Paris [*22*]. In combination with the deep parapet, these arches stress horizontal continuity to the point of visually severing the flying buttress piers from their supporting buttresses between the chapels. The only major vertical accents are traditional Norman Romanesque ones, the stair turrets at the junctions of the apsidal and straight parts of the choir. Considered in purely stylistic terms these and the similar turrets on other early 13th-century Norman chevets are no doubt instances of provincial conservatism, but when viewed in the context of early 13th-century Norman history, they become recognizable as signs of a defiant pride in the duchy's glorious past.

The Rayonnant style

The start of building at Amiens Cathedral in 1220 heralded the re-emergence of Paris as a major centre of Gothic architecture. In appointing the Parisian architect Robert de Luzarches (Luzarches is a small town 20km north of St-Denis) the canons of Amiens were acknowledging that their own region, Picardy, lacked a worthy tradition of recent great church building and that the capital was the best place to recruit the expertise that they needed. After a long period in the late 12th century when the centre of gravity of Gothic had shifted north-eastwards, Paris at the beginning of the 13th century was once again the scene of important activity. The main achievement of those years was the west end of Notre-Dame, begun around 1200–1210 and by far the largest and most ambitious two-tower façade yet conceived [92]. This and the many lesser projects proceeding at the same time were part of a renewed phase of growth which made Paris incontestably the greatest and most splendid city in France. As in the 12th century, the motor behind this expansion was the increased power of the crown. After the conquest of Normandy the royal revenues increased by seventy per cent, and after the victory over an English, Flemish and German invasion force at Bouvines ten years later the prestige of the French king rose to the point where he was for the first time accepted outside France as the pre-eminent ruler in Western Europe. The 13th century is dominated by the long reign of Louis IX (1226–70), who appeared to contemporaries, as he does to posterity, the very embodiment of the medieval Christian king: chivalrous, powerful and rich, yet also deeply pious and abstemious in his personal habits; a dutiful son to the institutional church but an indefatigable upholder of his own rights. Louis's court was austere, but since it was the seat of power it was inevitably a magnet to the great men of the kingdom, who increasingly found it advantageous to maintain an establishment in Paris. The concentration of so much wealth in the city stimulated its economic growth and assured its status as the pre-eminent purveyor of all manner of cultural commodities. Production of great church architecture could never of course be centred on any one city, but Parisian architects were undoubtedly beneficiaries of the prestige which soon came to be attached to almost anything connected with the capital. The 13th-century kings had no occasion to initiate new ecclesiastical projects more ambitious than Cistercian abbeys or palace chapels, yet the fact that Philip II and Louis IX paid for no great churches did not prevent people from associating the crown with the architectural style of Paris. After all, the French monarchy and Gothic architecture had risen to greatness together, during the same period and in the same region. Moreover, the single most influential project of the early 13th century, the

80 St-Denis, north side of the nave. The three nearest bays follow closely the design of the choir begun in 1231 [cf. *74c*]; the other bays date from *c*. 1250 and employ the system of graduated tracery orders first introduced in the south transept in the late 1230s [cf. *81*].

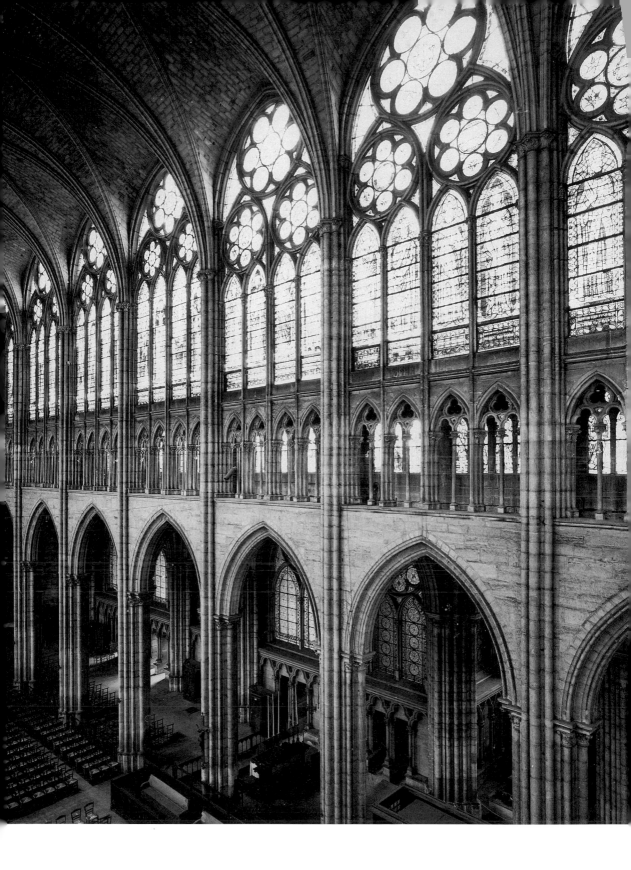

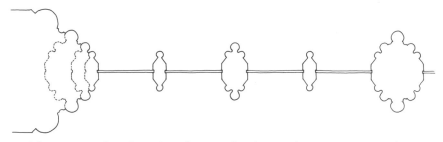

81 The system of graduated mullions and arches used in Rayonnant and Late Gothic tracery: horizontal section through one jamb and four lights of an eight-light window. For an application of the system see *135*.

seminal work of the Rayonnant style, was the reconstruction of the royal burial church of St-Denis [*80*].

Ever since the abandonment of Suger's scheme for replacing the 8th-century nave and transepts in 1151, the need to rebuild must have seemed more and more urgent. When work finally began in 1231, the eastern parts of the other great royal church, Reims Cathedral, were far advanced, and it may well have been awareness of Reims that spurred the St-Denis monks into entering the lists. Although St-Denis is considerably lower than any of the cathedrals so far discussed in this chapter – it could not have been otherwise without demolishing almost all Suger's work – its main inspiration was Amiens, then the tallest Gothic cathedral [*69, 70*]. St-Denis is in no other sense a more modest church than Amiens, and its innovations were to prove applicable in buildings of the largest size. Yet the fact that this most prestigious church could opt out of the high building race must have contributed to the general slowing down of that form of competitiveness after the mid-13th century.

The response of the first St-Denis master to Amiens was to enhance in every possible way the already exceptional prominence of window tracery. In his conception of tracery as an almost purely linear form he was less a follower of Robert de Luzarches than of the unknown architect who from around 1220 inserted new clearstorey windows in the choir of Notre-Dame in Paris [*33, 74b*]. As the *locus classicus* of the Parisian preoccupation with thin walls and attenuated mouldings during the Early Gothic period, Notre-Dame was the ideal context for tracery in which the roll moulding at the front takes precedence over the substantial chamfered member behind. This ultra-fine tracery enabled the St-Denis master to give his great clearstorey windows a more consistent character than those at Amiens (where the shafts on the smaller mullions are not answered by shafts on the jambs and central mullion); and in the south transept he initiated the concept of graduated orders of tracery, in which windows are built up from shafts and arches graded in gauge according to the size of the unit they belong to. The larger orders consist partly of magnifications of the smaller orders and partly of the smaller orders themselves [*81*]. More than in any High Gothic church, the vault responds take on the same fineness as the mullion shafts, and one is encouraged to make this equation by the perfect vertical continuity of the responds, which are interrupted neither by columnar piers nor by continuations of the string courses separating the storeys. It is rather ironic that full-length responds are achieved by reviving the Romanesque and proto-Gothic cruciform piers which but for the influence of Suger's choir would probably have remained the norm during the intervening century. An appropriate increase in linearity compared to the 12th-century examples is created simply by elongation.

The thin ribs in the vaults were easily assimilated to the linearity of the lateral elevations, and the pitch of the high vault is made even shallower than at Amiens so as to maximize the visibility of the clearstorey tracery. In the earlier campaigns at St-Denis, the prominence of the heads of the clearstorey windows is further promoted by making them much higher than the lights [80, right], a disparity probably intended to be mitigated by the enclosure of the glazed triforium within extensions of the clearstorey mullions. In actuality the contrast between glass and stone is such that one does not readily read the triforium arches as adjuncts to the clearstorey lights, and the second architect of St-Denis made his tracery heads shorter so as to give the windows more normal proportions [80, left]. Nevertheless, the linkage does effectively subordinate the triforium to the clearstorey by dividing it into small units each conforming to the subdivisions of the higher storey. The limited linkage of Amiens had allowed the paired tracery units in the triforium to be more elaborate and twice as wide as the smallest unit of the clearstorey. In the triforium at St-Denis glazed tracery takes the place of Amiens's solid backing wall and freestanding bar tracery is substituted for plate tracery. Both adjustments help assimilate the triforium to the clearstorey and thus further the aim of making window tracery pre-eminent in the interior. One may wonder why the triforium, with its primary aesthetic function of enlivening the wall fronting the aisle roof space was not abolished altogether. The case of Exeter Cathedral, where a triforium was inserted as an afterthought into a completed two-storey elevation, suggests that patrons still expected churches to have three storeys, either for symbolic reasons or merely out of conservatism. In aesthetic terms St-Denis's two-layer traceried triforium represents a convincing development from the Chartres type [60], for in addition to its role as an intermediary between the flatness of the clearstorey and the depth of the aisles, the middle zone now effects a transition between the complete translucence of the clearstorey and the much smaller amount of light reaching the central vessel from the aisle windows. The St-Denis scheme was to remain standard in France during the rest of the Middle Ages [187]. Not even Suger's choir can claim such a progeny.

No opportunities to implement the whole St-Denis system arose in the Ile-de-France during the later 13th century, but several incomplete High Gothic cathedral choirs were crowned with upper storeys which converted their main vessels into approximations of the Rayonnant manner. The most important instances are Tours (begun 1241), Beauvais [191] and Troyes, the

last an almost literal copy of St-Denis and presumably begun very soon after its model. For completely Rayonnant designs one must look further afield, to the Rhineland [84], Holland [183], Flanders [40, 83], Normandy [2, 82], central and southern France [87, 88] and Castile [118]. Most of these churches or parts of churches are Ile-de-France buildings in the sense that they owe nothing to local precedent and are designs by architects trained in or near Paris. If it were possible somehow to discern the motives behind each of these importations they would no doubt be very varied, yet in many cases there do seem to be strong undercurrents of allegiance to or rivalry with the French crown. The latter is clearest at Cologne Cathedral [84, 111], the most splendid of all Rayonnant churches, begun in 1248 by an architect named Gerhard in the documents but surely born Gérard. The patronage of Cologne is considered in the section on 13th-century Germany (pp. 151–2).

The choir of Cologne, the only part of the cathedral completed in the Middle Ages, is essentially a version of Amiens updated in the light of St-Denis. The uninterrupted vault responds of the latter are accepted, but their central shafts are given back the plasticity that they had at Amiens, with the result that the design as a whole gains in clarity and rhythmic variety. Similarly, the piers combine the cylindrical core of Amiens with St-Denis's multiplicity of differently gauged shafts, twelve in both cases. The retention of the cylindrical core in preference to the St-Denis stepped core generates heavy shadows between the shafts and so ensures vertical continuity between the piers and the main arcade mouldings, the latter very reminiscent of the deeply furrowed crossing arches at Amiens. Because Cologne is the outcome

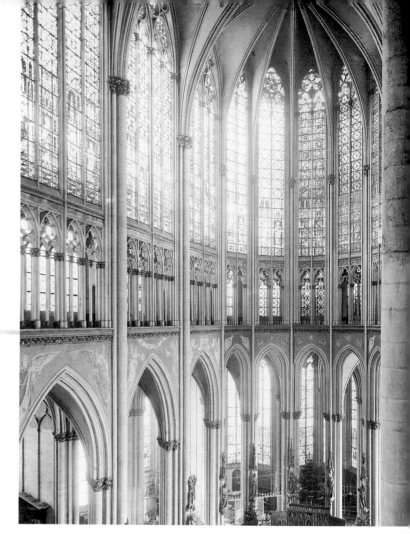

Opposite
82 Sées Cathedral, window in the north choir aisle, *c.* 1270.

83 Tournai Cathedral, choir ambulatory looking north-east, begun 1243. The walls of the radiating chapels are more completely given over to glass than at any other 13th-century cathedral. This is because their exceptional shallowness allows the buttresses receiving the flyers of the main apse to be placed entirely externally [*40*].

84 Cologne Cathedral, choir looking north-east, begun 1248, upper storeys *c.* 1280–1300, dedicated 1322. At 46m high internally, Cologne is just 2m lower than Beauvais, the tallest Gothic cathedral [*191*].

of judicious study of the greatest achievements of French Gothic during the previous quarter century, it has sometimes been branded as 'doctrinaire'. This highly unfair epithet is revealing only of 20th-century unease in the face of aesthetic perfection, for although Cologne is less obviously an innovatory building than its main sources, its individuality emerges from comparison with any contemporary Rayonnant church. Here, as in Rayonnant architecture generally, the main creative effort was channelled into ornament and proportion rather than into more basic aspects. It can hardly be doubted that the location of the masterpiece of Rayonnant cathedral architecture in Germany rather than France has had a bearing on the longstanding reluctance of French art historians to acknowledge the Rayonnant style as the culmination of 13th-century French Gothic.

The vertiginously tall clearstorey of the Cologne choir derives its proportions not from any earlier cathedral but from the Sainte-Chapelle in Paris, the most important ecclesiastical building commissioned by Louis IX (begun *c.* 1240). That a great church could owe so important a debt to such a relatively simple building type as a palace chapel is an earnest of a world in which the patronage of the secular powers would challenge that of major ecclesiastical corporations. The earliest indication that the great churches were beginning to lose their near-monopoly of architectural innovation dates from the late 1230s, when the architect of St-Denis gave the royal castle chapel of St-Germain-en-Laye rectangular tracery windows such as occur in no great church of the period. The implication is that 'private' commissions could be frankly experimental, whereas the high seriousness of great church design imposed constraints upon the architect's freedom.

The prime example of the sort of architecture which was disallowed by this sense of decorum is St-Urbain at Troyes, a collegiate church founded in 1262 on the site of his birthplace by Pope Urban IV [85, 86]. Although expensively finished, it was not a great church by current French standards, and hence the architect was free to treat it as a showcase for the most extraordinary bravura effects in all Rayonnant architecture. Here for the first time the Gothic system is being played with almost to breaking point. Every member is so fined down that we become anxious for its stability, while solid masonry is eliminated in ways which serve no other purpose than to assail our preconceptions about structural necessities. The skeletonizing of the flying buttresses has been mentioned already, and the gables over many of the windows are subjected to the same process. Gables over windows at least have a functional ancestry, but it is difficult to see their introduction into the tracery of the windows [86] as anything other than a gesture of defiance towards the rational articulation which had been hitherto one of the cornerstones of French Gothic. The spiritual heirs of the St-Urbain designer were not late 13th-century Frenchmen but 14th-century Englishmen and Germans.

Gothic great church architecture made its début in the very foreign milieu of southern France under the auspices of Urban IV's compatriot and successor, Clement IV. As Guy Foulquoi, Clement had been a trusted counsellor of Louis IX, so his appointment as archbishop of Narbonne in 1259 had served to reinforce the recently established royal authority in the region. In 1268, three years after his election as pope, and four years before the start of work on the cathedral, he issued a bull which noted that the reconstruction was to be undertaken 'in imitation of the noble and magnificently worked churches . . . which are being built in the kingdom of France'. Since it rises only 2m less than Amiens, the ambition of Narbonne is not in doubt. Although the design is far from orthodox in northern French terms [88], the architect is likely to have been the same anonymous northerner who around 1267 began the choir and transepts of the cathedral of St-Nazaire in the nearby royal city of Carcassonne, a comparatively small-scale project whose earliest parts are the first and last stylistically pure Rayonnant work in the south. The eastern parts of Carcassonne do not themselves rank as great church architecture since they follow the hall church format of the Romanesque nave to which they are joined.

85, 86 Troyes, St-Urbain: choir, begun 1262; upper parts of the transept, 1270s. *Above:* tracery in the apse of the south chapel. The contrived disparity between the two layers of pattern may have influenced the triforium at Sées [2], where one pattern is 'cut' by another, albeit in the same plane. The omission of capitals from the glazed tracery, one of many examples at St-Urbain, anticipates French Flamboyant architecture [187]. *Below:* view from the south-east. The detachment of the gables from the window walls recalls the separation of windows and vault at Auxerre and Dijon [76, 77].

Perhaps the most telling of the many traits common to Carcassonne and Narbonne is the distinctive treatment of their arcades. At Carcassonne these undergo an internal development ending with a solution very close to the strange Narbonne arrangement whereby finely profiled arches spring directly from the broad curved surfaces of the cylindrical pier cores. The only major difference is that at Carcassonne the piers are simple columns while at Narbonne they have eight shafts. In fact Narbonne's shafts amount to little more than ridges on the surfaces of the basic cylinders, quite unlike the closely spaced and boldly projecting colonnettes which almost conceal the cylindrical cores of most Rayonnant piers [84, 137], including the responds in the ambulatory at Narbonne. It would be natural to assume that Narbonne's arcade piers were originally to have been as richly shafted as the responds and that their present form represents a revision of the design. However, there is a good chance that at least their basic conception goes back to 1272, since columnar piers and many-shafted responds had already been combined at Carcassonne. Probably the original intention was to contrive an equally piquant contrast between bare arcades and richly Rayonnant upper storeys, a contrast which can still be savoured in the choir of Toulouse Cathedral. Toulouse was begun in the same style in the same year, 1272, and its patron was the bishop who had settled a dispute between the archbishop of Narbonne and his chapter about the siting of their new cathedral. Narbonne's upper storeys as finally built conform to the austere aesthetic of the piers. The range of possible explanations for the simplification is considerable, but adjudication between them is almost impossible since the date of the change is unknown. Lack of money almost certainly played a part, as the archbishop who ruled between 1295 and 1311 concentrated on building his palace, and in 1317 the southern French dioceses were subdivided, with the result that the revenues of both archbishop and chapter declined. The aesthetic preferences of Jean Deschamps, the architect in charge from 1286, are likely to have been a factor, since the choir of Clermont-Ferrand Cathedral, which he began 38 years earlier, had by this time been completed with a narrow clearstorey and an unlit triforium essentially similar to Narbonne's if not quite so drily detailed [87]. The aesthetic and practical preferences of the patron could well have determined that the windows be small so as to exclude more of the strong Mediterranean sun. This local usage was already being followed in the churches built in the region by the friars, the leaders of the fight against heresy in the cities of the south and main beneficiaries of the patronage of the local nobility and upper bourgeoisie. For a cathedral to be influenced by friars' churches was inconceivable in northern France, but a case of such a relationship already existed in the south, at Albi, where the severely simple aisleless cathedral begun in 1282 was essentially a mid-13th-century Toulouse friars' church writ large [194]. The bishop was a Dominican, preoccupied with the suppression of heresy, whose cool relations with the French crown may well

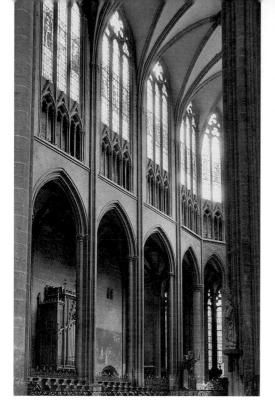

87 Clermont-Ferrand Cathedral, choir looking north-east, 1248–80. As in most Rayonnant cathedrals, large areas of predominantly white glass enable the refinements of the architecture to be seen clearly. Whether this was the intention behind the move away from deep colours is not certain, however, for white was also a symbolically favourable colour, connoting glory, virginity, purity, etc.

88 Narbonne Cathedral, choir looking east, begun 1272, at least one radiating chapel completed by 1289, main vessel completed by 1333.

have encouraged him to reject the Rayonnant style. Since the endemic anti-clericalism of the southerners deprived great church building of much popular support, the cheapness of Albi proved to be better suited to local needs than Narbonne's elegantly simplified version of Rayonnant. Narbonne itself remained only a choir; at Toulouse not even the choir was finished; and Rodez, the one other southern cathedral on the Narbonne model, reached completion only in the early 16th century.

High Gothic and Rayonnant façades

During the 12th century flying buttresses had managed to remain strangely immune from any kind of aesthetic control. It is difficult to believe that such brutally plain pieces of 'engineering' as the buttresses at St-Remi in Reims were not thought to look odd in relation to the smooth, elegantly detailed elevations which can only be glimpsed between them [42]. With the advent of the multi-tier buttresses needed to support the tall clearstoreys of the High Gothic cathedrals, the problem could no longer be ignored, and even the very first examples of the type, those on the nave at Chartres, carry statue niches excavated out of the buttress piers [62]. However, these towering excrescences needed more than a figleaf to make them decent, and the piers of

89 Cologne Cathedral, shrine of the Three Magi, attributed to Nicholas of Verdun, probably begun shortly after 1181. This is the most important 12th- or 13th-century shrine to have survived in the possession of the church for which it was made. At the dedication of the 13th-century choir in 1322 it was installed in the axial radiating chapel (see p. 152).

the slightly later choir buttresses are endowed with miniature imitations of the canopies in precious materials which it had long been customary to place over main altars and shrines. Altar canopies symbolize the vault of heaven, and a multiplicity of smaller canopies conjures up the dwelling-places of the saved in heaven (John 14:2).

The canopies on the choir buttresses at Chartres belong to a fairly widespread movement in French Gothic of *c.* 1180–1220 to enrich exteriors with borrowings from goldsmiths' work, traditionally the most esteemed form of church art by virtue of its association with altars and relics [*89*]. On the west portals of Notre-Dame at Mantes (*c.* 1180), figure sculptures inspired by the internationally famous metalwork of the Meuse region are accompanied by finials and crocketed gables clearly derived from those on reliquaries and shrines. The plinth of Notre-Dame in Paris shows further borrowings from this source juxtaposed with a version of a Classical triglyph-and-metope frieze [*90*]. The symbolic intent is unmistakable, for the pseudo-goldsmiths' work of the upper arcading frames figures of virtues and the metopes portray vices. Classical Antiquity, which could still inspire such minor elements in Early Gothic churches as the fluted columns on the clearstorey at St-Remi in Reims, is here anathematized as pagan and evil, of value only as an object lesson. The adoption of a decorative idiom based on a specifically Christian and Western art form is symptomatic of the hardening attitude of the early 13th century towards all alien cultures: Antique, Muslim, Jewish and heretical Christian. In 15th-century Low Countries painting 'Gothic is consistently equated with authentically Christian architecture, and although the earlier pictorial evidence is far less extensive, it is clear that this perception was already current in the 13th century.

How long metalwork-derived architectural forms retained their original connotation is not known. At Reims the buttress canopies are assimilated to the type used on the west front of Laon, whose ancestry was at least partly architectural [*49, 62, 63*]. At the Sainte-Chapelle, where the interior was treated to an exceptional degree as fictive metalwork, the external gables

90 Paris, Notre-Dame, west front, dado of the right-hand jamb of the central portal, c. 1200–1210. The diaper patterning below the figures resembles the background to the prophets on the lower tier of 89, and the spandrels of the trefoil arches enclosing the upper figures have what look like settings for imitation gems.

over the windows can be understood as an allusion to the gabled niches lining the sides of many Mosan shrines. What is more certain is that by the 1250s gabled windows had lost any specific meaning and had become just another fashionable motif [40, 95]. During the second half of the 13th century, the direction of the earlier influences was decisively reversed, and not only metalworkers but artists in all media regularly imitated the decorative architecture of the great churches.

Compared to internal elevations, major façades of c. 1200–1250 embody a less coherent evolution, no doubt mainly because relatively few opportunities for building them arose and expectations as to the form they should take were correspondingly undeveloped. Nevertheless, there is a parallel pattern of diversity and experimentation in the High Gothic period, succeeded from around 1245 by comparative uniformity. The transept fronts at Chartres are treated with unprecedented richness [62], as if to compensate for the west front not built when, as an afterthought, it was decided to retain the 12th-century façade. From the point of view of their creators, the most important attribute of the Chartres transept façades will have been their capacity to shelter the largest array ever seen in statuary of the battalions of the Church Triumphant. In their architecture both fronts are essentially adaptations of Laon's west front [49] to the enlarged scale and tall proportions determined by the internal spaces. The narrow arches flanking the central opening of the porch are a device for keeping the latter small enough to enable all three portals to have jamb figures of the same size and lintels at the same level. Limiting the height of the central opening also allows the introduction under the rose of long lancets which encourage a reading of all the windows as one composition, a five-light version of the clearstorey pattern. This encouragement is given only on the south front; the designer of the upper part of the north front included a string course between rose and lancets, a variation which indicates that he regarded the latter as a glazed version of the triforium. Most 13th-century French architects followed this line of thinking.

91 Amiens Cathedral, west front, begun 1220, completed up to the level of the rose window by 1243. The top storeys of the towers, the tracery of the rose and the gallery over the rose are 15th-century.

Among these was Robert de Luzarches. Unfortunately his west front at Amiens is as unsatisfactory as his nave is superb [91]. The extremely tall proportioning of the main vessel resulted in a huge gap between the rose and the central portal, which Robert filled with a gallery of kings *and* a 'triforium'. Skied above this plethora of arches the rose looks insignificant. No less unhappy is the squatness of the aisle windows and the way they lurk behind the huge side portals. The portals owe much to Laon [49], but their arches have become disproportionately tall compared to the jambs and the pinnacles between the gables appear ludicrously big in relation to the gables and to the buttresses of which they form part. In surface decoration as well as width these major vertical elements are extraordinarily inconsequential. Almost the only commendable feature of the Amiens façade is that when viewed frontally it conceals its worst defect, namely that the towers are shallow rectangular affairs standing not on the western aisle bays but on the hind parts of the truly cavernous portals. This bizarre arrangement was probably a device to overcome the problem of restricted length caused by the

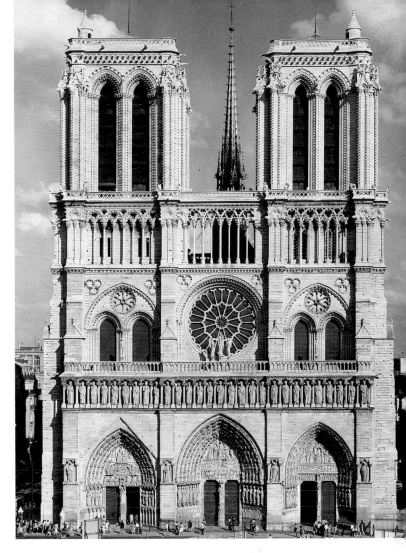

92 Paris, Notre-Dame, west front, c. 1200–1245. The unequal width of the towers results from the irregular setting out of the nave in the late 12th century [cf. *36c*].

presence of earlier buildings which could not be demolished; to have set towers over the west aisle bays would have given the nave very stunted external proportions, for its untowered part would have been barely as long as the main vessel of the choir [cf. *66e*].

The west front of Notre-Dame in Paris stands at an opposite pole from Amiens's shambling and congested façade [*92*]. That the familiar image of serene rectilinearity is partly fortuitous becomes clear when one adds in imagination the tall spires so obviously intended. The progressive tapering of storeys and deepening of buttresses can then be recognized as highly effective devices for making the transition from the cubic mass of the portal storey to the verticality of spires. A complementary sense of structural lightening is conveyed by the contrast between the kings' gallery and the traceried upper gallery and by the progressive enlargement of the openings in the towers. The pairing of all these openings is a minimal acknowledgment of the double aisles whose presence made the inclusion of large side portals so much more straightforward than at Laon [*49*].

Almost all that Notre-Dame takes from Laon is the deep arch framing the rose, a first tentative step towards offsetting its self-contained and hence fundamentally anti-Gothic character. Far less tentatively, the west front of St-Nicaise at Reims reduced the rose to being merely part of a magnification of the regular upright window design at Reims Cathedral [94, 67]. The cathedral masters had got as far as putting the transept roses within glazed pointed arches [63] but had declined to follow the designer of the south transept front at Chartres and treat the whole upper section as one window [62]. The St-Nicaise solution found few imitators, a consequence no doubt of the sheer accumulated weight of tradition. Another factor is likely to have been the general popularity of the normal type of rose. Present-day visitors like roses not least because their simplicity and integrity make them more easily comprehended than larger units of design such as bays. Only outside France did large windows of upright format become the usual centrepiece of major façades [110, 160, 169, 184].

St-Nicaise's other debt to the eastern parts of Reims Cathedral is the close match between the storeys of the towers and those of the internal elevations. However, the expression of structural realities is clearly not the guiding principle behind the design of the portals. There is no exact precedent for the way in which the gables zig-zag arbitrarily across voids and buttresses, although the sources seem clear enough. The north transept façade at Chartres must have suggested the pairs of open and blind arches between the

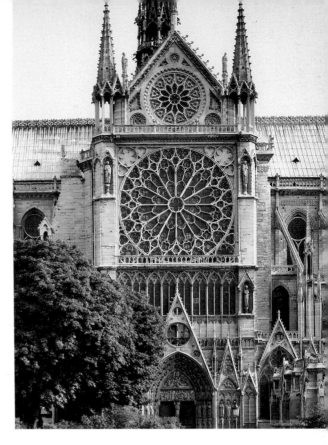

Opposite

93 Monument to Hugues Libergier (died 1263), originally in St-Nicaise, Reims, which he designed, and now in Reims Cathedral. The supervisory aspects of the architect's work are conveyed by the representations of tools used for checking workmanship: a measuring rod, a set square and a pair of calipers.

94 Reims, St-Nicaise, west front, probably begun *c.* 1240 (destroyed). This was the only major 13th-century French façade whose main window matched the tall proportions and pointed-arched profile of the interior space which it lit. The towers, based on Laon's [49], were the model for those of Reims Cathedral [63].

95 Paris, Notre-Dame, south transept front. The starting date (12 February 1258) and the name of the architect (Jean de Chelles, died *c.* 1260) are known from a contemporary inscription at the base of the façade.

central and side portals, and the pinnacles of the portal-dividing buttresses at Amiens [91] appear to be the inspiration for the sequence of seven gables, since the tracery under the latter is a modernization of that on the former. To the designer of St-Nicaise, Hugues Libergier [93], the tracery window of upright format was preferable not only to rose windows but to the traditional architecture of portals. His portals were unusually small and their modest allocation of sculpture was fitted into blind tracery so as to interfere as little as possible with its essential flatness and thinness. This solution also was too radical to find general acceptance, though it seems to have prompted the designers of the slightly later transept façades at Notre-Dame [95] to devise a more cautious reform of the archaic architecture of High Gothic portals.

The main debt of the Notre-Dame façades to St-Nicaise, their gabled portals, highlights the more disciplined approach of the Parisian designers, for whereas St-Nicaise's third and fifth gables overlap the buttresses in a rather disquieting way, at Notre-Dame the gables fit tidily into the main structural divisions. The line-up of statues flanking the central portal of St-Nicaise is retained at Notre-Dame, and although the portals themselves include the traditional sculptured tympanum, archivolts and jambs, they preserve the upright proportions of Libergier's portals along with his principle of containing figure sculpture within firmly delineated architectural settings. Comparison of the jambs on the north transept portal at Rouen (a fairly exact imitation of the south transept portal at Paris) with

96 Rouen Cathedral, north transept portal and forecourt, begun 1281.

those of the central Amiens portal shows the extent of this 'architecturalization' [96, 97]. Amiens's residually Romanesque weightiness and recession are eliminated at Notre-Dame and Rouen by reducing the arch orders from nine to three, and verticality is emphasized by elongating the overall proportions, by introducing continuously moulded arches between the jamb figures and archivolts and by breaking up the plinth into a series of upright pedestals for the jamb figures. These lose their quasi-columnar role and are fitted into deep niches. Thus the canopies, which at Amiens cut across the jamb shafts, become part of a larger and more coherent scheme. Amiens's additive, encrusted quality has given way to something as elegant and integrated as the Rayonnant interior, yet also distinctive in its minuteness, precision and delicacy.

The upper parts of Notre-Dame's transept façades owe almost everything to their slightly earlier counterparts at St-Denis, including the concept of squaring the rose. The treatment of the rim as just another tracery bar and the

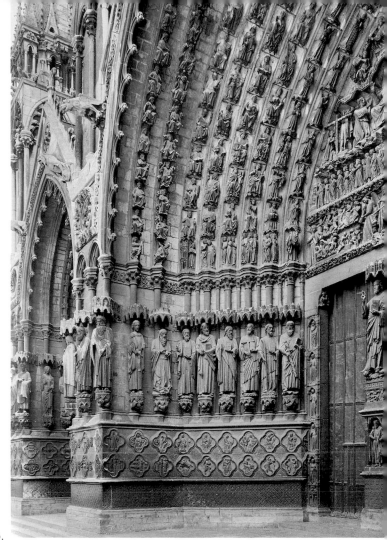

97 Amiens Cathedral, west front, left jamb of the central portal. This and many of the other Gothic portals whose sculpture depicts the Last Judgment are located on west fronts which face the setting sun and so recall the place of the Last Judgment at the end of earthly time. The gargoyles at the top left are 19th-century replacements but exemplify the vogue for grotesque marginalia in Gothic buildings, at its height in the period *c.* 1220–1350.

linking of rose and square by traceried spandrels are less extreme alternatives to Libergier's method of de-emphasizing the circle, since the rose still occupies a whole storey and remains the largest single element. The use of identical tracery in both glazed and solid spandrels is the most important instance yet encountered of the use of tracery to blur structural distinctions, a process anticipated in the glazed triforium of St-Denis and in the partly blind, partly open tracery of the porch at St-Nicaise. Below each rose at Notre-Dame is a triforium-like band of tracery linked to blind arcading in a way which invites comparison of its two-light units with those in the radial 'petals' of the rose. After their use here, 'petals' treated as two-light windows became a regular feature of Rayonnant roses. Not just the roses but the whole transept fronts of Notre-Dame inspired more imitations than any other Gothic façades, in places as far apart as London, Strasbourg and Clermont-Ferrand. Arguably the most impressive response was at Strasbourg [*100*].

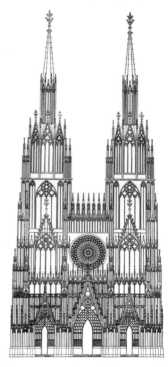

98, 99 Strasbourg Cathedral, west front. *Above left:* Scheme A, *c.* 1260–70. *Above right:* the more highly finished Scheme B, *c.* 1277. The precise functions of these drawings are not known. They may have been 'file copies' to guide future work or survivors from a larger number of designs made to enable the patron to choose between alternative proposals. A high proportion of the few surviving medieval architectural drawings show façades and towers, whose complete design could not be inferred from their lower parts if work was broken off for a long period. Drawings relating to the main bodies of medieval churches are far rarer, for the design of those parts was in principle established as soon as one bay had been completed.

Although Strasbourg was politically and culturally German until the 17th century, the nave of its cathedral (begun *c.* 1240–45) was as purely French as the Cologne choir, except for its breadth, the result of building onto earlier work. German-born masters were in charge by 1284 and possibly by 1277 when work on the west front started. Nevertheless, the pre-1300 parts of the west front stem so directly from French Rayonnant that they can best be considered within that tradition. The preservation of drawings showing preliminary schemes provides a unique opportunity to witness a design evolving 'on the drawing board' before a single stone was cut. 'Scheme A' of *c.* 1260–70 [98] is basically the Notre-Dame north transept façade made squatter to fit the breadth of the nave and extended to include towers with elevations much like those at St-Nicaise. The more fully worked-out 'Scheme B' of *c.* 1277 [99] is far closer to the existing front in having larger towers and a central section higher than the nave, and also in being sheathed in a profusion of mullions and pinnacles which break up most of the heavy horizontals inherited from Notre-Dame. Possibly for reasons of cost, 'B' was succeeded by the executed design, which preserves its essentials while reverting to some details of 'A'. The most original feature of the Strasbourg

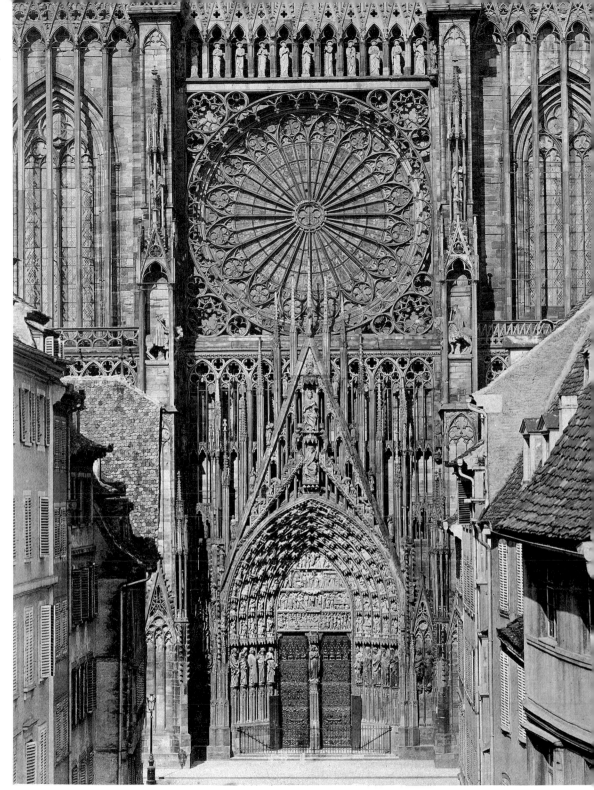

100 Strasbourg Cathedral, west front, begun 1277. The many detailed differences
between Scheme B [99] and the part of the façade shown here can be ascribed to the
architect Erwin who may have taken charge of work in 1284.

façade, the so-called 'harp' above the portals, is essentially a Rayonnant triforium built in the open air. Except perhaps for the extraordinary 'streamlining' applied to the south transept towers at Chartres [62], nothing in earlier Gothic façade design anticipates Strasbourg's tremendous surging verticals. The only convincing sequel is the west front of Cologne (p. 153).

The architects of the great churches

Despite the fact that information about cathedral architects and their procedures becomes somewhat more plentiful from the mid-13th century onwards, no consensus has yet been reached among specialists on the two central and interrelated issues of the social standing of the architect and the role of architectural drawing. It is often asserted that detailed designs drawn to scale were a novelty of the mid-13th century, and recently it has been suggested that their introduction brought architects enhanced prestige by enabling them to concentrate on designing while delegating to deputies the less glamorous business of translating designs into instructions for the executant masons. The view taken here is that scale drawings were probably not a new thing, that they helped raise the standing of their authors mainly through their affinity with the august discipline of geometry, and that the ability of architects to delegate the day-to-day running of sites was a consequence not just of the use of scale drawing but of the virtual ending of technical innovation in the Northern European Gothic tradition by around 1250. Because the processes of building became more a matter of routine than previously, there were likely to be far fewer unforeseen problems requiring the personal attention of architects. Thus architects of major projects were liberated from the need to be constantly present at a single site, and if their work was particularly in demand they became able to commute between several sites. Apparently the earliest documented instance of such a pluralist is Henry of Reyns, simultaneously architect of Westminster Abbey and several lesser buildings. The Master Aubrey who appears in the Westminster building accounts for 1249–53 was almost certainly acting as Henry's deputy, a function which within a decade or so was to become dignified with the title 'warden of the masons'. At each of Henry's other projects there would probably have been a counterpart to Aubrey. The employment of a German warden during the building of the lower parts of the choir of Cologne Cathedral would explain why, despite the impeccable Frenchness of the design, the jointing of the masonry was still being done in accordance with German Romanesque procedure.

Complex Rayonnant structures like the façades of Strasbourg or Notre-Dame in Paris were literally inconceivable without detailed preparatory designs drawn to scale. Some of the scholars who believe that such drawings were a novelty in the mid-13th century have suggested that it was their advent which caused architects to become preoccupied with linear patterning and miniaturized architecture more akin to small-scale drawings

101 Worcester Cathedral, wall arcade spandrel in the Lady Chapel, shortly after 1224. The architect sits back on the left, legs crossed, while what appears to be a small drawing on some kind of rigid support is scrutinized by a monk, probably the master of works (building administrator). The architect is shown holding large dividers of the type used for setting out the full-scale drawings needed to make the templates used by the cutting masons.

than to full-size buildings. However, it can equally well be argued that the survival of drawings from the mid-13th century onwards should be numbered among the effects rather than the causes of Rayonnant complexity; since the designing of the most elaborate Rayonnant buildings necessarily generated many more preliminary and working drawings than the equivalent High Gothic projects, the chances that some would survive were greater than hitherto. Indeed medieval architects must always have relied on fairly detailed drawings to communicate their proposals to their patrons, and what seems to be the only 13th-century depiction of such a drawing occurs in a pre-Rayonnant context [101]. Unfortunately, the one extensive early 13th-century collection of architectural drawings to have survived, the so-called 'sketchbook' of Villard de Honnecourt in the Bibliothèque Nationale in Paris, is not a representative sample. Villard's renderings of the eastern parts of Reims Cathedral are not merely crude but riddled with crass mistakes showing that he lacked such basic architectural skills as the ability to correlate cross sections and elevations. Equally revealing of his 'outsider' status is the series of diagrams showing formulas for setting out pointed arches, keystones and the like. Neither architects nor executant masons would have had any need of such a compilation; their procedures were enshrined in current practice and would have been transmitted orally and by example. But if Villard's drawings cannot be accepted as the work of a northern French cathedral architect, they do at least confirm that the main conventions of architectural drawing in use today were known by c. 1230. The purpose behind Villard's 'sketchbook' is still largely an open question.

The prestigious nature of architectural drawing was encapsulated in the now-destroyed labyrinth inlaid into the nave pavement at Reims Cathedral around 1290. This contained images of the four architects in charge of the work since its inception in 1211. Three out of the four appeared holding drawing instruments, and the first and last, Jean d'Orbais and Bernard de Soissons, were shown wielding large dividers to set out on the ground designs for the parts of the church with which they were particularly associated, namely the semicircular main apse and the circular west window. At least some observers would have made the connection with Plato's image of the divine craftsman and its centuries-old realization in Christian art as a stooping figure of God the Creator ('the Alpha and the Omega, the beginning and the end, the first and the last') using similar dividers to design the terrestial globe and the heavenly spheres. From the 13th century onwards dividers became a kind of professional badge for architects, as is evident from their appearance on tombstones and seals. But the most effective advertisement of the fact that the architect's art was founded on geometry was the precise, drawing-like linearity of the window tracery which so quickly dominated French architecture in the early 13th century. If the practical geometry of the medieval architect was far removed from the theoretical study which formed a fourth part of the university master's curriculum, the similarity was probably enough to engender respect among the many higher clergy who were university-trained. Admittedly, most of the clerical writers who expressed an opinion refused to classify architecture among the liberal rather than the mechanical arts, but the fact that the problem needed discussing at all is an indication that even a group usually reactionary in its social attitudes experienced difficulty in trying to evaluate an activity which had so much in common with one of the undoubted liberal arts. To those clerics who had first-hand dealings with architects these men would have seemed not lowly artisans to be condescended to but rather the specialist suppliers of an immensely prestigious commodity capable of transforming a religious corporation's public image. In the mid-13th century an architect described as famous could snub the unappreciative abbot of the important abbey of St-Trond in what is now eastern Belgium: 'If you do not like my excellent design [*id quod bene concepi*], I suggest you get yourself another architect.' To those who could afford it, artistic pride was evidently as important then as now.

The normal mode of address for architects in the 13th century, 'master', is attested from the Romanesque period onwards. Originally it meant simply the expert head and supervisor of a team of craftsmen, but by the 13th century it had probably come to have a rather grander ring to it since lawyers and university graduates used the same title. What seems at first sight a handsome acknowledgment of the Gothic architect's claims to be considered an intellectual worker is the title 'doctor lathomorum' (doctor or teacher of masons) which occurred in the epitaph of the important mid-13th-century Parisian architect Pierre de Montreuil (died 1267). However, this unique appellation cannot be used as evidence of a general advance in the standing of architects. It is primarily a piece of poetic licence intended to convey Pierre's status in the eyes of his admiring patrons, for the writer of the epitaph would have been a monk of the abbey of St-Germain-des-Prés, whose Lady Chapel Pierre had built and in which he was buried. By praising their architect the monks were praising their own judgment. A similarly flattering upgrading of the normal title occurs long before the advent of Gothic architecture in a late 11th-century text written at St Augustine's Abbey in Canterbury, where besides being called 'the most eminent master of the craftsmen' the architect of the abbey church is hailed as 'the remarkable *dictator* of the church'. (In the Roman Republic the *dictator* ruled in times of emergency along with the master (*magister*), his second in command.)

Another document often but wrongly adduced as evidence that French architects attained a quasi-academic status in the 13th century is the grave slab of Hugues Libergier, architect of St-Nicaise in Reims [93]. Certainly Hugues's cap is indistinguishable from the university doctor's *pilleus*, but it is his costume as a whole which pinpoints his status, for it exactly matches that shown in similar slabs commemorating the rich burgesses of northern French towns. It is in fact the 13th-century equivalent of the business suit. Although the bourgeoisie is the social stratum to which we may be certain that the designers of major Gothic churches normally belonged, by the 14th century outstandingly important architects like Peter Parler and Henry Yevele could be regarded as squires, the lowest rank of the nobility. Already in 1255 John of Gloucester, second architect of Westminster Abbey, was receiving livery robes equal in quality to those of the king's household knights.

Much the most remarkable feature of Hugues Libergier's monument is the simplified 'model' of St-Nicaise which he holds in his right hand. Derived from earlier portrayals of donors or founders of churches, this is a unique and potent symbol of the church building as the architect's 'artistic property'. The intention is still votive, but it is now the skill of the individual rather than his wealth which is being offered to God. A similar meaning was probably intended when around 1260 an inscription honouring the recently dead architect Jean de Chelles was cut into the base of the south transept façade of Notre-Dame in Paris [95]. This is among the earliest known instances outside Italy of a 'signature' on a building, although comparable inscriptions had long been placed on precious metalwork. The equally prominently sited late 13th-century labyrinths at Amiens and Reims paid homage to the cathedral masters in a slightly different way, for the maze motif was an allusion to Daedalus, the nobly born designer of the labyrinth of King Minos and the very symbol of the skilled artificer in the ancient world. Yet architects' memorials of any kind other than tombstones remained extremely rare, and it seems likely that inscriptions on churches came to be thought excessive assertions of the claims of individuals to what was first and foremost a symbol of the church 'built in heaven with living stones'. Far more numerous than the French churches inscribed with architects' names were the 13th- and 14th-century English churches where the most important men responsible for the building were discreetly commemorated in groups of uninscribed sculptured heads showing typically a king (God's deputy and the feudal superior of ecclesiastical landowners), a bishop or abbot, an architect and a clerical building administrator. Nearly all the medieval architects' names known today have been unearthed from the building records which begin to survive in quantity from the mid-13th century onwards.

So far as is known, all the men who became architects during the Middle Ages had risen from the ranks of the working masons cutting stone at the bench. The only certain exceptions, clerics who turned their hand to architecture, were of marginal importance in the Gothic period save in Italy. Naturally, the great majority of masons remained shapers of stones rather than originators of designs. Yet the advent of bar tracery changed the nature of their work as it had that of the architects, for if one compares the nave of Chartres with the choir of Sées it is obvious that the stonecutting skills needed to make the two structures are of a quite different order [60, 2]. The demand for a more conspicuously skill-absorbing architecture is part of a general movement in 13th-century French culture towards luxury and refinement. Any masons who were unable to adjust would have had no trouble finding work meeting the ever-growing need for stone buildings of less complex kinds.

Germany

Apart from the nave of Strasbourg and the choir of Cologne, German cathedral architecture during the first two thirds of the 13th century was conservative in style and modest in scope. Every major church built during this period incorporates French elements of some kind, but these vary greatly in their modernity and in their provenance. So whereas the nave of Bamberg Cathedral [102] has pointed arches and heavy moulded ribs which would have seemed familiar on account of the German Cistercians' use of them over a long period, the nave of the collegiate church of Limburg-an-der-Lahn has finely moulded ribs and a four-storey elevation which could not have failed to register as both novel and French [105]. The essentially Romanesque character of most of the churches where French Gothic borrowings occur is hardly surprising, given that Germany had had its own distinctive and continuously evolving tradition of great church architecture for longer than any other region of Northern Europe. And there is a sense in which early 13th-century Germans were not being much more conservative than their English contemporaries in their attitudes to French Gothic. That German churches of the period are less Gothic than English churches is indisputable, but the differences stem mostly from the different Romanesque traditions onto which Gothic ideas were being grafted. Whereas the central feature of Anglo-Norman and Early Gothic great churches is a long east–west vessel made up of numerous short bays and treated as an elaborate shaft-arch system [39, 145], the typical Romanesque great church in Germany is shorter and more compact and includes far fewer and simpler elements. Because of this

102 Bamberg Cathedral, interior looking north-east from the west liturgical choir, begun c. 1215. Double-ended churches with east and west choirs had been a major architectural type in Germany since the early 9th century. Both choirs at Bamberg were originally separated from the rest of the central vessel by massive stone screens. The west transepts are one of several reminiscences of the first cathedral, built in 1007–12.

tradition of treating central vessels as a broad volume whose extremities arc always clearly visible, there was no scope for the development of any equivalent to the English tradition of adding on long eastern arms radically different in style from the rest of the church. Thus the replacement west choirs at Worms Cathedral (after 1171) and Mainz Cathedral (c. 1200–39) are short structures incorporating only such Cistercian and Gothic elements as would not impair their ability to harmonize with the earlier naves to which they were joined.

Mainz and Worms were two of the three most ambitious Romanesque cathedrals in Germany. The recent and expensive renovation of their liturgically most important parts not only protected them from demolition and replacement by Gothic buildings but prolonged their life as general models for major new projects such as Bamberg Cathedral. At the two Rhenish cathedrals where total rebuilding in the Gothic style did take place during the 13th century, there were good reasons for destroying the earlier churches: at Strasbourg the severe damage caused by a fire in 1176, at Cologne the smallness and simplicity of the early 9th-century cathedral relative to many other churches in the city.

104 *Below:* Boppard, St Severus, south side of the nave, *c.* 1220–30. As at Limburg [*105*], the galleries are accessible via stairs in the aisle walls.

103 Limburg-an-der-Lahn, St George, from the north, begun *c.* 1190–1200. Among many features retained from local Romanesque usage are the 'helm' spires on the turrets and towers, the walkway under the choir gallery roof and the colour scheme (white over plastered rubble, carrot red with yellow and black trim over ashlar).

The nearest thing to a German reproduction of a French Early Gothic cathedral is the church of Limburg-an-der-Lahn [*103, 105*], begun some twenty years before Bamberg. Why Limburg should be the most French-looking building of its time is not known. To most modern observers the distinctive characteristic of the exterior is a quite un-French boxiness generated by the shortness of all four arms and by the sheerness of the wall surfaces, but early 13th-century Germans who had not seen French churches at first hand would surely have been most struck by the non-local features: the ambulatory, the two-tower west end, the flying buttresses and the Noyon-type clearstorey passage. Internally too the shortness would have seemed less remarkable than the tall proportions and the bay design, a combination of a four-storey elevation reminiscent of Laon with a Sens-like alternation of vault responds [*39, 30*]. No doubt the massive compound responds were included partly on the strength of their compatibility with German Romanesque tradition. The only radical departure from Early Gothic usage in the bay design of the main vessels is the substitution of stout square-sectioned piers for the columnar piers found in the majority of 12th-century French cathedrals. These allow the top-heavy effect of Laon or Paris to be eliminated in favour of a logical progression from robust main arcades

0   5   10   15   20m

105 Limburg-an-der-Lahn, St George, longitudinal section. One of two staircases to the nave galleries appears through the easternmost bay of the nave arcade.

to lighter and richer upper parts. The oldest and most famous of the many German buildings incorporating unmoulded arcades of the Limburg type is Charlemagne's Palatine Chapel at Aachen (c. 790–800) and it may be that there is a conscious echo of Aachen in the rather stark juxtaposition of the main arcades with the elegant arcaded 'screens' of the galleries. Aachen's gallery was used by the emperor and his suite, so there is at least a possibility that the analogous spaces at Limburg also functioned as privileged accommodation, in this case for the local noble and bourgeois families from which the priests forming the collegiate body were recruited. What is certain is that Limburg's galleries were meant to be much more accessible than those in the French Early Gothic cathedrals, for unlike the latter they are reached via straight staircases rising through the outer walls of the nave.

Among a considerable number of Rhenish buildings influenced by Limburg is the collegiate church of Boppard [104]. The nave here shows the same restless and quirky linearity as the upper parts of Limburg's west towers, and in fact this is a common characteristic of early 13th-century Rhenish architecture. Cusped 'fan' windows of a well established local type [cf. 108] pierce the base of a tunnel vault overlaid by sixteen radiating ribs, a capricious and unique variation on sexpartite vaulting. The vault seems all the odder for being so unrelated to the stolidly Romanesque arcade and gallery, although the disparity is no greater than that between the two lower storeys at Limburg. If Limburg had been destroyed, Boppard would not now be recognizable as a twice-Germanicized version of Laon.

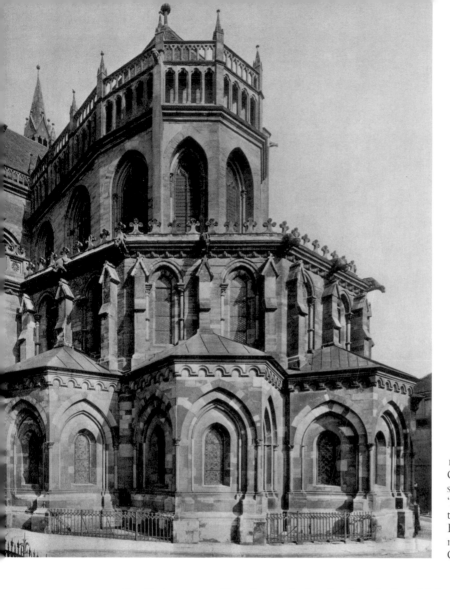

106 Magdeburg Cathedral, choir from the south-east. The 'horizontal scalloping' on the gallery cornice is a Burgundian Romanesque motif disseminated by the Cistercians.

Stylistic anomalies abound also in the choir of Magdeburg Cathedral in Saxony, although here the main cause is the far commoner one of interruptions in construction giving rise to changes in the design. This is the only early 13th-century German choir with both an ambulatory and radiating chapels, yet in style these parts of the building are far from being French. The prismatic exterior [106], the pointed arcade arches [107] and groin vaults, and above all the elephantine massiveness, derive from Basle Cathedral in Switzerland, rebuilt from c. 1189 on traditional German Romanesque lines but including a leavening of Burgundian Cistercian influences. Magdeburg's gallery is a more committed essay in French Early Gothic (though this is only fully apparent from within the gallery), and was designed by an architect whose earlier work included several Cistercian buildings in south-west Germany. The clearstorey reverts to the unbuttressed sheerness of the lowest storey and is surmounted by a Gothicized

107 Magdeburg Cathedral, choir looking north-east: first stone laid in 1209; concerted building work begun *c.* 1219; gallery, *c.* 1225–35; clearstorey, *c.* 1235–45 (tracery inserted in 1567). The clearstorey windows show the influence of French High Gothic [cf. *60*] and may have superseded a scheme providing for low windows and a triforium.

version of the German Romanesque eaves gallery. The un-German narrowness of the main vessel must have been intended to evoke the French cathedrals. The actual height (*c.* 30m) is less than that of the highest French churches, but closely matches Speyer Cathedral and the Palatine Chapel at Aachen, the other two German churches whose imperial associations equalled those of the 10th-century cathedral at Magdeburg, the grandest church of its age and the showpiece of Otto I's 'capital' and bastion against the Slavs. Oddments salvaged from this and other structures are worked into the main elevations: niches for relics previously walled into the Ottonian cathedral, Antique marble and granite column shafts from the same source, and figures from the first German attempt at the French Gothic type of sculptured portal. With its formal coherence so compromised by these mementos of its illustrious past, Magdeburg had no real chance of becoming a pattern for future German cathedrals.

The nave of Bonn Minster, begun *c.* 1210, is perhaps the one building of its time which achieves a genuine fusion of the French and German traditions, though since these traditions were so divergent there was no possibility that their contributions would be of equal weight [*108*]. The basic aim at Bonn was to imitate the cathedral of Geneva in Switzerland, a member of the 'family' of Early Gothic designs represented in this book by the Trinity Chapel at Canterbury [*58*]. The German elements – round arches, long bays, domical vaults, pilaster-like responds – all increase the autonomy of the individual forms and so immobilize the Gothic qualities of Geneva. High arching flyers ruffle the exterior calm somewhat, but the nave is sandwiched between earlier apsidal transepts and an apsidal westwork, traditional Rhenish Romanesque features treated in the traditionally massive and smooth-contoured way.

The non-French traits of the Bonn nave derive from the enormously prolific Lower Rhenish 'school' centred on Cologne, most of whose products were not great churches. The influence of these buildings was felt in Westphalia to the north, where the most notable 13th-century great church is Münster Cathedral [*109*]. Hence the strongly Lower Rhenish flavour of the domical vaults with ridge ribs, the wall passage in the apse, the triple clearstorey lancets, and the eccentric placing of the triforium openings. Many of these elements, with others of similar provenance, were appropriated not directly but via the only other early 13th-century Westphalian great church, Osnabrück Cathedral, begun in 1218. At Osnabrück, double bays of the standard 12th- and early 13th-century kind incorporate the non-standard feature of blind arches enclosing each pair of arcade arches, and these were undoubtedly the basis of the enormously long arcades at Münster. However, the main aim behind Münster's wall-voiding arches was probably a desire to assimilate the basilican scheme as far as possible to the hall church type, which by *c.* 1230 had been employed for a number of important Westphalian churches, including two cathedrals. By the end of the 13th century the hall was well on the way to replacing the basilica as the normative type of church throughout Central Europe [*112*].

The fact that every one of the very different great churches designed by early 13th-century German architects failed to become a model for general imitation is not too surprising, as none of them embodied a vision as authoritative and coherent as that developed in northern France during the same period. And even if German architectural traditions had been less inimical to Gothic aesthetics, the cultural and political climate of Germany after *c.* 1200 was not favourable to the creation of a unified national tradition of Gothic cathedral design, for centralized authority was everywhere in retreat before regional particularism and the bishops had become notorious for their preoccupation with extending their temporal powers. From around 1220 virtually all the more architecturally active cathedral authorities were tacitly acknowledging the failure of the native tradition by employing

108 Bonn Minster, nave looking north-east, begun *c.* 1210. The squat cusped windows in the aisles derive from Rhenish Romanesque.

109 Münster Cathedral, interior seen from the site of the western liturgical choir, begun *c.* 1230, dedicated 1264.

French architects to extend, complete and embellish works begun by Germans. More or less sudden stylistic about-turns were effected at Mainz, Bamberg, Naumburg and, most tellingly of all, at Strasbourg, where completion of the Lower Rhenish Romanesque-cum-Cistercian Gothic transept with a tall Chartres-type clearstorey *c.* 1220–30 was followed, after about a decade, by the start of work on the purest of French Rayonnant naves. The adoption of a French design for the complete rebuilding of Cologne Cathedral from 1248 was thus virtually inevitable, although to the inhabitants of Cologne the new work must have come as a shock, for it was effectively a declaration that the hallowed architectural traditions of Germany's greatest city had been found inadequate for the highest purposes [*84, 111*]. The clergy of the other churches in Cologne and of other German cathedrals would have realized at once that their own buildings had been outclassed, but there is the possibility that the size and modernity of Cologne Cathedral's architecture embodied a more interesting form of competitiveness.

Although technically the patron at Cologne was, as usual, the chapter, it is clear that the driving force behind the project was Archbishop Conrad von Hochstaden (1238–61) who, after the pope's deposition of the Emperor

110 Cologne Cathedral, west front, designed *c.* 1300–1310: the two lowest storeys of the south-west tower, *c.* 1310–1410; the remainder mostly of 1842–80. It is unlikely that the original designs would have been adhered to if work had reached the upper levels during the Middle Ages.

Opposite

111 Cologne Cathedral, choir from the south-east, begun 1248, dedicated 1322. The general scheme is an enriched version of the choir of Amiens Cathedral (*c.* 1236–67). Variations in the detailing of the flying buttress piers indicate revisions to the design as work progressed from north to south.

Frederick II, assumed the role of 'kingmaker' in Germany. The ceremonial foundation-laying in August 1248 was attended by the king designate, William of Holland, and six weeks later Conrad exercised his traditional right of crowning at Aachen in his diocese. The fittings of the choir [*84*] were begun only around 1300, when the structure of the eastern arm had been completed, but the general outline of their iconography may well have been planned during Conrad's lifetime as it complements the architecture in presenting what from his viewpoint was an ideal image of the relations between the emperor and the German church, an alliance on the lines of that actually achieved only in France. The high altar is dedicated to St Peter, the first pope, and beyond it stands the shrine of the Three Magi [*89*], whom the Middle Ages regarded as the first Christian kings. At the east end of the northern range of choir stalls was once a statue of Pope Sylvester, precursor of the archbishops of Cologne in having baptised the first Christian emperor, Constantine, an image of whom stood in the corresponding position opposite. On the piers are statues of Christ and the Virgin leading the twelve Apostles (the pillars of the church) and below them, painted on the wall

behind the northern stalls, are all the archbishops of Cologne lined up behind the Sylvester image. On the south side – the less honorific side, God's left – are the emperors led by Constantine. Below the paintings sat the living archbishop and his chapter. In 1049 Pope Leo IX and the Emperor Henry III had sat in the equivalent stalls to those under the Sylvester and Constantine images, and thereafter the ruling pope and emperor had been honorary members of the chapter entitled to seats in the choir. Valuable as this unique iconography is for the insight it affords into the motives of the archbishops for rebuilding their cathedral in the style associated with the French monarchy, it in no way impinges on the architecture, which could equally well have contained a quite different scheme.

Independence from the inhibiting traditions of French Gothic façade design, allied to perfect mastery of the Rayonnant idiom, enabled the architect of the west front at Cologne to conjure a sublime vision of verticality unequalled in Gothic architecture [*110*]. His designs remained largely unbuilt, and the translation of vision into actuality was only made possible by the survival into the 19th century of a splendidly detailed

112 Verden-an-der-Aller Cathedral, interior looking east, begun 1274.

elevation drawing of *c.* 1300–1310, perhaps made as a 'file copy' to be referred to during what would inevitably be a protracted campaign. His consistent use of windows of upright format acknowledges what outside France was an obvious fact, namely that roses are an insurmountable obstacle to designing façades which are perfectly integrated systems in the same sense as Gothic interior elevations. In the horizontal-breaking gabled windows of the Cologne choir [*111*] he recognized the ideal Gothic *leitmotiv*, and the bristling buttress piers of the choir became the basis for the complex pinnacles which so perfectly effect the transition from square towers to octagonal spires. The pierced tracery of these spires is a more inventive stroke than one can find in any northern French façade design later than *c.* 1270.

Around 1300, when the Cologne façade was being designed, it probably looked as though the future of Rayonnant cathedral architecture lay in Germany. The Rayonnant style did indeed gain universal acceptance there, and the process of assimilation was so rapid and thorough as to suggest the existence of a general recognition that the gulf separating Rayonnant from early 13th-century German Gothic was too wide to admit of compromise. Yet the late 13th and early 14th centuries were no more propitious for great church building than the period *c.* 1200–1250. Except for the choir begun at Regensburg Cathedral in 1275 as an enlarged and less sophisticated version of St-Urbain in Troyes, almost all the most important works of German Rayonnant are buildings of simpler and distinctively German formats. A case in point is the cathedral of Verden-an-der-Aller near Bremen [*112*], where the hall church type is modernized by means of windows derived from the Cologne choir and piers appropriated from St-Nicaise in Reims via

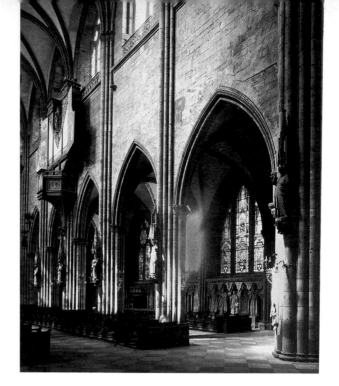

113 Freiburg-im-Breisgau Minster, north side of the nave, begun *c.* 1250. The bare walling above the main arcades was probably intended to be covered by paintings. The two bays in the foreground are earlier than the others.

St Elizabeth at Marburg, the earliest German hall church built in a purely French Gothic style. Verden thus combines the familiar and the fashionable, although unlike most such combinations from the early 13th century [104, 105] it is stylistically homogeneous. The modestly endowed chapter at Verden probably never contemplated building a French-style great church, but if they did, the spectacle of the slowly advancing choir at Cologne would surely have been enough to deter them. The far quicker rate of building at Strasbourg would not have been seen as an incentive to build grandly, for there, following the military defeat of the bishop by the rich and powerful municipality, the latter took over responsibility for the funding and direction of the works, an arrangement unique at a major Northern European cathedral. The widespread tendency of German bishops to conduct themselves like autonomous secular princes after the collapse of imperial power in 1250 can only have helped speed up a general gravitation of the laity's enthusiasm and money towards church building projects initiated by the towns, the most enduring and purposeful powers in late medieval Germany.

The minster at Freiburg-im-Breisgau and St Mary's at Lübeck are arguably the finest 13th-century examples in south and north Germany respectively of the 'burgher cathedral', that is an urban parish church which aspires to the condition of a cathedral. The nave at Freiburg [113] is a simplified version of the nave of Strasbourg in which Rayonnant luminosity gives way to the blank walling and small windows of German Romanesque tradition [102]. Freiburg and Lübeck were both new towns founded in the 12th century by commercially minded local rulers, but unlike Freiburg's merchants, those of Lübeck achieved full control over the government of

114 Lübeck, St Mary, choir, begun 1277. The height (39m internally) is surpassed in 13th-century German architecture only by Cologne Cathedral. The comparatively small clearstorey windows and the extremely thin walls through which they open have north German antecedents, for example the apse of Münster Cathedral [*109*].

their city. By the time that the choir of St Mary's was finished around 1290 [*114*], Lübeck's long-standing domination of the trade between the Baltic and the North Sea was consolidated by its assumption of the leadership of the Hanse, the league of towns soon to achieve a near-monopoly of Northern European trade. The strong trading links between Lübeck and Flanders, and the Flemish origin of many of its citizens, could well account for the Soissons-derived fusion of the ambulatory and radiating chapels [*66c*], for this scheme had been adopted in the three most ambitious church buildings of 13th-century Flanders, the choirs of Tournai Cathedral [*83*], St John's in Ghent (now St Bavo's Cathedral) and St Salvator's in Bruges, the latter two partly remodelled in the 15th century. Although Lübeck does not reproduce their Rayonnant elevations, the distinctive linearity of the style is effectively suggested by the fine-gauged masonry-based forms of its moulded brickwork. St Mary's was clearly judged to be a successful modernizing of the local brick tradition, for in the following decades a series of slightly simplified copies, all in brick, arose in the Baltic coastal towns founded from Lübeck around 1200 (Rostock, Wismar, Stralsund), at the Cistercian abbey of Doberan, at Schwerin Cathedral (completed by 1327) and at Our Lady in Copenhagen (begun 1316, destroyed). Lübeck's own cathedral was left two stages behind St Mary's, with a Gothic hall choir and Romanesque nave almost identical to those demolished to make way for the church which formed the real focal point of religious life in the 'capital' of Northern Europe's greatest mercantile Empire.

Spain

Until the early 16th century great churches were built in Spain only by exceptionally important cathedral chapters. This pattern predated the arrival of Gothic architecture, for out of hundreds of substantial Romanesque churches put up in the 11th and early 12th centuries none is a great church except the cathedral housing the national shrine of St James at Santiago de Compostela [3]. The prestige of Santiago was such that it became the chief model for late 12th- and even early 13th-century cathedral architecture in north-west Spain and Portugal. Castile's one great church from the late 12th century is Avila Cathedral, where tall proportions, false galleries and a St-Denis-like chevet were combined with Cistercian detailing. In being not merely French stylistically but the work of a French designer, and in lacking Spanish precursors or successors, Avila anticipated the three major cathedrals begun in the 13th century – Burgos, Toledo and León. A continuous tradition of Spanish cathedral architecture did exist before 1300, but only at a much less ambitious level. The minimally gothicized scheme represented in Germany by Bamberg and Naumburg had its counterpart in Spain, at Lérida [117], Ciudad Rodrigo, Salamanca (Old Cathedral), Tarragona, Tudela, and Zamora. The two-storey elevations, quadripartite vaulting on powerful responds, long bays, unambulatoried apses and broad, compact plans all derive from Castilian Romanesque, the pointed arches and rib vaults from French sources, mainly Cistercian and Angevin. Variously modernized, the Lérida scheme remained in use throughout the rest of the Middle Ages.

It cannot be a coincidence that Burgos and Toledo were based on Bourges [71–73b] and begun practically at the same time, Burgos in 1221 or 1222, Toledo in the latter year. Rivalry between the two sees went back to 1085, when Toledo was reconquered by the Christians and an archbishopric established, only eight years after the king of Castile had proclaimed Burgos 'mother and head' of all churches in his kingdom. Burgos was the main seat of the Castilian court, whereas Toledo was the largest and most sophisticated city then in Christian hands. The architectural debt of Burgos to Bourges is limited, as was inevitable in a church only two-thirds as high and with single aisles. The main borrowings are the 'split' piers and the very high triforium, the latter with plate tracery akin to that in the nave at Bourges. The disparity between the heavy enrichment of the triforium and the sobriety of the rest of the elevations foreshadows the late medieval Spanish penchant for extreme contrasts of rich and plain. A tall, basically Reims-type clearstorey and round Norman Gothic abaci hint at the possible peregrinations of the architect before his arrival at Burgos. His recruitment and indeed the whole idea of rebuilding are usually and very reasonably linked to a journey through France which the bishop of Burgos made in 1219.

Toledo [115, 116] is a far more ambitious building, for it imitates the staggered double-aisle scheme of Bourges, augmenting it with non-projecting transepts and no fewer than fifteen radiating chapels, seven of

115, 116 Toledo Cathedral. *Above left:* north side of the choir, begun 1222, completed late 13th century. *Above right:* inner north choir aisle from the west, with part of the early 14th-century choir enclosure on the right. The joints in the stonework were covered with gilded lead in the 18th century.

conventional size alternating with eight very small ones. Detailing is perhaps fractionally less close to Bourges than at Burgos but the distinctive piers are reproduced faithfully enough. The most remarkable passages of detail are the triforia. The oculi and arcades of the lower triforium are very like those in the transept end walls of Beauvais, a fellow member of the Bourges 'family' of designs, but the arcades, which were not back-lit originally, are discreetly islamicized with paired marble shafts and cinquefoil arches such as can still be seen in Toledo's Mudéjar buildings. The upper triforium [*115*] is more obviously Islamic in its overlapping lobed arches reminiscent of the Great Mosque at Córdoba. From a non-Spanish viewpoint it might seem strange that Islamic forms were tolerated in so important a church, but Toledo was the most orientalized city in Christian Spain and its main mosque had served as the cathedral since 1085. The Mudéjar style was patronized by Christians, Jews and Muslims, and what mattered most to the Christians was the recovery of their ancient sites, not the authorship of the beautiful and serviceable mosques which had come to occupy those sites since the Islamic conquest in the 8th century. After the christianizing of the Great Mosque of Toledo, a royal burial chapel was added at the east end. This was perpetuated in the 13th-century cathedral where until *c.* 1500 the apse was designated a royal chapel and separated from the single rectangular bay of the choir by a high solid wall. Eastern funerary chapels have a pedigree extending back to the 4th century, but here the aim was apparently that the kings of Castile be commemorated as leaders of the reconquest in a manner which echoed the setting of the relics of St James (the patron of the reconquest) in the apse of his

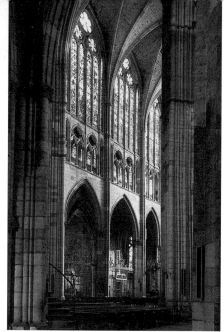

117 Lérida Cathedral, interior looking north-east, begun 1203.

118 León Cathedral, north side of the choir, begun soon after 1255. León was the first and last Rayonnant church in Spain, although a less fully glazed version of its upper storeys occurs in the nave of Toledo Cathedral (begun *c*. 1300).

cathedral at Santiago de Compostela. At Toledo, as at Santiago, the presence of a funerary chapel in a very short eastern arm necessitated using the crossing as part of the sanctuary and placing the choir stalls in the east bays of the nave. Choir enclosures in naves eventually became a normal feature of Spanish cathedrals [*208, 219, 220*].

After the final union of León with Castile in 1230, it must have seemed imperative that the mother church of the older kingdom be rebuilt as impressively as Burgos. In fact León Cathedral is even more straightfor-wardly French than Burgos. It was begun in 1255 to a design which Spanish scholars have always accepted as the work of a Frenchman [*118*]. Certainly no church in Spain anticipated León's pure Rayonnant style. Built of a rather coarse stone which necessitates the omission of such refinements as pierced cusps, its most original feature is the glazed lancets which prevent the traceried heads of the broad clearstorey windows from becoming too high relative to the lights, as they are in the earlier parts of St-Denis [*80*]. The slight recessing of the central section behind the flanking lancets derives from the late 12th-century western nave bays at St-Remi in Reims. No doubt a desire to outdo León was the spur to the bishop of Compostela who in 1258 laid the foundation stone of an immense eight-bay French Gothic choir intended to replace the short choir of the Romanesque cathedral as the setting for the shrine of St James. Work seems not to have progressed beyond the lowest walls before being abandoned some time after 1276. The failure of so prestigious a project must help explain why no further schemes of such high ambition were conceived in 13th-century Spain.

The Early English style

The reconstruction of the choir of Canterbury Cathedral from 1174 started a spate of great church building in England which, within a few years, had swollen to a flood rivalling in volume the productivity of France in the High Gothic period. The motor behind this activity was the familiar one of institutional competitiveness. Thomas Becket was perceived by the English clergy as having died in the cause of protecting the liberties of the church from the incursions of a tyrannical king, and his cult was seen by everyone to have brought real power and prestige as well as riches to the monks of Christ Church, Canterbury. Almost inevitably, many religious communities were encouraged to dust down the relics and reputations of their patron saints and to provide new shrines in purpose-built extensions to their Romanesque churches. Often the liturgical choir was moved out of the crossing and into the eastern arm, thereby emphasizing solidarity between patron and community and distancing the latter from the laity in the nave and transepts. But apart from being a vehicle for corporate self-aggrandizement, the growth of interest in native saints was also a symptom of increasing nationalism, a movement accelerated in ecclesiastical affairs by renewed papal determination to exploit the revenues of the English clergy. Resentment of the expansion of French power under Philip II, particularly after the conquest of Normandy in 1204 and the invasion of England in 1216, helped engender a mood of xenophobia which must account in part for the virtual drying up of French influences on English architecture after the completion of the Canterbury choir in 1184. However, another cause of the divergence of English and French Gothic at this time must be the unique character of the Canterbury choir itself. It was not only the most lavishly finished of all 12th-century Gothic buildings; it was also uniquely rich and diverse in invention and hence well able to feed the two main currents of early 13th-century English Gothic, the so-called Early English style: a 'national' version stemming from Lincoln Cathedral, and that of the south and south-east, whose main monument is Salisbury Cathedral. English architectural self-sufficiency is strikingly demonstrated by the almost complete absence of French influences in the years after 1214 when many prelates returned from six years of exile in France during the suspension of church services imposed by Pope Innocent III. This isolation is all the more remarkable for having begun at the very moment when most of Western Europe was taking its first lessons in French cathedral Gothic.

The choir of Lincoln (begun 1192) belonged to the only scheme for complete rebuilding to be undertaken at an English cathedral between Wells (begun c. 1180) and Salisbury (begun 1220). When an 'earthquake' caused great but unspecified damage to the Romanesque building in 1185, Lincoln lacked its own saint, but like other major English churches in the post-Becket era it set about manufacturing one. The claims of the founder, Bishop Remigius, were not particularly impressive, but it seems likely that his relics were to have been installed in a hexagonal chapel at the east end of the choir. Only the plan of this structure is known from excavation, for together with the rest of the eastern termination, it was demolished in 1255 to make way for an extension housing the relics of Lincoln's bona fide saint, Hugh of Avalon, bishop from 1186 to 1200 [*119*]. Not only the hexagonal chapel but the apse to which it was attached, the eastern transepts and the general elongation were all based on Canterbury [*56*]. In fact there is very little in the surviving parts of the Lincoln choir that was not inspired by either the Gothic or the Romanesque parts of Canterbury.

The first Lincoln master's admiration of Canterbury was tempered only by his readiness to improve on it by taking its richest and most complex variants as models for the regular forms in his design [*120*]. Thus the five-part vaults used throughout the aisles at Lincoln had been at Canterbury the solution to a problem which occurred in the aisles of only one bay; the partly freestanding responds receiving these vaults and the multiplication of clearstorey lancets had both been reserved for the most hallowed part of Canterbury, the Trinity Chapel [*58*]; and the use of a different design for almost every pair of piers imitates a pattern which had arisen at Canterbury partly as a result of revising the design and partly from the desire to indicate relative proximity to the saint's shrine [*57*]. Clearly the Lincoln master neither knew nor cared how unorthodox Canterbury was in French terms, for many of his borrowings are features which from an English standpoint seemed to confirm traditional usage. Important instances are the clearstorey passage and the low, Durham-like springings of the high vault. Most of his departures from Canterbury are reversions to English usage pure and simple:

119 Lincoln Cathedral, from the south-east. From right to left: Angel Choir, begun 1256; eastern transepts and St Hugh's Choir, begun 1191; west transepts, *c.* 1200–1220; crossing tower, after 1237 and *c.* 1307–11; nave, *c.* 1220–35; western block, late 11th-century, mid-12th-century and late 14th-century. All three towers carried lead-covered timber spires, that on the crossing 160m high.

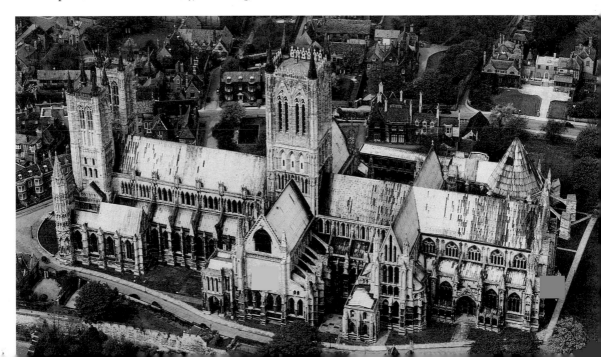

120, 121 Lincoln Cathedral, St Hugh's Choir. *Left:* north side. The high vault responds were originally linked to the piers. *Below:* wall arcade in the north aisle. The foliage on the capitals is 'stiff-leaf', usual in early 13th-century England.

the greater depth and profuseness of the arcade mouldings and the single shaft receiving all the vault ribs, perhaps modelled on the single shafts and flanking corbels which are known to have received the ribs of the Romanesque nave vaults at Lincoln. Yet despite these anglicizings it would be a mistake to categorize Lincoln simply as some kind of atavistic throwback. In common with Canterbury and all its French sources, the main arcades are far thinner than the upper walls, and before the building of the high choir stalls in the 14th century this storey must have conveyed a similar sense of structural slightness. The Frenchness of the effect permitted by the false bearing technique is not diminished by the fact that the latter is less competently done than at Canterbury.

As a technician, the first Lincoln master was, it must be admitted, weak; the numerous irregularities and botches suggest a workshop barely able to cope with the complexities of the design; and in 1237 or 1239, some thirty years after their completion, the eastern piers of the crossing failed and brought about the partial collapse of the central tower and western choir bay

122, 123 Lincoln Cathedral. *Above left:* pier in the west arcade of the south-east transept. *Above right:* vault of St Hugh's Choir. The longitudinal emphasis was originally underscored by bands of painted pattern flanking the ridge rib.

As a formal innovator, however, the author of the Lincoln choir is in the first rank. His work is very far from being the enterprising selection and reshuffling of older motifs which the discussion of sources in the preceding paragraph might suggest. The integrity as well as the singularity of his vision is instanced by the circular abaci and bases which he took over from the eastern transepts at Canterbury. At the time these must have had considerable novelty value, but their inclusion here is surely due to their value as complements to the softly rounded modelling and non-planar quality of the arch and jamb mouldings and to their inability to indicate the axis of the arch or rib they receive. At his most original, the first Lincoln master transforms his sources so completely that the historian cannot be confident of having traced his creative processes in anything more than the faintest outline. This applies to two of the most celebrated and characteristic of his devices for enlivening structure: the crocket piers in the eastern transepts [*122*], which owe to Canterbury all their basic elements except the crockets, and the aisle wall arcading [*121*] whose 'syncopated' rhythm of arches develops from the much more discreet arrangement of layered arches in the east triforium of the choir at Chichester Cathedral, the earliest southern sequel to Canterbury. Yet in terms of eccentricity even these designs pale beside the high vault of the choir [*123, 172p*].

The earliest high vaulting surviving at Lincoln, that in the eastern transepts, is already unconventional by 12th-century French standards. It is sexpartite but set over single rather than double bays, in the manner of the west bay of the choir at Vézelay [*29*]. There is some evidence that the original intention was to build a similar vault over the choir at Lincoln, but this plan

124 Lincoln Cathedral, nave looking east.

was abandoned, possibly out of dissatisfaction with the obstruction to the clearstorey caused by the intermediate ribs and webs. The vault actually built has been dubbed the 'crazy vault' on account of its asymmetry as well as the sheer oddness of its conception. Instead of converging at the centre of each compartment, as in all the rib vaults discussed so far, the lateral cells end at two different points, both roughly one-third of the way from opposite ends of the compartment. The lopsided rhythm set up by this arrangement effectively destroys any sense of the vault as a series of distinct compartments defined by transverse ribs and corresponding to the bay divisions on the side walls. Instead, the emphasis is placed firmly on the individual groups of four ribs and their staggered meetings at the longitudinal ridge. This bay-softening aspect of the vault is compounded by the introduction of a longitudinal ridge rib, the first prominent appearance of the motif in a great church. The longitudinal emphasis of the Lincoln choir vaults proved to be an influential development of that tradition of long receding vistas discussed in the preceding chapter in relation to Wells and Canterbury. The asymmetry of the crazy vault was ignored by English architects, although it foreshadows and may actually have influenced the even more conspicuously lopsided 14th-century 'jumping vaults' of northern Germany and Poland [172p, h].

The crazy vault is so unlike any earlier high vault that it might seem a forlorn hope to enquire as to its possible sources. Probably its non-converging cells were to some extent conceived as counterparts to two features of the aisle wall arcades, the 'syncopated' layers of arches and the refusal of the near layer to respect the bay divisions. The actual pattern of the diagonal ribs is not wholly unprecedented in Gothic vaulting, for it can be broken down into Y shapes or triradials. The head-to-tail arrangement of the triradials at Lincoln recalls that of the triangular compartments which make up the vault over the ambulatory of Notre-Dame in Paris [36c], a design quite possibly known to the Lincoln designer. Alternatively, inspiration may have come from the English tradition of centralized chapter houses. The extension to the city walls at Lincoln which the building of the choir necessitated also left room for a chapter house as large as the existing decagonal structure built c. 1230, so the architect of the choir may well have prepared a scheme for a chapter house during the 1190s. The scanty evidence available for other early centralized chapter houses suggests that the vault of such a building designed at the end of the 12th century would be of the simple pattern still used at Westminster in the 1240s [134]. To adapt the constituent triangular compartments of a Westminster-type vault for use over a longitudinal space would have involved little more than joining two opposite compart-ments along one of their longer sides [172g]. Some corroboration for an 'internal' theory of the origin of the crazy vault comes from the high vault of the nave [124], which was undoubtedly a direct response to the crazy vault.

The high vault of the Lincoln nave exploits the decorative potential of the sheaves of four ribs on the longitudinal surfaces of the crazy vault by increasing the number of ribs to five and by adding a further pair in each lateral cell. This first tierceron vault, so called from the purely decorative ribs between the transverse, diagonal and wall ribs, has a plan like four-pointed stars [172q], but from most viewpoints it resembles rather a series of palm fronds. The centres of each compartment are stressed by short transverse ridge ribs, but the boundaries between compartments are made indistinct by the sheer number of ribs on the longitudinal surfaces, in spite of the slightly heavier gauge of the tranverse ribs. As in the choir, a continuous longitudinal ridge rib underscores the horizontal aspect. Perhaps in order to avoid crowding the vault surface with the extra ribs, the bays are made considerably longer than in the choir. This adjustment also avoids the incipient congestion in the richly shafted upper storeys of the choir bays [120] and gives the nave arcades a generous length consistent with the breadth of the main vessel itself. The lengthening of the bays contributes further to the remarkable consistency of effect in the nave by increasing the visibility of the aisles from the central vessel. The process of looking is principally one of following the length of these three broad parallel spaces, and whether we look along or across, our line of vision passes supports of complex profile and arches whose undersides are richly textured. Large-scale vertical accents, especially the high vault responds, are too lightly stressed to do more than offset the major horizontals. The nave of Lincoln presents a vision of Gothic which is arguably as integrated and compelling as anything in contemporary French architecture. Comparison with the nave at Amiens [69] reveals how far the two main European traditions of Gothic had diverged during the forty years following the completion of the Trinity Chapel at Canterbury.

The cost of building one bay at Lincoln must have been considerably greater than at any of the French High Gothic cathedrals. Amiens is more than half as high again as the Lincoln nave, but most of the additional height is achieved by elongating supporting elements which are much simpler and therefore much cheaper than their counterparts at Lincoln. The cost of the extra courses of masonry in Amiens's simply profiled piers and mullions and the increased cost of building at very high levels cannot have equalled the greater outlay needed to realize Lincoln's far more elaborate design; and of course Lincoln, despite its relative lowness, necessarily includes in each bay as many arches and vaults as Amiens, elements which are much more time-consuming and costly to build than walls and vertical supports. Probably the most extreme variation in cost is that between the elementary profiling normally used for arches in the French Gothic cathedrals and the astonishingly complex and varied mouldings which occur throughout Lincoln and other early 13th-century English great churches [125]. It would not be surprising if one arcade arch of the English kind took twenty times longer to make than its French counterpart. The impact of this variation on

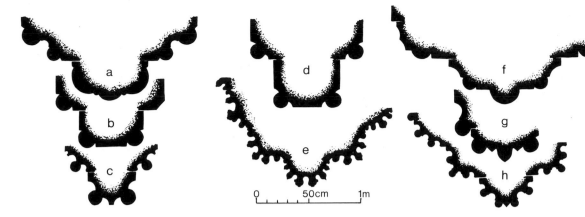

125 Sections through French and English main arcade arches: (a) St-Denis, west bay of west block; (b) Sens; (c) Bourges; (d) Chartres; (e) Ely, east part of eastern arm; (f) Durham, choir; (g) Ripon, choir; (h) Wells, transept.

the total building cost must have been considerable, for even in the Middle Ages craftsmen's wages were a very large component of building costs. This point requires some emphasis because the comparative smallness of the 13th-century English cathedrals is too often assumed to have made them cheaper than the French High Gothic giants. Indeed, the sumptuousness of the English buildings is amazing given the small size and population of the country. In the 12th and 13th centuries England was generally thought of as a rich country, particularly by foreigners, but more obviously relevant to cathedral building was the concentration of wealth in the hands of a few bishops and cathedral chapters. The number of English dioceses was still basically that fixed in the early Middle Ages when England was a far smaller, poorer and more sparsely populated place. Like Western Europe generally, England was experiencing an agricultural boom in the 13th century, and since ecclesiastical wealth derived mainly from land it is not too surprising that towards the end of the century papal tax collectors found that out of Europe's forty richest dioceses twelve were in England.

The ability of 13th-century England to support a tradition of Gothic rivalling that of France in both economic and artistic terms was thus due largely to the wealth of the major bishops' sees. Of course not every corporate patron of great church building was rich, but because their prestige was involved, the less well endowed bodies found themselves building more ambitiously than they would have done if their richest peers had not set the stakes so high. The emphasis of English Gothic on elaboration of detail rather than size was also a matter of cultural tradition, however, for the great post-Conquest Romanesque churches which were being altered, extended or replaced in the 13th century were at once a brake on the scale of new work and an incentive to demonstrate the modernity of that work by contrast with the comparative roughness and simplicity of what was being added to. Yet English expectations in regard to great church architecture were so

126 Wells Cathedral, west front, *c.* 1230–40 (upper parts of the towers, late 14th- and early 15th-century). The numerous statue-filled niches are a particularly elaborate evocation of the 'many mansions' of the heavenly Jerusalem (John 14:2), and the smallness of the portals was presumably inspired by the Sermon on the Mount (Matthew 7:13): 'Enter ye in at the strait gate.' The towers stand outside the westernmost bays of the aisles rather than over them [cf. *53*]. The lancets in the towers were originally open. Influence from contemporary French façade design is confined to details: the plate tracery quatrefoils above the lowest tier of statues [cf. the buttresses between the portals in *91*] and the trefoil-headed and three-sided canopies.

effectively fixed by the prestigious choir of Canterbury that they were conformed to even in projects such as Salisbury and Lincoln whose scale was not physically constrained by surviving Romanesque work.

Lincoln exemplifies another fundamental difference between English and French Gothic, namely the much greater readiness of English designers and patrons to countenance departures from original designs. We have seen already that the crazy vault of the choir was an afterthought; and at the moment when that change was decided on, the design of the gallery openings also underwent a fairly thorough revision [*120*]. These adjustments raise the unanswerable question of whether permission to make them would have been sought from the patron. If the authorities at Lincoln did indeed give their sanction to the crazy vault this would suggest tremendous self-confidence on their part. Lincoln's western transepts are the work of a second architect, a much less original mind than his predecessor, and again one can only ask whether the stylistic about-turn represented by his work reflected the wishes of the Lincoln clergy, who might well have had second thoughts about the choir design, or whether it was accepted that a new architect would automatically expect to be able to impose his own tastes. The almost reverential attitude of Gervase of Canterbury towards William of Sens and the tactical advantage any specialist has over his clients both suggest that the architect of a major project would encounter few obstacles to getting his way. However, it must be significant that at Lincoln the major changes of design coincide fairly closely with the start of work on the next main vessel to the west. Thus the main vessels of the western transepts are by the second architect and the nave is the design of a third. Apart from the adjustments made to the choir gallery by the first master, radical change within each main vessel seems to have been avoided. Nevertheless, the variety of Lincoln is extraordinary by comparison with any French High Gothic cathedral. It is possible that the three architects of Lincoln were simply exploiting the fact that the long and low main vessels of English Gothic churches were relatively self-contained and hence far less a single simultaneously visible interior than the main vessels of French cathedrals. However, it is tempting to associate the individualism of the Lincoln architects with a deeper cultural difference between England and France, one pinpointed at the time by the illustrious soldier-statesman William Marshal, who knew both kingdoms well. He was not paying the English a compliment when on his deathbed he observed that there were no people in any land like those in England, where each man had his own opinion. While France was becoming a nation newly united behind its kings, England was deeply divided about where ultimate political authority should lie. It seems legitimate to invoke the well-attested picture of England's inhabitants as excessively individualistic, factious and anti-authoritarian when attempting to explain why, despite its creative vigour, early 13th-century England produced no equivalent to the 'mainstream' tradition extending from Chartres to the reconstruction of St-Denis.

By around 1230 the architectural vocabulary of Lincoln had gained acceptance throughout England except in London, the south-east and the far south. In the south-west it displaced the Early Gothic manner of Worcester and Wells. The main outlet for invention was in the introduction of Lincoln motifs into schemes of varied format, for the individual forms of Early English Gothic, unlike those of French High Gothic, underwent no drastic transformation. The greatest concentration of churches influenced by Lincoln is in northern England and southern Scotland, although this may be partly an accident of survival due to the remote situation of many of the northern monasteries. The simplifications which the Lincoln styles underwent at the hands of their northern imitators can be set down to the more restricted means of the institutional patrons, to their conservative taste or sometimes to both these factors. A case in point is the only new cathedral choir completed during the period in the north of England or Scotland, that of Glasgow Cathedral [127, 128]. The Glasgow choir is by no means a cheaply finished building, but it omits three expensive features of Lincoln [cf. 124]: the masonry high vault, the marble shafts and the arcading on the aisle walls. The main vessel is spanned by a late medieval wooden tunnel vault perpetuating at least the basic form of the original covering. The omission of a stone vault can be ascribed to the survival of Anglo-Norman Romanesque tradition, but the tunnel form, like the banded effect which its continuously horizontal lower limit promotes in the upper storeys, probably derives ultimately from Byland [51]. The series of such vaults in northern England seems to have started with Fountains (begun in the late 1140s) and reached a climax of size and ambition in the transepts of York Minster, after the abandoning of successive projects for stone vaulting and a flat ceiling. Another feature of Glasgow understandable as a reversion to Romanesque usage reinforced by Byland influence is the rejection of false bearing in favour of piers as thick as the upper walls. Indebtedness to Yorkshire is evident in the similarity of Glasgow's four huge eastern lancets to the five in the north transept at York, and also in its simple rectangular ambulatory, a type disseminated from the Burgundian Cistercian abbey of Morimond to Byland and other Cistercian abbeys throughout Europe. Apparently the only borrowing direct from Lincoln is the plate tracery in the aisle windows. This kind of design is very reminiscent of Lincoln's nave triforium but was probably paralleled even more closely in the great west window at Lincoln before it was remodelled in the 14th century.

At Beverley Minster, in eastern Yorkshire, Lincoln's inventiveness is diluted by an even stiffer dose of neo-Cistercian puritanism than at Glasgow [129]. Beverley was a rich collegiate foundation and functioned to some extent as a kind of sub-cathedral in the York diocese. However, money was no doubt short in the aftermath of the collapse of a crossing tower which, had it been completed, would have been the last stage of the remodelling of the Romanesque church after a fire in 1197. Around 1220 it was decided to destroy both new work and old and to make a completely fresh start; hence the restricted use of expensive trimmings such as foliage capitals. The architect of Beverley had earlier designed the eastern extension of the Cistercian abbey of Fountains, and it seems likely that his appearance at Beverley was due to his having been in charge of the very large new church begun in 1207 at Fountains's daughter house of Meaux only 5km away (destroyed). The Cistercians had been participating intermittently in the development of northern great church architecture from around 1170 when Byland was begun, and echoes of Byland are still detectable in Beverley's banded upper storeys and slim vault shafts [51]. The clustered piers are also part of the architect's Cistercian heritage, but their detailing, like that of the

127, 128 Glasgow Cathedral. *Above:* view from the south-east: choir probably begun *c.* 1240, transept and nave early 14th-century, spire early 15th-century. The crypt under the choir exists partly to level up the sloping site, but, unlike that at Bourges [*64*], it also fulfilled important liturgical functions. The door in its south wall gave pilgrims direct access to one of two shrines of the cathedral's patron, St Kentigern. The extra space for chapels which the crypt provided probably explains why the transepts are short and without chapels. The crypt projecting from the south transept belongs to an abortive scheme for lengthening the transepts. *Right:* choir looking north-east. The high altar and the main shrine of St Kentigern stood in front of the pier below the east window.

rest of the design, is modernized in accordance with the innovations of Lincoln. Beverley's one obvious borrowing from Lincoln is its triforium modelled on the 'syncopated' wall arcading in the choir [*121*], although the debt only highlights the Beverley master's spiritual remoteness from the wayward and fantastical first Lincoln master. Along with the extravagant depth of the Lincoln arcading, its bay-disrupting character has been toned down, for the front layer contains complete arches rather than arches halved by the vault shafts. If this comparison is to the advantage of Lincoln, the same is hardly true of that between the nimbly stepping five-part arcade in Beverley's clearstorey and its source in the Lincoln choir [*120*]. Perhaps the single most important contributor to the energetic grace characteristic of Beverley is the exceptionally elevated level of the high vault springings. It is not absolutely impossible that the banded triforium and the extension of the clearstorey below the high vault springings were inspired by French High Gothic architecture; however there are local precedents for both, that for the latter being the architect's own earlier choir at Fountains, where high-springing vaults were practically forced upon him by the exigencies of building onto the 12th-century transept and nave. The level of the springings at Beverley demanded flying buttresses of much bolder profile than the roof-skimming flyers of Lincoln and Canterbury, but nothing in their design suggests personal knowledge of French High Gothic buttress design. Although direct French influences are unlikely, Beverley comes nearer than any other example of the Early English style to the austerely·cerebral beauty of Soissons or Amiens [*65, 69*].

Beverley's visual clarity is complemented by a very coherent system of proportions partly reliant on the ratio $1:\sqrt{2}$ (1.4142), a ratio used in Antiquity and perhaps even more widely throughout the Middle Ages. The square root of two arises naturally in the design process, for it is the length of the diagonal of a square whose sides are one unit long. Ready-made approximations to this irrational number were available to medieval mathematicians and architects, and one of these, 71:100, governs some of the basic dimensions of Beverley. The height to the wall heads of the main vessels and also the total width of the choir, including the thickness of the aisle walls, is 71 English imperial feet; the height up to the ridge of the roofs over the main vessels, 100 feet; the internal length of the main transepts, 171 feet (100 + 71). The other 'key' numbers besides 100 are 32, the width in feet of the central vessels of the choir and main transepts, measured between the centres of the high walls, and 27, the clear width of the main vessels. Many of the important dimensions in the church can be expressed as either a fraction or a multiple of one of these three numbers, or one of the latter multiplied or divided by the square root of two, or a compound obtained by addition or subtraction of numbers in these two categories. The dimensions derived from 100 and 32 or from 32 by itself include: the length and width of the aisle bays, 16 feet (32 ÷ 2); the height of the arcade piers, 23 feet (16 × $\sqrt{2}$); the

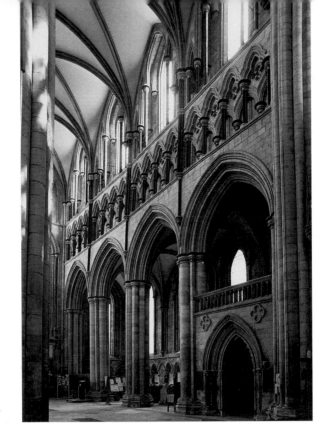

129 Beverley Minster, east
side of the north-west transept,
designed *c.* 1220.

height to the top of the triforium, 45 feet ($32 \times \sqrt{2}$); the total internal height,
to the underside of the high vault, 68 feet ($100 - 32$); the internal length of the
choir, 123 feet ($100 + 23$). The last dimension must surely have been chosen
for the value of its parts as a symbol of the Trinity and of the Creation (see pp.
65–6), an interpretation corroborated by the clear width of the main vessels
of the choir and western transepts, 27 feet (3^3). Dimensions based on 27
include the height of the central arch of the clearstorey, 19 feet ($27 \div \sqrt{2}$) and
the height of the shafts flanking this central arch, $13\frac{1}{2}$ feet ($27 \div 2$). However,
one or two of these relationships may be fortuitous since it is clear that the
heights of the storeys in the main elevations are determined by that universal
proportional tool, the Golden Section. Two of the standard approximations
to the Golden Section used in the Middle Ages were 52:32 and 35:22; hence
the springing level of the high vaults, 52 feet, and the relation between the
height of the main arcade, 35 feet, and the height of the clearstorey, 22 feet, or
$32 - 10$, 32 being the width in feet of the central vessel and 10 the height of
the triforium and square root of that other key number, 100.

Unfortunately, not enough analyses of the dimensions of other 13th-
century Gothic churches have been published to enable one to say whether
the Beverley architect's use of proportions was typical of the period.
However, two things that can be stated with some confidence are that $1:\sqrt{2}$
and the Golden Section were the most favoured ratios in the Middle Ages,
and that the width of the eastern arm was quite often used to generate other

dimensions. Obviously, all major churches were designed in accordance with a proportional system of some kind, since to have failed to follow the Creator in disposing 'all thing in measure, number and weight' would have been to lapse into a spiritual and psychological limbo. Equally obviously, the devising of proportional relationships took place only after decisions had been reached from aesthetic and practical standpoints regarding the approximate size and prominence of individual elements. Indeed the most remarkable aspects of the Beverley master's use of proportions are the ingenuity and determination he displays in integrating them into his highly personal artistic vision.

The one English great church begun in the early 13th century and completed in accordance with the original designs is Salisbury Cathedral. Salisbury is also unique in a still more fundamental sense, for it was the only English cathedral built on a virgin site in the Gothic period. The abandoning of the cramped hill-top at Old Sarum had been contemplated for many years, but it is very appropriate that the successful transplantation of the cathedral community to its present spacious setting [130] coincided with the confident and reformist mood which took hold of the English bishops immediately after the Fourth Lateran Council of 1215, the high point of the medieval Church Triumphant under papal leadership. The driving force behind the new building was the bishop, Richard Poore, who secured papal permission for the move from Old Sarum within a few months of his election in 1217. Poore had earlier been dean of Sarum while his older brother was bishop, and it may be that these personal ties account for two idiosyncrasies of the new building which, it will be suggested below, are possible reminiscences of the Romanesque cathedral. Nevertheless, Salisbury was clearly not conceived in a retrospective or nostalgic spirit. There can be no doubt that to all those involved in the formulation of the design, it was intended to be the very model of Gothic modernity.

In drawing up his design, the architect of Salisbury had access to detailed information about Lincoln and Wells, the two most important English cathedrals then under construction. The elongated and comparatively low proportions of each limb of the building and the resultant compartmented quality are in line with English tradition generally, but the inclusion of two sets of transepts both with only eastern aisles is a debt specifically to Lincoln [119]. Another Lincoln feature is the arrangement of lancet windows, two in the aisles, three in the clearstorey. The influence of Wells [53] determines that the clean external contours are not disturbed by any flying buttresses (those existing now are later additions) and that the only arched abutments are kept hidden below the aisle roofs. Lincoln's apsidal east end was rejected in favour of a rectangular ambulatory giving access to three rectangular chapels, the central one of which projects eastwards by two bays. In a simpler form, this kind of termination had been used in southern England from the early 12th century, and among the main Romanesque examples was the choir of Old

Sarum Cathedral. The destroyed late 12th-century east end at Wells was probably of this type.

Although Salisbury's rectangular ambulatory and projecting eastern chapels appear to follow in outline the equivalent features of Old Sarum Cathedral, their main importance is that they exemplify one of two types of east end widely used at English great churches in the 13th and 14th centuries, the other being choirs whose central vessel and aisles end with a straight east wall [119, 145]. The Salisbury scheme predominated in the south, straight east ends in the north. It is not certain that the 13th-century popularity of square ambulatories and projecting chapels was due to influence from Salisbury, but a circumstance favourable to such influence was the widespread and longstanding admiration for Salisbury's liturgical customs, an admiration which culminated late in the century with the more or less wholesale adoption of the Sarum Use by numerous English and Scottish cathedrals.

No influence whatever was exerted by Salisbury's west front. Its simple screen form derived from local Romanesque antecedents, and in this respect at least it was comparable to the far more elaborate and impressive screen fronts at Wells [126] and Peterborough, the greatest achievements of English façade design in the early 13th century. The decision not to build a towered façade at Salisbury was no doubt mainly an economy measure to assist rapid

130 Salisbury Cathedral, from the south-east, begun 1220, dedicated 1258 (crossing tower and spire probably completed by 1328); cloister and chapter house completed by 1266.

completion, but it might also have stemmed from a wish to avoid competing with the tower planned to rise over the central crossing. The great steeple which now occupies this position is early 14th-century above the level of the main roofs, but parallels yielded by other 13th-century English crossing towers suggest that its lower storey approximates to the full height of the lantern tower originally planned. The kind of spire intended in the early 13th century need not have been less needle-like than the present one, but it would almost certainly have been of lead-covered timber rather than stone. Considerations of safety no doubt dictated that the bells were hung in a separate free-standing belfry. This existed until the late 18th century.

The interior of Salisbury is more unified than that of any other English cathedral [131]. The only major variation in the design, the use of four-shaft piers in the nave in place of the eight-shaft choir type, is less likely to be a simplification of the original designs than a comparatively subtle expression of the lesser importance of the publicly accessible nave relative to the canons' choir. The extensive use of marble (readily available from nearby Purbeck) does nothing to lessen the overall impression of decorum and restraint created by the use of plain moulded 'bell' capitals and simple quadripartite vaulting. As at Beverley, where economic considerations also impinged, there is no simplification of arch mouldings, for these were clearly regarded as indispensable ingredients of great church architecture. The ultimate source of this sober aesthetic was the very plainly treated crypt of the Trinity Chapel at Canterbury, a building much in the public eye as the resting place of Becket's relics until their translation into the Trinity Chapel proper in 1220. The 'retrochoir' of Winchester Cathedral (begun *c.* 1202) [166], the choir of St Mary Overie, London, now Southwark Cathedral (begun in 1212), and the eastern parts of Rochester Cathedral (completed by 1215) are all heavily indebted to the Canterbury Trinity Chapel and especially to its crypt, and all anticipate to a greater or lesser extent the style of Salisbury.

By including so few decorative flourishes, the architect of Salisbury raises our expectations regarding the large-scale organization of the design. Unfortunately, this is exactly where he lets us down. The fault lies with the middle storey, a false gallery crammed into a low space of approximately the same proportions as that occupied by paired units at Canterbury and most early 13th-century English great churches [57, 120]. The resulting obtusely pitched arches and squat shafts are completely at odds with the erect proporting of the two other storeys and of the central vessel. Perhaps Salisbury's middle storey was due to the intervention of Bishop Poore or another member of the chapter. If the bishop was involved, he may have wished that the new cathedral should imitate a feature of his previous cathedral at Chichester, where galleries of more conventional proportions had been built in the recently finished eastern extension to the galleried Romanesque church. Another possibility is that the false galleries of Salisbury perpetuate the form of those in the early 12th-century choir at Old

131, 132 Salisbury Cathedral. *Above left:* interior looking east. The crossing was originally intended to be lit by the windows of a lantern tower, but was vaulted over in the 15th century. The piers are of Purbeck marble, their cores unpolished and coursed, their shafts polished and edge-bedded. *Above right:* axial chapel looking east, begun 1220, dedicated 1225.

Sarum. Yet neither Romanesque precedent nor the similarly plate-traceried and roughly contemporary false galleries in the transepts of York Minster explain the depressed proportions or the way in which the jambs of adjacent arches are fitted together too tightly to leave room for continuations of the high vault responds. The stubby proportions of the latter are so strongly reminiscent of those in the nave at Wells [55] as to suggest that the Salisbury designer was attempting to achieve a compromise between the banded effect of the Wells elevations and a traditional-looking false gallery. Whatever the thinking behind it, this highly unfortunate feature deprived Bishop Poore's new cathedral of the exemplary status that could have been expected to follow from the almost ideal conditions under which it was built.

Despite the Englishness of all the basic premises of Salisbury's design, it includes a handful of elements which seem due to influence from French High Gothic. The plate tracery of the false galleries could, at a pinch, derive from English sources, but the progressively greater prominence of the form in the façades of the east and west transepts and the nave suggests a growing awareness of the importance of tracery in France. The four-shaft piers used in the east wall of the choir and throughout the nave may have been intended for approximations to the normal High Gothic pier, although again there are alternative south-eastern English sources. The shafts of the Salisbury piers are not integral with the cores, as at Chartres or Reims, but edge-bedded, and the cores are in plan four segments of a circle rather than a single circle. The monolithic piers carrying the vault of the axial chapel may also combine a French concept with English handling [132], for their audacious slenderness is equalled only in the 'screen' before the equivalent chapel at Auxerre [76]. From a Continental point of view, what is more remarkable than the presence of French elements at Salisbury is the fact that there are so few. Probably it was inevitable that English Gothic would sooner or later be subject to a renewed wave of French influence, for most English prelates were aware of the number and splendour of France's new churches, and the Early English style could show nothing comparable to the formal evolution embodied in northern French Gothic of c. 1200–1240. It seems very apt that English insularity in architecture was first seriously breached by the rebuilding of Westminster Abbey [133] on the orders of Henry III, a king far more international in outlook than his subjects.

England and the Rayonnant style

Westminster is unique among Gothic great churches in having been paid for by an individual. All the other abbey churches and cathedrals discussed in this book were funded by the corporations which owned them, albeit with the help of donations from the faithful at large. The most ambitious churches built wholly at the charge of other 13th-century kings were Cistercian abbey churches which, although generally less austere than their 12th-century forerunners, came nowhere near the extraordinary richness of Westminster. In fact Westminster is, internally at least, the most lavishly finished great church of the 13th century, and it is not surprising that the cost per bay works out at around twice that of Salisbury Cathedral. Salisbury cost almost £27,000 (including the chapter house and cloister), whereas the three-quarters of Westminster finished before Henry III's death in 1272 cost over £42,000. The average normal annual income of the crown, in other words the English state, has been put at around £35,000 during Henry III's reign. Such exceptional expenditure served an exceptional purpose. Westminster Abbey embodied Henry's elevated view of the place of kingship within the divinely established order. To his English subjects it was intended to proclaim the king's role as God's anointed vicar and lord of all men in the kingdom, clergy as well as laity. To Europe it asserted Plantagenet parity with the Capetians by combining the functions and some of the architectural features of the three churches most closely associated with the French kings: Reims Cathedral, the coronation church; St-Denis, the royal pantheon and repository for the coronation regalia; and the Sainte-Chapelle, the setting of the relic of the Crown of Thorns and chief showpiece of the French crown in the capital.

If Westminster succeeded in enhancing Henry's prestige on the Continent it would have been because it was the setting for the shrine of Edward the

133 Westminster Abbey, north transept (on the right) and nave (liturgical choir),
looking north-west, c. 1250–72. The lower storeys of the easternmost nave bay were
built with the west side of the transepts, and before the building of the rest of the nave
they served as buttresses absorbing thrusts exerted by the north and south crossing
arches. The iron tie bars attached to the main arcades were probably meant to be
temporary. Those which cross the aisles prevented lateral thrusts from the aisle vaults
pushing the slender main arcades inwards before the clearstorey and triforium had been
built. Once completed, the upper storeys provided a vertical thrust which enabled the
main arcades to resist thrusts from the aisle vaults without tie bars.

Confessor, the last native-born English king. The German emperors already had such a patron in Charlemagne, but the French crown lacked its own saint until the canonization of Louis IX in 1297. The English seem to have viewed the abbey merely as the chief product of Henry's rather obsessive personal piety. While the French crown became steadily more powerful and more 'absolutist' during the 13th century, the same period in England saw the birth of Parliament and a baronial movement to limit royal power. To Henry's far more popular and effective son, Edward I, the ideological content of Westminster was comparatively unimportant, and at his coronation, the first in the new church, the unfinished lantern tower, which his father had intended should bathe the coronation 'theatre' in a flood of highly symbolic light, was temporarily boarded up. That neither Edward nor any of his successors saw fit to complete the Westminster lantern is interesting: the late medieval English kings were in general far less assiduous than their French cousins in promoting the mystique of royalty.

Westminster was the most French-looking example of great church architecture built in England since the Canterbury choir, but, unlike Cologne and León, it was not a pure French Rayonnant design executed on foreign soil. Its polygonal apse and radiating chapels, its north transept façade with large portals and rose window, its tallness and comparatively great internal height (31.5m) are all unmistakably French, but everything about its detailed handling reveals the English background and training of its architect, Henry of Reyns. Certain English features, the use of Purbeck marble for example, could reflect the king's wishes, but some things which set Westminster apart from French Gothic are surely too inconspicuous or too technical to be plausibly ascribed to the intervention of the patron. One such is the construction of vault webs in sloping courses forming angled meetings at the ridges [134], as against the French technique of horizontal coursing [69]. A French architect would have frowned on the greater thickness of the shafts in the gallery relative to the more important shafts which divide the bays and receive the ribs of the high vault, but exactly the same 'solecism' can be seen at Lincoln [124]. Here again, it is difficult to believe that such a detail can have been included in order to satisfy the king. The thinness of the high vault shafts was partly dictated by the small amount of space left on the capitals of the main piers by the deep and typically English arcade arches. Not only the arcades but the entire structure of the high walls is of a thickness consistent with English usage, although the elongated proportions of the elevation successfully distract attention from this.

In French terms the main elevations at Westminster were far less up-to-date than those of Cologne or León, yet it seems clear that this disparity had more to do with the role of the abbey as the English coronation church than with conservative taste. In place of the four-light windows which Amiens had made obligatory in France [70], the Westminster clearstorey has simple two-lighters which, along with the similar windows in the aisles, are unmistakably an allusion to Reims [68]. The ideological function of the abbey as an assertion of parity with the French crown was clearly more compelling than the normal urge to be abreast of contemporary fashion. One or two Reims elements are used with no sense of their original significance. An example is the thick transverse ribs confined to the aisle vaults here but used throughout Reims and in conjunction with massive responds [66d, 67]. At Westminster the high vaults have the horizontal emphasis traditional in English Gothic, for the bay-defining transverse ribs are thin and there are longitudinal ridge ribs. Notwithstanding Henry of Reyns's inconsistent use of Reims motifs, it seems likely that his surname commemorates a personal visit to Reims.

Alongside forms clearly of French High Gothic parentage, like the bar tracery and the two-tier flying buttresses, Westminster includes others which are English, yet which seem to have been adopted on the basis of their compatibility with the French format of the church. In this category are the piers, which, while approximating to the standard four-shaft High Gothic pattern [69], are actually much closer to those in the nave at Salisbury [131]. The gallery, well lit perhaps for the benefit of those stationed there to shout the formal acclamation at coronations, conforms to the general scheme of Canterbury and Lincoln [120] in its elevation towards the main vessels, but encouragement to follow such prototypes could have come from the two-unit triforium of Amiens [70]. The single oddest departure from French precedent in the main elevations is the narrowness of the clearstorey windows. The residue of solid wall around them presumably reflects conformity to normal English usage as exemplified by Lincoln and Salisbury, but if Henry of Reyns's putative visit to Reims had taken in the sumptuous Benedictine abbey church of St-Nicaise (begun 1231), he would have found sanction there for the smallness of his windows. It hardly need be added that St-Nicaise's clearstorey was utterly unorthodox in a northern French great church.

Although part of Henry of Reyns's response to French Gothic may have been the rather grudging one of seeking authorization for adhering to certain English conventions, the building itself is evidence of a willingness to borrow from some of the most modern works of Parisian Rayonnant. This is particularly evident in those tracery designs which were not based on the main elevations at Reims. To give only one example, the trefoil-cusped lights in the tracery of the gallery had first appeared in window tracery in the Sainte-Chapelle, begun no more than five years before Westminster. The Sainte-Chapelle may also have inspired the most distinctive ornamental feature of the internal elevations, the carved diaper pattern of stylized flowers which was originally brilliantly gilded and painted and thus assimilated to the parent form of repoussé diapering on reliquaries and shrines [89]. The interior of the Sainte-Chapelle does not actually feature diaper, but, uniquely among major Gothic buildings, its walls were gilded and inlaid with glass simulating enamels so as to make the masonry resemble as far as possible the golden shrine enclosing the relic of the Crown of Thorns. The long-destroyed shrine of Edward the Confessor can be assumed to have resembled virtually all surviving 13th-century shrines in incorporating diaper, so it seems that Westminster was imitating the Sainte-Chapelle in assuming a brilliantly polychromatic guise based on the shrine which it housed. Such an inspiration lay outside the sources regularly drawn on by mid-13th-century architects, but Henry of Reyns would surely have been aware of the only important precedents in Gothic architecture for large areas of carved surface patternings: the foliate diaper covering most of the west front of St-Nicaise, and the simple trellis, not at all reminiscent of goldsmiths' work, on the spandrels above the crossing arches at Lincoln [124]. In fact the diapering of the main elevations was an afterthought, for it is absent from the very earliest section of a main arcade spandrel to be built, that above the south respond of the east arcade in the south transept.

The first part of Westminster Abbey brought to completion was the chapter house [134]. Its octagonal plan places it within a specifically English tradition of centralized chapter houses, yet despite its English form, this splendid room is Westminster's only convinced exposition of the 'glass cage' effect perfected in the clearstoreys at Amiens and St-Denis and in the main upper room of the Sainte-Chapelle. In one way the chapter house is even more extreme than any French building in the priority which it accords to windows, for whereas the relatively low springings of the rectangular-planned high vaults of great churches inevitably obstruct the traceried heads of the clearstorey windows to a greater or lesser extent [68, 80], here the octagonal plan results in perfect visibility for all windows. Clearly Henry of Reyns wished to give windows greater prominence than in earlier centralized chapter houses, for their arched heads coincide exactly with the curvature and springing level of the vault, a relationship not found in the Lincoln chapter house and virtually unknown in the clearstoreys of 13th-century great churches. A comparison of the Westminster chapter house with any part of early 13th-century Lincoln [124] shows how windows have prevailed not only over vaults but over the English tradition of richly modelled walls and piers. Nevertheless, the vault is important as the single most accessible example of a type of design which was eventually to exert a profound influence on late medieval great churches in England and probably in Central Europe also [156, 172a–e].

Neither the abbey church nor the chapter house at Westminster was a satisfactory exemplar for great church architecture in England. No doubt the chapter house elevations were thought too specialized to have any useful applications, and the French tallness of the church could not be emulated in the major English projects of the late 13th century, almost all of which were additions to existing churches. The French chevet was imitated only at two other abbeys, both of royal foundation: Hailes, whose patron was a brother

134 Westminster Abbey, chapter house, begun 1246. The vault (a careful restoration dating from 1866–73) shows the typical 13th-century English construction of the webs from courses of masonry which meet at an angle along the ridges.

of Henry III, and Battle, which had been William the Conqueror's thank-offering for his victory over the English. The lack of further imitations suggests that Westminster's French High Gothic scheme had become tainted through association with Henry's unpalatable insistence on the sacral character of his kingship and his supranational political ambitions.

The English response to Westminster is typified by the Angel Choir at Lincoln, which superseded the late 12th-century apse and provided space for the shrine and cult of St Hugh [135]. Almost all that was welcomed from Westminster was the traceried window, and even this had to take its chances within a scheme based closely on the earlier work adjoining to the west [120]. To endow tracery with the profuse mouldings and clustered marble shafts customarily applied to lancets was a natural development from the richly moulded gallery tracery at Westminster. Where this comfortable process of acclimatization went awry was in the clearstorey, which retained the two-layer structure and generous ornamentation of the earlier Lincoln clear-storeys, with the inevitable result that the inner layer of tracery crowds out one's view of the actual windows. Judging by the lack of imitations of the Angel Choir clearstorey, it was considered a failure. Far more impressive is the 17m-high window in the east wall, one of the very earliest eight-lighters

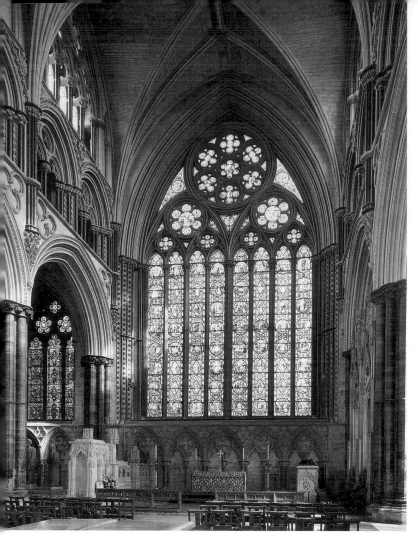

135 Lincoln Cathedral, Angel Choir looking north-east, begun 1256. This extension to the recently completed cathedral [119] takes its name from the sculptured spandrels of the gallery, which, like much else here, were inspired by Westminster Abbey. The focal point of the Angel Choir, the shrine of St Hugh, stood in the third bay from the east. The still surviving base for the small shrine containing St Hugh's head is in the easternmost bay on the left.

in Europe. The design can be seen as a development of the clearstorey windows at Amiens [70], in which the final enlargement of the basic two-light-and-circle unit produces a circle so large that it can no longer contain only cusps. The preference for flat eastern terminations in major late 13th-century English churches, along with the absence of any strong tradition of rose windows, left the way open for the development of extremely ambitious tracery compositions, and by the last decade of the 13th century English tracery design had become the most inventive in Europe (see p. 194). Yet enthusiasm for the Rayonnant tracery window in the post-Westminster decades was not accompanied by any acknowledgment that it could be more than a spectacular decorative set piece. The awkward stretches of residual wall between the head of the Lincoln east window and the high vault testify to late 13th-century English architects' indifference to one of the basic premises of Rayonnant design, namely that entire elevations should fit together with the same precision and clarity as tracery itself, where of course there can never be any left-over spaces.

136 Exeter Cathedral, north side of the choir, *c.* 1288–1310. The window tracery is typical of the late 13th century in its rich formal vocabulary, but the number and diversity of the patterns used is exceptional. The chapels projecting from the choir aisles each contain two altars and thus fulfil the same liturgical function as the far larger eastern transepts at Salisbury [*130*] and Lincoln [*119*].

Although the thirty years following the death of Henry of Reyns in 1253 saw a steady increase in the employment of Rayonnant motifs by English architects, their borrowings were virtually confined to tracery patterns and moulding profiles. The thick-wall structure remained unchallenged everywhere, even in the growing number of major churches from which clearstorey passages were omitted. At Exeter the extraordinarily inventive and varied tracery of the choir can be seen with ease only on the exterior [*136*]: from inside it is rendered almost invisible in diagonal views by the deep window embrasures and by the conoids of the exceptionally elaborate vault [*138*]. The interior of the Exeter choir is in fact the prime late 13th-century instance of the kind of composition invented in the Lincoln nave [*124*], where both supports and arched elements are converted into diagonal planes endowed with a richly 'fibrous' texture by a profusion of complex moulding profiles. The tierceron vault includes no fewer than thirteen ribs above each springing where Lincoln has seven. In this setting it is hardly surprising that so flat and linear a form of ornament as tracery failed to compete. Probably the only thing here which can be regarded as a move towards Rayonnant norms is the height of the clearstorey, though it is still too low not to seem overwhelmed by the conoids of the low-springing vault. In the first part of the choir built from *c.* 1288 the elevation was two-storeyed, but it appears

137 York Minster, north side of the nave, begun 1291. The simple French-style quadripartite vault planned when the stone springers were set in place was never completed. The present timber lierne vault is a 19th-century reproduction of one begun in 1354, except that the latter was decorated with blue paint and gold stars reinforcing its role as a symbol of heaven. Subventions from the Yorkshire aristocracy are commemorated, with unique assertiveness, by statues of laymen in the triforium and, more conventionally, in glass and stone heraldry. The internal height matches that of Westminster Abbey and the nave of St Paul's Cathedral, London (102 feet/31 m), and thus embodies York's self-image as the second city of England.

that the prominent and steeply sloping sills of the clearstorey were disliked, for in 1318 they were replaced by an arcaded triforium. Perhaps the insertion of a third level was also seen as remedying the failure of the two-storey design to measure up to the normal requirements of great church architecture.

In 1286 a former theology professor in Paris University was elected archbishop of York, an appointment which probably explains why the nave begun at York Minster in 1291 was 13th-century England's only whole-hearted essay in Rayonnant great church architecture [137]. The tallness and flatness of the clearstorey and the extension of the mullions of its tracery to form the supports of a triforium must have seemed revolutionary, especially in York, where the large church begun in 1271 at St Mary's Abbey followed the minster's early 13th-century transepts in having a high false gallery under a low clearstorey with lancets and a wall passage. The minster nave as a whole was clearly intended to be no less French than the combined clearstorey and triforium. Hence the very acutely pointed arches of the main arcades, the vault responds continuous with the piers, and the simple quadripartite form of the intended vault (finished much later in timber and to a more complex design). The details of tracery, mouldings and foliage sculpture show a grasp of the ornamental vocabulary of Rayonnant unrivalled in England when the design was drawn up some time in the late 1280s. Yet just as at Westminster, the design includes many things, both important and trivial, which prove conclusively that the designer was an Englishman convinced of the superiority of certain traditional usages. Some of the important features carried over from the Early English style are the broad proportioning of the central vessel, the height of the main arcades, the failure of the clearstorey to extend below the capitals receiving the high vault, the thickness of the walls, and the richness of the mouldings, especially those on the arcade arches. Admittedly, the great width of the central vessel was partly dictated by the re-use of Romanesque foundations, and if there had not been an early 13th-century tower over the crossing it is likely that the height of the nave would have risen beyond 31m. The number of channels through which the idea of a relatively narrow clearstorey could have been transmitted is greater than in the case of Westminster, for further major churches incorporating this feature had been designed in the intervening four decades, most notably Clermont-Ferrand Cathedral [87]. Clermont has an unglazed triforium of the York kind, a feature found only rarely in northern French Rayonnant, and one which should probably be bracketed with narrow clearstorey windows as instancing conservatism in regions more or less culturally remote from Paris. On the other hand, the gablets decorating the triforia at York and Clermont indicate that their designers were fully conversant with Parisian fashion.

In one sense, York provides a sequel to Westminster, for just as Henry of Reyns made the chapter house more purely Rayonnant than the church, the York nave master used full-width Rayonnant windows in the slightly earlier vestibule to the minster chapter house. Yet the vestibule, like the nave, lacks one major Rayonnant element, in this case the linkage of the window mullions with those of the blind tracery on the dado below. One can only conclude that for the designer of these buildings Rayonnant was less an all-embracing architectural system than a repository of novel motifs. Certainly he was very well informed about a great range of Rayonnant buildings, as witness the extremely close similarity between his upper storeys and the aisle windows and dado at Sées Cathedral in Normandy [82] and the perfect match in the decorative tracery of the Cologne choir stalls for the curious 'windmill sails' pattern in the clearstorey tracery. The Cologne stalls were made c. 1308–11, but since there are precursors of this pattern in the Rhineland and none in England, it seems more likely that the influence was travelling from Germany than the other way about. Exactly how such accurate long-distance transmission of ideas worked will never be known. It is at least a possibility that drawings could be circulated among the most important cathedral architects so as to obviate the need for personal travel and study.

The response to the French scheme of the York nave was as negative as it had been towards Westminster. Only Guisborough Priory, north-east of

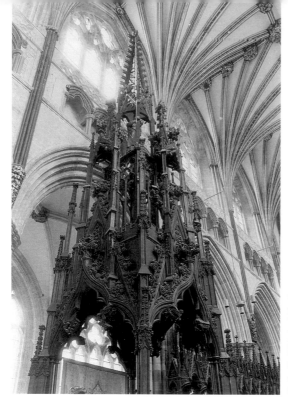

138 Exeter Cathedral, south side of the choir, c. 1288–1310; canopy of the bishop's throne, 1313–17. Unlike the lantern at Ely [146], the Exeter throne canopy seems to have owed its masonry-derived detailing to the architect, the carpenter being responsible only for its execution.

York (begun c. 1300; mostly destroyed), repeated the general disposition of the York elevation, but even here the resemblance was very superficial. There was a tall clearstorey and a triforium formed of arches separated by narrow uprights, but the clearstorey windows were recessed behind a wall passage of traditional type and thus divorced from the triforium. The rejection of York's powerful mast-like vault responds in favour of very slim shafts corbelled out from the spandrels of the main arcades brought Guisborough's overall design closer to Exeter [138] than York. Where the Guisborough master's admiration for York was unqualified was in the rich decorative architecture and sculpture which lined the ample wall surfaces beside and below the aisle windows. The general arrangement of this part of the York nave derived from the Angel Choir of Lincoln [135] rather than from the very simple aisle elevations usual in Continental Rayonnant churches, although all its individual elements were drawn from recent French sources. The Guisborough master's reaction to York anticipated that of Yorkshire generally, and during the next four or five decades designs of highly traditional kinds were enlivened by York-derived finery. The reason for the enormous popularity of the decoration in the aisles at York and the reason for the indifference to the main elevations are the same: the blind tracery and gablets in the aisles rejuvenated an existing tradition of complex and varied ornamental effects, whereas the linked upper storeys of the nave stood diametrically opposed to that tradition, stressing overall unity at the expense of richness and diversity. It was only many years later that overall unity captured the imaginations of English cathedral architects.

CHAPTER III

Late Gothic

UNTIL THE VERY END OF the Middle Ages, the cathedrals and greater abbey churches continued to fulfil their traditional role as the most conspicuous symbols of the might and cohesion of Western Christendom, the flagships, so to speak, of the Church Triumphant. But in the same way as the magnificence of flagships is not necessarily a true guide to the strength of a fleet at large, so the outstanding examples of great church architecture chosen for discussion in this chapter betray nothing of the disenchantment which by 1300 had overtaken almost all the most ambitious enterprises fostered by the institutional church during the previous two centuries – the reformed monastic orders, the friars, Scholastic philosophy, the Crusades. Of course the great churches, like the institutions they served, continued to be regarded as immutable facts of life by the vast majority of people, but there is at least one distinctive characteristic of late medieval architecture which can reasonably be connected with the decline in the universal church. Though Gothic had never been in any sense a papally directed movement, its fragmentation after 1300 into many varied and almost autonomous regional styles must have been greatly assisted by the solidarity which developed between national governments and the higher clergy once it had become apparent that the popes had failed in their efforts to fashion the Western church into a supranational state. However, the increasingly secular outlook of the prelates is just one manifestation of a general laicization of society during the late Middle Ages. Another is the rapid growth in the power and wealth of towns, and this too must have been among the main causes of the regionalization of Gothic, for the cultural horizons of townspeople were still on the whole narrow in the critical years around 1300. A further development which may have acted as a catalyst to the formation of national styles, the growth of anti-French sentiment from the late 13th century, has already been touched on at the start of the previous chapter.

There can be no doubt that it was the diversity and ambition of lay architectural patronage which was at the root of another feature common to all the national traditions of Gothic great church architecture: their indebtedness to other, lesser building types. Up to the end of the 13th century the great churches had led and other classes of building had followed, but in the last two and a half centuries of the Middle Ages important architectural innovations increasingly often made their début in secular buildings or major parish and friars' churches. Although the nature and extent of borrowings by cathedral designers from extraneous sources varied markedly from region to region, their near-universal presence is a sure sign that the great churches had lost some of their overwhelming pre-eminence in the hierarchy of architectural genres. And in a practical sense too the major churches could be affected by the growing lay patronage of lesser church building types, as these must often have attracted funds away from the cathedrals and abbeys. However, few generalizations apply to all of late medieval Europe, where patterns of patronage varied as much as styles, and there are numerous instances of great churches which would never have been begun but for the readiness of ambitious municipalities to take over responsibility from unenthusiastic or under-endowed clergy. Civic pride could also be a significant factor in those great church building projects – outside Italy and the Low Countries, the vast majority – where the clergy retained control of financial administration.

Like many other artistic traditions, Gothic architecture becomes aesthetically more complex in its later phases. No doubt the phenomenon is explicable partly by reference to immanent evolutionary processes whereby certain new solutions turn into well established formulas that can only be developed further by refining and elaborating – a point reached in Northern European Gothic by the mid-13th century, when technical problems ceased to be a major preoccupation. But the greater richness of Late Gothic relative to what preceded it is not only an artistic development: it is yet another symptom of the laicization of late medieval society. The loosening of the medieval social order by the Black Death brought about a new emphasis on display as a means of asserting distinctions of status, a change particularly striking in the field of dress. Whereas from *c.* 1200 to the early 14th century civilian costume remained simple and relatively static, the late Middle Ages witnessed an explosion in cost, elaboration and variety. Ostentation in dress was also a sign of the increased individualism which showed itself in religion as a preoccupation with the welfare of the individual soul. Indulgences, masses for the souls of the dead and pious benefactions designed to secure remission of time in Purgatory were all at the peak of their popularity in the period *c.* 1300–1550, and their impact on the great churches was dramatic. Private funerary chapels and grandiose tombs proliferated, and pre-existing churches were often almost transformed by completions, extensions and embellishments – typically, towers, porches and elaborate internal fittings – all of which served to advertise the worldly standing as well as the piety of their individual donors. These additions are frequently important works of architecture in their own right, something which can hardly ever be said of the component elements of 12th- and 13th-century Gothic great churches.

The diversification of architectural genres within the ambit of the major churches is only one of the impediments to quantifying late medieval great church building with a view to learning whether it attracted less investment than in the earlier centuries. The general sluggishness of the European economy in the century *c.* 1350–1450 is unlikely by itself to have caused any overall reduction in activity, for the fall of the population by a third during the Black Death meant that the individual survivors had more wealth at their disposal. Probably the single greatest disincentive to build was political instability, when the energies and resources of the ruling classes were diverted into military channels. Yet in France the pace of great church building had slackened well before the onset of the Hundred Years War and the Black Death. Partly this was due to the drying up of opportunities for new building, but at those many churches where construction had been halted after the completion of the choir, a major obstacle to the prosecution of the work was at the same time psychological and aesthetic: lack of enthusiasm for continuing with a project whose most important part had already been built in an outdated style. But the French experience was untypical. The English tradition of partial rebuildings allowed innovation to continue untrammelled by any undue regard for overall unity, while away from the heartlands of Gothic completely new territories were being opened up to the style – in Central Europe, northern Italy, the Low Countries and Spain. It is the achievements of these 'frontier states' of Gothic which shorten the odds against any easy presumption that great church architecture was a contracting concern during the late Middle Ages.

England: the Decorated style

England is the natural starting point for any discussion of the great church in the late Middle Ages. This is partly because most of the vocabulary of the Late Gothic style was invented there but also because England was the one area of Europe with an outstanding 13th-century achievement in great church design where the creative effort was kept up after 1300. The name 'Decorated', traditionally applied to English Gothic of c. 1300–1350, suits the majority of great church projects of this period, whose most obvious trait is complex and varied ornament. In England Gothic had always been perceived primarily as a means of transforming thick walls into rich and lively decoration, but what seems to have triggered the renewal of inventiveness in the field of ornament was the sudden exposure of the English to an aspect of French Rayonnant with which they were previously unfamiliar, namely the miniature canopies found on portals and buttresses. This 'microarchitecture' had no obvious applications in a country where large sculptured portals and tall flying buttresses were shunned, but around 1290 two English architects, evidently working independently, lighted on the idea of making it a major component of internal elevations, precisely where the French had never used it. Although an innovation in artistic terms, it has to be remembered that this canopy-enriched architecture was in essence only a variation on the age-old idea of the church building as an evocation of heaven's 'many mansions'. The normal medieval term for a canopy, 'tabernacle', means 'little house' or 'hut' and also recalls the tented sanctuary built by the Jews in the desert, one of the precursors of church architecture.

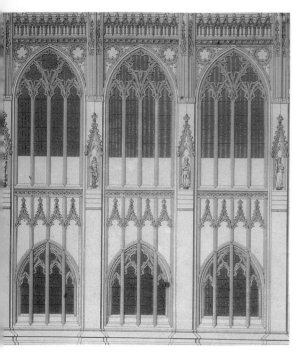

139–141 St Stephen's Chapel, Westminster Palace, London, begun 1292. *Left:* exterior bay design. *Opposite, left:* interior elevation of the north side of the easternmost bay of the upper chapel. *Opposite, right:* stalls in the upper chapel (detail of *140*).

142 *Opposite, below:* Noyon Cathedral, right portal of the west front, canopies over jamb figures, *c.* 1235.

By a narrow margin, the older of the two earliest buildings to make use of Rayonnant microarchitecture is the chapter house at York Minster, where the stalls for members of the chapter are dignified not with the shallow arcading generally used in this position but with a series of overhanging canopies clearly recognizable as enlarged and slightly elaborated versions of the hexagonal canopied niches first used on the jambs of the transept portals of Notre-Dame in Paris and imitated at Strasbourg, Rouen and elsewhere [*96*]. However, the initiation of England as a whole into the delights of microarchitecture came from a quite different quarter, namely the twelve crosses erected from 1291 to the memory of Edward I's queen, Eleanor of Castile. The Eleanor Crosses were based on simpler monuments built twenty years earlier to commemorate Louis IX of France, and these in turn were based directly on the microarchitecture of great church portals and buttresses. In 1292, only a year after the start of work on the Eleanor Crosses, one of the four main architects involved in their design, Michael of Canterbury, began a building which took from the crosses the concept of an architecture centred on sculptured images and deriving its character from the canopies over those images. This was St Stephen's Chapel at Westminster, the main chapel in the main English royal palace, a belated sequel to Louis IX's Sainte-Chapelle and like it a two-storeyed structure [*139–141*]. But whereas the Sainte-Chapelle had contributed comparatively little to the stylistic development of French Gothic, St Stephen's is the key to understanding the great church architecture of early 14th-century England. The lower storey survives, badly restored, but the main, upper storey is now known only from drawings.

The stalls in St Stephen's [*141*] were more elaborate and more eclectic than their York equivalents. Their uppermost components are a crenellated cornice and narrow tracery lights unmistakably based on jamb figure canopies such as those on the west front at Noyon Cathedral [*142*]. The basic shape of the overhanging trefoil-arched canopies of the stalls derives from an early 13th-century English type of statue canopy, the best-known examples of which occur on the west front of Wells [*126*], but the double-curved or 'ogee' arches which form their central parts had appeared on the west portals of Auxerre Cathedral (*c.* 1260–80) in company with several metalwork-derived motifs [cf. *90*], an association which suggests that the ultimate source of the ogees was the same. Ogees were certainly being used by metalworkers earlier than by architects (e.g. the canopy of the now destroyed mid-13th-century bronze tomb of Queen Ingeborg of France, died 1223) and indeed they convey the sense of being formed by bending metal strips.

The constituent motifs of the microarchitecture at St Stephen's were extremely influential. One of the most obvious applications for them was in church furniture, which for the first time became a major architectural genre, almost rivalling the great church itself as a vehicle for formal inventiveness. The prodigious bishop's throne at Exeter of 1313–17 [*138*] has on its lowest stage overhanging trefoil arches derived from those at St Stephen's, but the upper stage includes some of the very earliest examples of a more advanced variant not found at St Stephen's. This is the 'three-dimensional' or 'nodding' ogee, in which the outer and central parts of the overhanging arches have merged into a continuous sequence of curves which imply an unstable, forward-swelling movement. Perhaps more than any other single motif, the nodding ogee arch encapsulates the fantastic and anti-rational element in Decorated architecture. In full-scale architecture its natural habitat was over images on buttresses [*143*].

The most important example of this process of liberating microarchitecture motifs from their original settings is the introduction of ogee arches into window tracery. The cross-shaft of the Eleanor Cross at Hardingstone bears a blind tracery pattern whose use of ogees is so free as to entitle it to be called the earliest curvilinear or flowing tracery, the type of tracery which eventually became the norm in European Late Gothic. The lower chapel at St Stephen's had the earliest known English examples of actual windows incorporating ogees [*139*]. The tracery in the upper chapel was unfortunately destroyed before any detailed records were made, but a window at Canterbury Cathedral, where Michael was architect in the 1270s and 1280s and probably later, is apparently a near-replica of the great east window of St Stephen's [*144*]. Its general layout follows late 13th-century precedent, but its detailing includes the same wide ogee cusps as the lower chapel tracery. The strange concave-sided triangular or 'split' cusps embody the conceit of apparent pliability even more vividly than ogees, whose metalwork ancestry they probably share. Both appear side by side on the Auxerre west portals. Split cusps were not widely used outside south-eastern England, but the commonest and simplest kind of flowing tracery, ogee-reticulated tracery, so called from its net-like mesh of ogees [*148*], was probably also invented by Michael of Canterbury, in the east cloister at Westminster Abbey (*c.* 1300). An origin at Westminster Abbey would be highly appropriate, as the only earlier tracery which anticipates ogee-reticulation is the blind pattern on the tympana of the lateral portals of the mid-13th-century north transept. This is an all-over pattern of tangential circles arbitrarily cut off by the arches enclosing the tympana. To convert tangential circles into ogee-reticulation one has only to omit their upper and lower sixths.

Ogee-reticulated tracery rapidly became established as an 'everyday' kind of flowing tracery, but by around 1320 far more ambitious ogee-based compositions were being essayed in the eastern and northern regions of England. Almost the only characteristic common to all of the huge number

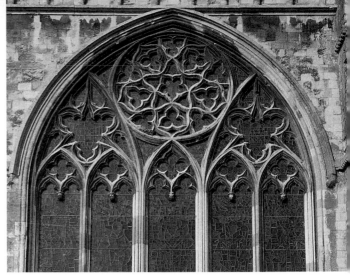

143 Beverley Minster, easternmost bays of the north nave aisle, *c.* 1330–40.

144 Canterbury Cathedral, window in St Anselm's Chapel, 1336. In the late Middle Ages the architectural setting of imagery could often be far more expensive than the imagery. The stonework of this window cost £28 14s. 6d., the stained glass £6 13s. 4d.

of flowing patterns created in the forty-year heyday of the form is a sense of swirling or flickering upward movement around a central axis [*143*]. The interiors which show flowing tracery to greatest advantage are those of major parish churches like Boston and Hull, where the absence of vaulting permitted extremely thin piers and walls offering only minimal obstruction to the visibility of the windows. In the greater churches, as in their late 13th-century predecessors [*135*], the traditional thickness of the lateral walls meant that the only parts of the interior where tracery predominated were the end walls of main vessels. The prime examples of flowing tracery in this position all appear to date from the 1330s: the east windows at Carlisle Cathedral and Selby Abbey, the west window of York Minster and the south rose of Lincoln Cathedral.

For vaults, as for window tracery, Decorated architects devised new and more complex kinds of linear patterning. Here again, St Stephen's Chapel was in the vanguard, for the vault of its lower chapel was probably the earliest important example to incorporate liernes, short decorative ribs at the crown of the vault which are not connected directly to any of the springing points [*172r*]. These liernes were evidently generated by a process internal to St Stephen's though not without parallels elsewhere. It appears that Michael of Canterbury was taking as his point of departure a tierceron vault like that in the nave of Lincoln [*124*, *172q*]. However, the two-bay chancel was bounded to east and west by a triplet of windows and a tripartite chancel screen, both of which required that the adjacent parts of the vault be divided into three. The two kite-shaped arrangements of liernes in the centre of the chancel make sense as a way of echoing the rib arrangement at the east and west extremities of the chancel while at the same time including tiercerons. In the nave the kite shapes are extended to every vault compartment on the longitudinal axis. Among the vast progeny of the St Stephen's vaults are those in the choir aisles at Wells [147], where the kite shapes have become hexagons set on the lateral axes as well as on the longitudinal axis. The scope for variations in lierne vaulting was as great as in flowing tracery.

So far, St Stephen's Chapel has been considered simply as the source of the novel vocabulary of Decorated architecture. It was in reality much more than that, for it embodied an empirical approach to design which was quite new in Gothic architecture. The processes by which the lierne vault of the lower chapel was arrived at were only the final stages in a kind of chain reaction of problem solving triggered by the attempt to give the features of the chapel reasonably upright proportions despite the extreme overall breadth of the room. The same readiness to approach a problem without preconceptions and to embrace unorthodox solutions can be seen in the other parts of the chapel. In the main upper room the point of departure was the requirement that there be statues of Apostles on the lateral walls. The analogous figures in the Sainte-Chapelle had been bracketed out from the vault responds very much in the way that High Gothic portal figures project from jamb shafts [97], but that arrangement was evidently unacceptable in England since it was never used. Given the strength of this prejudice, it is perhaps not surprising that Michael of Canterbury saw the inclusion of statues as necessitating the elimination of a vault as well as vault responds. To a French architect in charge of a comparably prestigious project such a step would have been as unimaginable as the decorative treatment which the omission of vaulting allowed, namely a magnification above the windows of the crenellated cornice and blind tracery on the canopies of the stalls [140, 141]. The only feature of the upper chapel which in France would have been thought appropriate to its situation is the simplified form of Rayonnant linkage, the descent of the mullion shafts down the dado under the windows. The full-dress version of linkage applied to the exterior [139] would certainly have earned French disapproval, for it obscures the internal disposition of the building. The only horizontal element between the ground and the parapet does not, as one would naturally presume, correspond to the level of the floor between the storeys, and the presence of windows lighting the lower chapel is played down by recessing their tracery well behind the freestanding parts of the mullions of the pseudo-triforium. Perhaps the strangest feature of the lower chapel exterior is the moulding which frames the openings and intersects with the mullions. It shows that Michael was ready to attempt a compromise between masking the windows and admitting their presence. One can only assume that he relished this self-imposed and fundamentally impossible task of balancing illusionism and structural truthfulness. By comparison, the screening of the windows in the west towers at Strasbourg [100] seems the very embodiment of sweet reason.

Michael of Canterbury's radical and exploratory approach was followed by only a small handful of early 14th-century English architects. The great

145 Ely Cathedral, longitudinal section. From right to left: part of the nave, early 12th-century; octagon, 1322–34; three west bays of the east arm, *c*. 1322–36; east bays, 1234–50 (with later windows). The continuity in scale between Romanesque and Gothic parts is typical of English cathedral architecture [contrast *191*].

majority were content that the innovatory detailing generated by this approach should be used within the context of highly traditional schemes. Of Michael's spiritual heirs, one of the most distinguished was whoever conceived the octagonal crossing built at Ely Cathedral after the fall of the Romanesque tower in 1322 [*145*, *146*]. If this disaster had occurred in 1222 or 1422, or even in 1272 or 1372, the new tower would no doubt have been of the same square plan as the old one. It took a stroke of genius to see the basis of a new tower in the octagonal area ruined by the collapse of the four piers that sustained the Romanesque crossing. Even if the inspiration came from the hexagonal crossing at Siena Cathedral [*197*] or the octagonal dome at the centre of the as yet unrealized designs for Florence Cathedral [*201* left] – possibilities which can be neither confirmed nor excluded – this would still be a tribute to the designer's capacity to detach himself from the traditions of English Gothic. The monks of Ely believed that the idea came from the brother responsible for the upkeep of the fabric, Alan of Walsingham, and a reason for not dismissing this as a piece of monkish chauvinism is the improbability that a master mason would of his own accord have proposed a solution which involved making over responsibility for the most impressive part of the structure to a master carpenter. Admittedly, wooden vaults were becoming more common in late 13th-century England, though it is not clear in any instance whether their use was due to their comparative lightness, their cheapness or their speed of construction. What is certain is that the Ely crossing vault is of a form which could not have been realized in stone. A Gothic rib vault, unlike a dome, could not have been open at the centre to this extent nor could it have carried the walls of a masonry lantern. However, the illusion that the Ely vault is of stone is wholeheartedly enacted, and when its original painting and gilding were still intact the great majority of observers

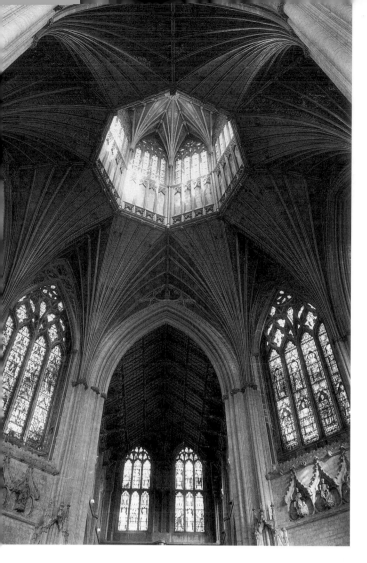

146 Ely Cathedral, octagon looking south, 1322–34. The statues of Apostles under the windows (now 19th-century replacements) evoke the quasi-apostolic life of the monks whose choir stalls stood below. Stylistic differences between the stone and wooden parts of the octagon indicate that the fictive masonry treatment of the latter was the responsibility of the master carpenter William Hurley.

would have been deceived. It hardly need be added that the huge timber 'brackets' which actually support the lantern bear no relation whatever to the inscrutably conventional tierceron vault which hides them from view [145]. The stone-built lower parts of the octagon reveal their designer's knowledge of Michael of Canterbury's work, but this is even more obvious in the case of the lantern, whose internal elevations are based on the exterior of St Stephen's [139]. The designer of all the wooden parts of the Ely octagon was William Hurley, the chief royal carpenter, active at St Stephen's from 1326. Wooden vaults continued to be built over major English churches until the end of the medieval period, but in one sense the Ely octagon had no sequel, for all the later works of fictive masonry architecture at the English cathedrals could have been carried out in real masonry just as readily as in carpentry. The sophistication and resourcefulness of the English late medieval carpenters found their main outlet in secular architecture.

The innovatory spirit of St Stephen's Chapel could also inform great church buildings of less exceptional format than the Ely octagon. The exterior and the two interiors of the chapel had been conceived by Michael of Canterbury as three separate design problems, each capable of radically different solutions. The complex canopy-encrusted upper chapel, the sturdy supporting architecture of the lower chapel and the traceried 'streamlining' of the exterior have so little in common that there can be no doubt of Michael's deliberate intention to generate three distinct modes. Perhaps the most impressive demonstration of the possibilities for great church architecture inherent in Michael of Canterbury's architecture of multiple modes is the eastern parts of Wells Cathedral [53, 147–151]. As in many 13th-century English churches, the motive for rebuilding at Wells was the desire to gain greater privacy for the liturgical choir by transferring it from the crossing into the eastern arm. This necessitated lengthening the main vessel of the east arm and providing replacements for the ambulatory and axial chapel demolished in order to achieve the lengthening. But whereas the late 12th-century east parts were evidently as simple and consistent in their design as the surviving transepts [54], the overriding aim of the new work was to endow the axial chapel (Lady Chapel), ambulatory and choir with distinct identities expressive of their different functions and status. These can best be considered in east to west order, the sequence followed by the builders.

Uniquely among the chapels at the east ends of English cathedrals, the Wells Lady Chapel is an elongated octagon with its three eastern sides longer than the three at the west end. There is a possibility that this quasi-centralized plan was consciously conceived within the ancient if increasingly intermittent tradition of Marian rotundas which started with the Roman Pantheon as rededicated in 609. The most impressive feature of the Wells chapel is its vault [149]. Essentially this is a dome whose lowest parts are cut away by penetrations – fragmentary tunnel vaults of the same curvature as the wall ribs. In fact it is more complex than this, for between the penetrations the dome bulges outwards. The only Gothic vault which approximates to this shape is the wooden one in the York Minster chapter house, where a saucer-like dome at the centre is bounded by a sixteen-sided polygon of ribs which causes relatively inconspicuous outward bulging between the eight penetrations. Perhaps the Lady Chapel architect had access to a collection of English chapter house designs assembled in preparation for the building of the octagonal chapter house at Wells in the 1290s. The similarities to the three-dimensional geometry of the York vault are not matched in the extraordinary surface pattern. The central star shape with points balanced on the inner end of each penetration creates the impression of a complex lierne vault, though in fact only some of the ribs forming the points of the star are true liernes and all the rest are intersecting tiercerons. The strongly centralized character of this cat's cradle pattern enhances the spatial integrity of the chapel, and in this it is aided by the repetitive, non-axial character of the window tracery.

147, 148 Wells Cathedral, east end, *c.* 1320–40. *Left:* north choir aisle looking east. *Above:* view across the ambulatory towards the north-east chapels and Lady Chapel. The window on the left has ogee-reticulated tracery, the commonest early 14th-century English type.

The Lady Chapel is only the largest and most elaborate of five chapels at the east end of the church [*149, 150*]. The other four are all rectangular and of the same height as the choir aisles, two consisting of projecting quasi-transepts, the other two being housed in continuations of the choir aisles flanking the west end of the Lady Chapel. The space between all five chapels and the high east wall of the choir is the ambulatory, whose liturgical function was as a kind of anteroom or vestibule. Approaching from either of the choir aisles, one anticipates that rectangular bays like those one can see ahead [*147*] will be continued behind the high east wall. However one's first sight of the ambulatory confutes any such prediction [*148*]. Not even the boundaries of the space are very clear, for windows of differing patterns appear at different distances and the angling of the heavy arcade which defines the west end of the Lady Chapel further complicates matters. At a more or less uniform distance due west of the four piers carrying this arcade are set the four very slim piers which sustain the ambulatory vault, a relationship which is only obvious when seen in plan [*150*]. Neither the piers nor the rib clusters they carry give any clue as to orientation; on the contrary, they are as much an invitation to circulate as the chapter house piers and conoids from which they derive [*134*]. Since this is the very part of the building where one most needs some help to orientate oneself – after all, the route to three out of the five chapels involves crossing the ambulatory diagonally – it has to be assumed that the disorientation was intended and that one's preconceptions are being deliberately flouted. However, there is just one place from which the ambulatory seems symmetrical and comprehensible: the only bay of normal rectangular plan, situated immediately before the axial opening into the Lady Chapel. If, as seems very likely, this bay was the intended site of the shrine of Bishop William Marsh,

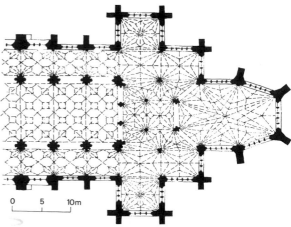

149, 150 Wells Cathedral. *Left:* Lady Chapel looking east. *Above:* plan of the east end.

whose canonization was being energetically canvassed while the east end was in building, the serenity attained here would have been symbolic as well as visual. The only close parallel in Britain for such a setting of a saint's shrine is the rectangular bay over St Kentigern's tomb in Glasgow Cathedral. The Wells and Glasgow arrangements both recall the canopy on four columns which throughout the Middle Ages marked the burial place of St Peter, Christendom's most famous saint.

When the ambulatory and eastern chapels were designed it was probably intended that the choir aisles would be covered by simple tierceron vaults like those over the two bays to the east of them on either side. In the event they received much more unusual vaults which look as if they were deliberately contrived to contrast with those in the ambulatory [147, 148]. Whereas in the latter conoids predominate and liernes are inconspicuous, in the choir aisles the emphasis is reversed so that while the liernes occupy an almost horizontal diamond-shaped area equivalent to half the area of each bay, the conoids are flattened and pushed so far back into the corners of the bays that they have become effectively halved inverted pyramids, a reading facilitated by the omission of diagonal ribs. The aim seems to have been to give each compartment the spatial distinctness of the Lady Chapel vault without its domed shape.

A different aspect of the Lady Chapel vault is developed in the high vault of the choir [151]. This is a tunnel vault with lateral penetrations, a longitudinal version of the centralized scheme used in the chapel. But though the resemblance is almost certainly deliberate, the main source of the Wells vault is the transverse tunnel vaults over the aisles of the choir of St Augustine's, Bristol, begun in 1298, around twenty years before Wells. There one can see similar penetrations bounded by the lower parts of diagonal ribs which traverse two bays. It is not clear whether Bristol or Wells owed anything to the timber tunnel vaults without penetrations which were built in northern England and Scotland during the late 12th and early 13th centuries [128]; what seems certain is that the Wells vault was the first masonry high vault in England to combine the increased visibility for clearstorey openings which the timber tunnels had permitted with the longitudinal emphasis of tierceron vaults such as those at Exeter or Lincoln [124]. Inconspicuous transverse ribs pay lip-service to the traditional concept of bay divisions in vaults and maintain token continuity with the strong verticality of the full-length responds. No doubt in northern France a tunnel vault would have been regarded as an unacceptable departure from Gothic principles, almost a reversion to the Romanesque, but there was no obstacle to acceptance of the Wells solution in England, where for almost a century vaults had been valued for their decorative properties. Judged simply as linear decoration the high vault at Wells is undoubtedly a resounding success, but as in the other vaults of the choir, the surface pattern also complements its three-dimensional form. The unbroken longitudinal continuity of the central part of the tunnel receives an all-over pattern of hexagons alternating with squares. The springings are treated as long radiating panels appropriately suggestive of upward growth, but a plan [150] reveals that these panels are only projections of the same hexagon and square pattern used in the rest of the vault. The Wells designer's careful study of the totally different vault over the central vessel at St Augustine's, Bristol is evident from his borrowing the motif of cusping and also from his concern that the surface pattern of the vault be echoed in the tracery of the central section of the east window.

The greater importance of the central vessel relative to the peripheral spaces is demonstrated by the greater formality and richness of its elevations, for these include no residual stretches of plain wall such as occur in the aisles and chapels. The overall scheme preserves continuity with the main elevations of the late 12th-century church – a necessity since the walls of the three west bays of the old choir were retained, with only their upper storeys refaced internally. The originality of the elevations stems from the adoption of an idea used earlier but in more primitive guise in the entrance wall of the chapter house at Wells, namely the scooping out of the substance of the wall above the main arcades. The space thus vacated is occupied at triforium level by a delicate openwork screen which ranks as the most important application in great church architecture of the canopy-encrusted mode of the main chapel at St Stephen's Chapel. The ultimate source of this design is the standard Rayonnant triforium, but its elevation and open structure betray its derivation from the St Stephen's stalls [140, 141]. Familiarity with the fountainhead of the Decorated style is evident from several other borrowings, including the extension of the clearstorey mullions behind the triforium screenwork. The way in which these uprights continue down

151 Wells Cathedral, choir looking east, completed c. 1340. The storeys follow the 12th-century transept and nave elevations [54, 55] in height, but surpass them in richness and thereby indicate that the choir is a more honorific place. The view through the three arches behind the high altar was originally impeded by a high canopied screen similar to that still surviving at Durham [159]. On the right is the bishop's throne of c. 1340.

where one would expect to find spandrels over the main arcade arches is strongly reminiscent of the exterior elevations of St Stephen's between the upper and lower windows [139]. Apparently the only earlier English examples of statues standing in the openings of a triforium are those portraying lay donors in the York nave [137], where there is just one per bay. The twenty-five Wells statues, which would have been religious (Christ, the Apostles and twelve prophets?), were confined to the sanctuary in the three easternmost bays, and must have conveyed the sense of leading the worship of the clergy seated in their canopied stalls in the less sacred liturgical choir to the west.

The open-minded and exploratory approach which inspired the Wells choir, the Ely octagon and the other greatest monuments of Decorated architecture grew directly out of Michael of Canterbury's work, especially St Stephen's Chapel. Michael's sense of artistic freedom must in turn have stemmed at least partly from his awareness that being able to draw on both main national traditions of 13th-century Gothic gave him a range of options far beyond anything open to earlier architects. However, this is not likely to have been part of the experience of the architects who followed him during the next forty years or so, for their work gives no indication that they took an interest in French Gothic as such. Michael of Canterbury's exploitation of Rayonnant sources was sufficient to keep an entire generation of architects supplied with raw material from which to create their own innovatory designs. Where Michael's experience and that of his followers did coincide was in their patrons – extremely rich and self-confident individuals and corporations; and in their opportunities – projects of comparatively limited scope, and in any event not total rebuildings of entire great churches. The greatest Decorated buildings represent a phenomenal intensification of creative effort and resources and hence are less distinguishable by their size than the main works of any previous period of medieval architecture. It is significant that no enduring influences were exerted by the York nave, the one English building contemporary with St Stephen's which was on a scale large enough to permit a straightforward synthesis of the French and English traditions of great church design. Forty years later the same French concept as appears at York was employed in the south transept at Gloucester Cathedral in the eminently un-straightforward spirit of Michael of Canterbury's work, and the outcome was one of the most permanent changes ever effected in medieval architecture.

England: the Perpendicular style

Although the remodelling of the south transept of Gloucester Cathedral from c. 1331 is the earliest example of a style of architecture which was to remain in use for over two hundred years, it resembled the Ely octagon and the eastern parts of Wells in being conceived as a 'one-off' solution to a particular problem [152]. The problem was in essence how to modernize the main interior elevations of the late 11th-century choir and transepts without demolishing the galleries, whose chapels had only just been refurbished. The method adopted was to remove the Romanesque ashlar facing and replace it with a veneer of Gothic tracery masking the old wall surfaces and openings. The peripheral spaces – the aisles, galleries and crypt – were left virtually unchanged. The inspiration for this approach was undoubtedly the exterior elevations of St Stephen's Chapel [139], for the openings of the galleries are screened by descending mullions in exactly the same way as the equally obtrusive and necessary lower windows at St Stephen's. Even the mouldings framing the openings are reproduced. The name of the Gloucester architect is not recorded, but the fact that his design includes features indicating that he knew every centimetre of the chapel makes it likely that he was Thomas of Canterbury, second architect of St Stephen's and probably the son of Michael of Canterbury. The remodelling of the transept was the first stage in the modernizing of the whole east end of the church in honour of Edward II,

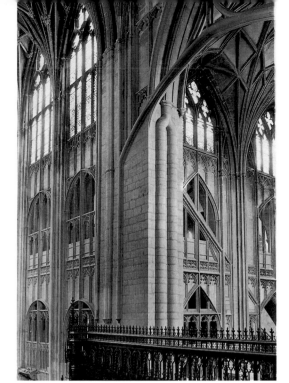

152 Gloucester Cathedral, south side of the choir (left), begun c. 1337, Romanesque south-east crossing pier, and east side of the south transept, c. 1331–6. The 'flying' arch at the top right, which carries down the line of the vault responds and so enables the wall above to be treated as two bays similar to those of the choir [154], is parodied in the bizarre drainpipe-like linking of shafts on the crossing pier.

murdered in 1327 and buried north of the high altar in a tomb which quickly became the focus of a popular cult. Presumably the young Edward III, who several times visited his father's tomb as a pilgrim, recommended that the remodelling be directed by the architect in charge of the most important royal church-building project then in hand. It is from around this time that documentary evidence becomes relatively plentiful for architects having more than one major project under their control, often at places geographically quite far apart.

An attribution to Thomas of Canterbury would account for another aspect of the design, namely the greater Frenchness of some of its detailing as compared to the equivalent elements of St Stephen's. The most important instance of this is the use of the Rayonnant graduated tracery system discussed in the previous chapter [81]. It seems inherently likely that the start of work on the Eleanor Crosses and St Stephen's in the early 1290s was the occasion for the acquisition by the embryonic royal works office at Westminster of a collection of drawings of 13th-century French designs. In this situation there would have been no need to travel in order to study the linked upper storeys which had inspired the external treatment of St Stephen's [80]. Perhaps it was because the architect of the Gloucester south transept was restoring this scheme to the interior setting where it originated that he chose to revert to the graduated tracery system which earlier English architects had only rarely allowed to escape from the confines of tracery proper [cf. 135, 137]. The boldness of the vault responds is equally French, although the main source for their complex section is the lower chapel at St Stephen's. Access to French designs other than those whose influence can be

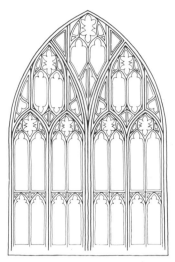

153 Gloucester Cathedral, south window of the south transept. The concave-sided hexagons and the 'split' cusps inside them are two among many details of the south transept which betray the Kentish and London background of its designer [cf. *144*].

0   5m

traced at St Stephen's is suggested by the tall blind tracery lights separating the vault responds from the openings of each bay. Their function is partly to conceal the bulky Romanesque supports of the two lower storeys, but they also resemble their fully glazed equivalents at León in keeping the tracery heads of the clearstorey windows in proportion to the lights. Yet in Rayonnant terms, the Gloucester clearstorey is far too low relative to the overall height. Although it is the only storey totally rebuilt in the 14th century, its upper limit does not exceed that of its Romanesque predecessor.

French elements are completely absent from the vaulting and tracery, the fields where English Gothic was pre-eminent in the early 14th century. The high vault is a rather over-elaborate lierne vault, which exerted no influence. The clearstorey tracery is a simple flowing pattern, but the large window in the south wall is the earliest extant example of Perpendicular tracery, hesitant in its detailing but including the diagnostic verticals carried straight up to meet the enclosing arch [*153*]. The embryo of the idea is present in the series of freestanding mullions contained within the arches framing the lower windows at St Stephen's, although that registers less as a tracery design in its own right than as a subordinate part of a larger whole [*139*]. The Gloucester window has tracery made up of vertical units based on the component lights of the Rayonnant-style triforium. In the bay next to the crossing these lights are also beginning to take over the arcade level of the lateral elevations.

The south transept was not the most obvious place to begin remodelling the eastern parts of the church. Perhaps it had been damaged by the southward settlement of the crossing tower which necessitated the visually disruptive internal flying buttresses in the east and west walls. Alternatively, it may have been felt that the approach adopted by the architect was so untried as to require a full-scale experiment in a comparatively unimportant part of the church. What is clear is that the Gloucester south transept belongs to the same empirical tradition as the Ely octagon. The point deserves some emphasis, for whereas Ely had no sequel, the south transept at Gloucester was the first fruit of a new architectural dispensation which limited imaginative freedom in the interests of overall unity. In many ways this was a recurrence of what had happened a century earlier in France when High Gothic diversity was supplanted by the relative uniformity of Rayonnant; and it is probably no accident that the redirection of 14th-century English architecture resulted from the belated acceptance of at least some Rayonnant principles. Credit for this aesthetic reformation cannot be awarded entirely to Thomas of Canterbury or whoever designed the Gloucester south transept. There was a London branch of Perpendicular also stemming from St Stephen's Chapel whose first exponent was Thomas's successor as architect of the chapel, William Ramsey. The main works by Ramsey, unfortunately surviving only in drawings, were relatively small-scale, but their influence on later Perpendicular great church architecture in the southeast is unmistakable (see p. 215). Thomas of Canterbury died in 1336, and the attribution of the Gloucester transept to him would explain why the choir, which was begun c. 1337, was entrusted to another architect. This second Gloucester master remained faithful to the basic conception of the south transept, but his work differed from that of his predecessor in being to a limited extent influenced by south-western Decorated architecture.

The choir of Gloucester is beyond question more impressive than the south transept [152, 154]. The clearstorey ascends to a new height, far above the hunched upper windows in the earlier work, and the whole gains in rhythmic and textural consistency by the introduction of additional horizontals and their spacing at more or less regular intervals. The *leitmotiv* of this design is now the upright arch-enclosing rectangle or 'panel'. The all-over grid formed of tiered panels is indeed so insistent that its derivation from Rayonnant triforia would be less than obvious if we did not have the 'first draft' which the south transept represents. It is possible that part of the appeal of this scheme was its affinity with the tiered arcading so popular in England in the 12th and 13th centuries, especially on façades [126]. But whereas these were often additive in composition and rather busy in effect, the Gloucester choir elevations entail a rigorous subordination of detail to overall effect – a reversal of the emphases of most Decorated architecture. The arches at the top of each panel are varied enough to avoid monotony, but the horizontals are played down by making them equal in gauge to the thinner uprights rather than to the thicker ones, as had been the case in the south transept. Verticality is further stressed by banishing all horizontals from the tall panels flanking the vault responds, an adjustment necessitated by the drastic reduction in the bulk of the responds. This and the reception of many ribs by one shaft represent a partial reversion to one of the main traits of 13th-century English great church architecture [120]. The vault itself is a tunnel vault with penetrations, like that at Wells [151] but overlaid with an extraordinarily dense mesh of ribs which resembles Wells only in its inclusion of diagonal ribs traversing two adjacent bays and defining the limits of the penetrations. Its almost unfathomably complex yet even-textured pattern provides an ideal foil for the lateral elevations. There are few more poetic effects in Gothic architecture than the way in which the powerful verticals of the Gloucester responds dissipate themselves into the conoids and finally give way to the longitudinal surge of pattern along the crown of the vault.

The climax of the choir is the east window, the largest window in medieval Europe. Its apparent weightlessness, combined with the matching of its panelled treatment to that of the lateral elevations, suggests that this is the system of the choir realized in ideal, transcendental form, an interpretation in accord with traditional theological speculations on the spiritual significance of light and also with the subject matter of the stained glass: the celestial hierarchy set above the earthly ecclesiastical hierarchy. The limpidity of the architecture finds a perfect complement in the near-monochrome figures imitating the niched statues of the great altar screens then coming into general use [159]. The three-part form of the window was no doubt inspired by Bristol or Wells [151], but more particularly it reflects the exigencies of inserting two new bays in the position previously occupied by the apse and ambulatory of the Romanesque choir. The eastern corners of the extended main vessel had to be planted on the outer wall of the crypt ambulatory; this entailed canting the outer sections of the east window in relation to the centre and making the side walls of the easternmost bay swing outwards before joining the eastern corner piers. Because the east window is wider than the main vessel and because the side walls of the easternmost bay are invisible from the west end of the choir, the illusion is created that the east wall floats unattached to the sides of the choir. Only the Ely octagon equals this feat of a sublime effect attained through brilliantly sustained improvisation.

During the second half of the 14th century the influence of Gloucester spread throughout the West Midlands and south-western England. Perhaps even more than the choir, the building which caught the imagination of patrons and architects was the cloister, apparently begun a little before the completion of the choir around 1360 [155]. The east walk of the Gloucester cloister contains the earliest known fan vault, a kind of vault which can be seen as the culmination of several lines of thought pursued by English architects during the previous century. The concept of matching the patterning of vaults and tracery has already been discussed in relation to the choir at Wells, but that example seems very tentative by comparison with the Gloucester cloister, where the vault is given parity with the walls and windows as a surface for the display of the repetitive and infinitely extensible tracery panelling invented in the Gloucester choir. The actual tracery pattern on the vault is anticipated only in Rayonnant rose windows [95], a

154 Gloucester Cathedral, choir looking north-east. The concept of glazed, open and blind tracery set in a single plane derives from Rayonnant architecture [cf. 2, 177].

155 Gloucester Cathedral, east walk of the cloister looking north, *c.* 1351–64. Except in the first bays to be completed (in the foreground), the joints in the masonry of the vault are standardized, as in window tracery [cf. *74*].

relationship which helps substantiate the claims of Perpendicular to be considered as the ultimate development of Rayonnant. The flat traceried ceilings between the rims of the 'roses' are foreshadowed only in south-western vaults like those in the choir aisles at Wells [*147*]. The aspect of fan vaulting which has the deepest roots in English Gothic is its three-dimensional shape, like halved trumpet bells. These are normally and appropriately compared to the freestanding conoidal rib clusters at the centre of polygonal chapter houses like Westminster [*134*], but it must not be overlooked that there had been intermittent attempts in the 13th century, notably in the nave of Lincoln [*124*], to adapt the peripheral conoids of chapter house vaults to bays of the regular rectangular format. However, in the Gloucester cloister the bay-softening aspect of the Lincoln vaults is exactly balanced by the bay-emphasizing quality of the flat diamond-shaped ceilings between the conoids. It is hard to imagine a more complete contrast than that with the choir vault at Gloucester, probably still under construction when the cloister was begun. All that the two vaults have in common is the ready visibility of all their surfaces and the omission of prominent, window-obstructing diagonal ribs such as occur in the majority of 13th-century vaults.

156 Sherborne Abbey, choir looking north-east, probably begun *c.* 1425. The setting of the clearstorey windows and arcade arches within recesses permits Rayonnant-inspired flatness to be combined with traditional English thick wall construction.

What is quite new about the Gloucester fan vaults is their constructional technique. The traditional distinction between ashlar ribs and rough masonry webs [*17*] is abandoned in favour of large ashlar blocks, every one of which includes parts of the surface tracery and parts of the intervening plain surfaces [*165*]. Given the labour and expense of carving cusps which stand proud of the webs, like those in the high vault at Wells, this technique of all-ashlar shells was an obvious step to take once it had been decided to treat vaults as a specialized form of blind tracery. The Gloucester fan vaults were very widely imitated in cloisters, whose square bays were the ideal context for a type of vault based on conoids of semicircular plan. To fit fan vaults into the rectangular bays normal in great churches was far less straightforward and was attempted comparatively seldom. The very varied solutions devised testify to the heavy demands which this problem made on the skill of the individual designer. The oldest surviving fan vault over the main span of a great church is that in the choir at Sherborne Abbey (probably begun *c.* 1425) [*156*], although it is likely that earlier essays have been lost.

The exceptional length of the bays covered by the Sherborne vault no doubt reflects the designer's anxiety to retain as much as possible of the appearance of fan vaults built over square bays. The same consideration surely explains why he refused to cut the fans on the transverse axes so that their rims would meet along the longitudinal axis, as in the central part of the early 16th-century vault in Henry VII's Chapel at Westminster[*163*]. The central strip vacated at Sherborne by the use of fans of smaller radius could obviously not be filled with traceried ceilings like those at Gloucester, whose flat-arch construction was only suitable for use on a small scale. It was decided instead to continue the conoids of the fans inwards, decorating them with conventional bosses and liernes. The dilution of the fan vault concept was not confined to the surface detailing: the construction is almost entirely in the traditional rib-and-infill technique with fairly roughly built webs. Economy is unlikely to have been a factor at Sherborne, which is near to several quarries yielding good ashlar, so it seems that the architect did not care or dare to use Gloucester's novel shell construction for a high vault. In fact the only surviving example of the systematic use of that technique in a high vault is at Henry VII's Chapel [165].

By around 1360, when the Gloucester choir was nearing completion, the Perpendicular style had begun to supplant the Decorated in all the architecturally most active regions of England. There was probably no single cause for this *volte-face*. Gloucester was certainly by far the most impressive great church design built so far in 14th-century England, but another explanation has to be found for the influence exerted by the main monument of the London version of Perpendicular, the small chapter house and cloister of St Paul's Cathedral (begun in 1332 by the royal master mason William Ramsey; destroyed). Something which the Gloucester and St Paul's designs shared and which seems to have commended them generally was that they both embodied a coherent, imitable and flexible architectural system. Perpendicular lacked the capacity to generate strongly contrasted modes, and it eschewed much of the huge vocabulary of Decorated, but these were evidently things which patrons and architects were willing to sacrifice. The decisive rejection of Decorated licence in favour of an eminently purposeful style must have been something more than just a swing of the pendulum of fashion. Since Perpendicular began to gain a general currency only after the Black Death of 1348–9, it is at least possible that it appealed to people who felt themselves chastened by what was universally interpreted as a visitation of divine wrath. We cannot be sure, since no contemporary commentator mentions the change, but it is very likely that the sculptural luxuriance and rich colouring of Decorated came to appear ostentatious and worldly and that Perpendicular was welcomed as a soberer and more spiritual style. The restrained aesthetic of the architecture proper was accompanied by a marked concentration of figure sculpture near altars and other focal points [158, 159] and, as has been mentioned in relation to Gloucester, by the use of more and lighter stained glass. The systematic deployment of the arched panel motif would probably have seemed a more effective evocation of heavenly mansions than walls encrusted with few but elaborately niched figures, for imagery was less essential than arches in the conveying of this meaning. Another possible factor in the rapid acceptance of Perpendicular is that the royal associations of the style enabled it to ride on the back of the wave of patriotic fervour which swept England in the wake of Edward III's spectacular victories over the French at Crécy (1346) and Poitiers (1356). Or again it may be that during the century after the rebuilding of Westminster Abbey by Henry III the English had come to expect a measure of leadership in architectural matters from the crown.

157 Canterbury Cathedral, nave looking east, *c.* 1378–1405. The bulkiness of the high vault responds and the (apparent) thinness of the main arcades represent a reversal of the priorities of 13th-century English architecture [cf. *124*]. Typical of the Perpendicular style is the virtual elimination of minor decorative sculpture.

In the hundred years which followed the building of the Eleanor Crosses and St Stephen's Chapel, the royal works organization became a permanent institution despite fluctuations in the scale of royal building activity. It came to be recognized as England's premier repository of architectural expertise, and increasingly often the richest ecclesiastical patrons turned to royal architects. The involvement of William Hurley at Ely has been mentioned already, but the single most important instance during the later 14th century, unfortunately supported only by circumstantial evidence, is the designing of the nave of Canterbury Cathedral [*157*] by Henry Yevele, chief royal architect from 1360 until his death in 1400. Yevele was the archetype of the successful late medieval architect, owning a mansion by London Bridge besides numerous other properties in the City of London and two country manors. He was architect to Westminster Palace, Westminster Abbey and St Paul's Cathedral, he had a profitable tomb-making business and he was an important contractor and supplier of building materials. He enjoyed the rank of esquire, one degree below knight.

Like the nearly contemporary remodelling of the nave at Winchester Cathedral, the Canterbury nave succeeded a crudely finished early Romanesque structure whose replacement would have been considered an urgent necessity. At Canterbury, as in late medieval Europe generally, there was no thought of replacing earlier Gothic work, whose essential affinity with contemporary architecture seems to have been acknowledged and respected. Indeed great care was taken in designing the new nave at Canterbury to ensure that the upper limits of each storey were set at the same level as those in William of Sens's choir [*56*]. (Internally the impact of this

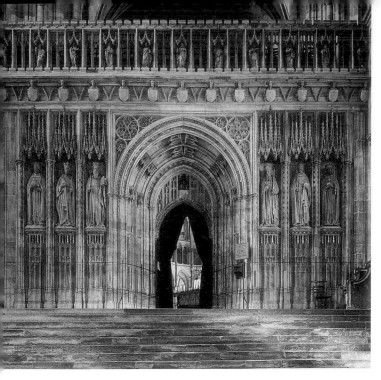

158 Canterbury Cathedral, choir screen, *c.* 1450. The statues of English kings flanking the entrance to the choir represent a selection of ancient and recent benefactors to the cathedral. The designer was probably the London architect Richard Beke.

horizontal continuity was later blunted by the introduction of a tall choir screen and other obstructions.) Since the choir stands on a high crypt and the nave does not, the main arcades and aisles in the new building become extraordinarily tall in relation to the clearstorey and the token triforium. Such proportions were obviously liked for themselves, and it cannot be accidental that tall arcades and low clearstoreys were by this period normal in English friars' churches and major parish churches. Perhaps there was a conscious aim to impart a demotic flavour to that part of the church regularly accessible to the laity at large. Not that the Canterbury nave is simply a parish church nave writ large; English parish churches were nearly always wooden-roofed, whereas at Canterbury the presence of a high vault makes itself felt to an exceptional degree through the responds which are so prominent in axial views that they block out all sight of the intervening walls. The term 'respond' is in fact rather a misnomer for what are better understood as the upper parts of piers shared between the high vaults on the one hand and the main arcades and aisle vaults on the other. This is strongly reminiscent of Bourges [*71*], and indeed the thinness of the main arcade arches when seen from the main vessel would seem to confirm a French origin. Towards the aisles, however, the main arcade arches are considerably deeper, an imbalance which occurred in one of the most important sequels to Gloucester, the remodelling of the choir of Glastonbury Abbey (completed by 1374; mostly destroyed). At Glastonbury the divided piers and asymmetrical main arcade arches perpetuated features already present in the late 12th-century choir, although this does not diminish the probability that they were the model for Canterbury's piers. The Gloucester choir could not serve as an exemplar for

159 Durham Cathedral, reredos of the high altar, erected 1376–9. Made in London and probably designed by the royal architect Henry Yevele, this structure exemplifies the kind of prominent gift favoured by prestige-conscious late medieval patrons. The arms of the donor, head of the most important noble family in the region (the Nevilles), appear above the two doors leading to the now-destroyed shrine of St Cuthbert. The images were removed from the niches in the mid-16th century.

pier design since its supports were massive cylinders inherited from the Romanesque choir. The source of the detailing of the Canterbury piers was the cloister of St Paul's in London, the masterpiece of William Ramsey, one of Yevele's predecessors as chief royal mason. The triple vault shafts flanked by hollows and continuous 'double ogee' mouldings are exact enlargements of those which received the vault of the cloister. In fact the Canterbury nave as a whole typifies late 14th- and early 15th-century south-eastern Perpendicular in its faithful adherence to the formal vocabulary invented by Ramsey, a vocabulary which allows for somewhat greater emphasis on the integrity of individual members than was possible in the diaphanous tracery screening of the Gloucester choir. The beauty of the Canterbury nave resides not in formal inventiveness but in the skill with which other men's innovations were exploited in the service of an essentially original idea.

By the late 14th century the number of major new undertakings on the scale of the Canterbury nave was dwindling rapidly. Besides Canterbury there were the remodellings of the Winchester nave and the Glastonbury choir already mentioned, to which can be added only the choir of York Minster begun in 1361. Apart from its Perpendicular tracery, the main vessel at York was conceived as a continuation of the nave begun sixty years before [137]. Since the nave was based on the same kind of Rayonnant designs as Gloucester, the result was a kind of short-circuiting of the original creative processes behind Perpendicular. The aisles and east front of York display a more quirky and inventive side of the designer, the local man William Hoton, but it is indicative of how the cultural and economic centre of gravity of England was shifting southwards during the late 14th century that the work of Hoton's successors at York came more and more into line with southern, and specifically London, ideas. When the London-based royal architect William Colchester took charge of the minster works in 1405 he was badly beaten up by aggrieved local rivals, yet his southern style remained entrenched. At Durham Cathedral Priory, the north's other major patron of first-class Perpendicular, the picture is broadly similar [159]. A graphic illustration of this process of 'deregionalization' is the west front of Beverley Minster [160]. Above the lower stages begun c. 1380 in the rich and vigorous style of William Hoton, there is a clear though adroitly managed switch to a far smoother and less idiosyncratic manner. Since the great west window was glazed by 1399 the change cannot have been due to a protracted pause in the work.

The towers on the Beverley west front exemplify one of the characteristic achievements of late medieval great church architecture everywhere. Like the upper parts of the west towers at Wells [126], they are carefully considered contributions to the façade as a whole rather than virtuoso performances. That role was more appropriately assumed by crossing towers, although in England continuity with the Romanesque tradition of crossing towers ensured that the emphasis was more on grandeur of effect than exuberant fantasy, as in Germany [56, 175]. The first of the extremely high crossing towers carrying timber spires was at St Paul's, London (completed in 1221), and apparently the next was at Lincoln (completed in 1307). The needle-like stone spire of Salisbury [130] was barely finished when work started on the lantern of the Ely octagon [145], the first of countless late medieval English flat-topped towers. Many of the finest of these owed as much to the vagaries of patronage and finance as to any one architect's vision. Even the suave west towers of Beverley are much slighter than those provided for when the front was started.

The 15th century saw a continued reduction in the number of new great churches begun. From the first half of the century there is a handful of major monastic churches, of which Sherborne Abbey is the most impressive survival. The choir is an entirely new building [156] whereas the nave is a thorough remodelling of a Romanesque structure. The only complete rebuilding of a first-class monastic church in the late 15th century – Bath Abbey, begun in 1499 – was really a sign of exceptional decadence, for it replaced a far larger Romanesque church which had been allowed to fall into serious disrepair. The two grandest English great churches of the 15th century were not monastic or cathedral churches but a parish church and a royal chapel. St Mary Redcliffe in Bristol has been famous ever since its completion around 1480 as England's one cathedral-like parish church. The main incentives for the rich merchants of the locality to build a church combining elements of the two most ambitious great church choirs near Bristol – Wells and Glastonbury – would have been an awareness of the 'burgher cathedrals' of the Continental cities with which they traded and

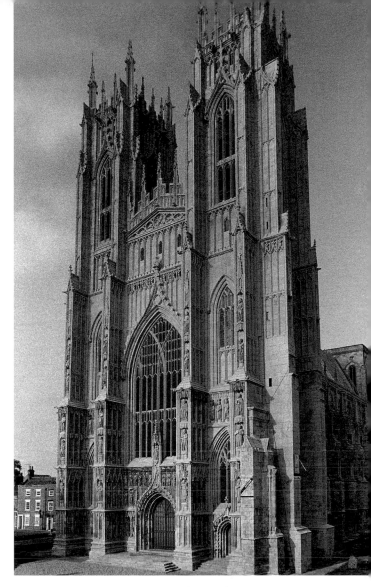

160 Beverley Minster, west front, *c.* 1380–1420. The irregularities at the lower right are the result of building the façade up against an earlier chapel (demolished in the 16th century).

pride in the fact that what was in effect a millionaires' suburb had once been a separate entity from Bristol. One should not be too ready to regard this as a characteristically late medieval phenomenon, for it is clear that the previous early 13th-century church also transcended the comparatively modest norms of English parish church architecture. Consciousness of the challenge posed by the achievements of predecessors can also be detected in what must rank as the most distinguished new church of the 15th century, King Edward IV's chapel of St George in Windsor Castle, begun in 1475 [*161, 162*].

Ever since Edward the Confessor rebuilt Westminster Abbey from *c.* 1050, the initiation of major church building projects had come to be regarded as an attribute of effective kingship in England. Only the late medieval kings who were most successful in war could safely neglect the tradition. Up to a point, medieval monarchs were by definition patrons of church building in that they needed to be seen encouraging what was almost

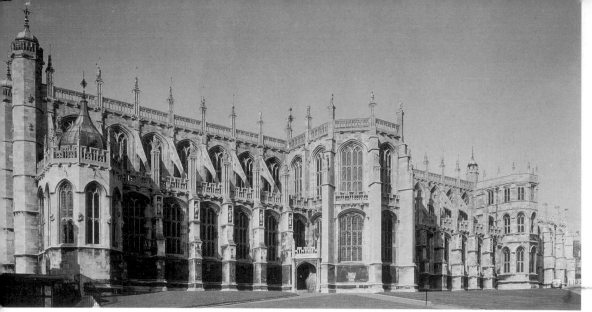

161 St George's Chapel, Windsor Castle, from the south-west, 1475–1511. The great church aspect of the chapel is less apparent than if the planned crossing tower had been built. The likeness of the transepts to the bay windows common in late medieval English domestic architecture was more obvious before the addition of buttresses in the 1920s.

universally regarded as pious work. Nevertheless, the far smaller importance which the French crown attached to this activity is evident from Louis XI's only large-scale church building project, the collegiate church of Cléry on the Loire, for though handsome Cléry has virtually none of the attributes of a great church. The fact that the English kings, taken as a whole, were uniquely lavish patrons of great church building has been obscured by the destruction in the 16th century of much of what they achieved in this field. For most 15th-century English kings finding the wherewithal was harder than for their ancestors. Henry VI's twin educational foundations at Eton and Cambridge, whose centrepieces were churches of cathedral scale though not cathedral format, were endowed from the property of suppressed monasteries dependent on French abbeys; and the funding of St George's, Windsor derived mainly from a huge bribe by which Louis XI hoped to ensure that Edward IV would not invade France – a fine irony in view of the chapel's status as the seat of the Order of the Garter, the premier English chivalric order.

Although the English royal tradition of great church building must be most of the explanation why the Garter had the grandest permanent setting of all European chivalric orders, there were special reasons for the cathedral-like form of St George's. The location of the chapel in the main royal residential castle and its function as a royal mausoleum would inevitably have invited comparisons with Westminster, and Edward must have read Arthurian romances where Camelot is made to house not only the Round Table, the prototype of all chivalric societies, but a magnificent minster or cathedral. The great church format provided a pretext for including twenty-six piers, the same number as there were Garter Knights. Twenty-six was the

162 St George's Chapel, Windsor Castle, nave looking north-west, completed by 1506. The design follows that of the late 15th-century choir with only minor changes. Four-centred arches were part of the Perpendicular style from the beginning [cf. *152*] but are used here with exceptional consistency.

normal total of knights needed to form two tournament teams of thirteen, and thirteen is the number of Christ and the Apostles, so it seems clear that the piers in St George's embodied a specifically chivalric variation of the ancient idea of the Apostles as pillars of the church. This symbolism was lost later when the nave was built one bay longer than originally planned, but it must lie at the root of the main architectural peculiarity of the chapel, the small scale of the lateral elevations and aisles relative to the width of the main vessels. Since the overall length of the chapel was limited by sloping ground to the west and pre-existing structures to the east the requisite number of piers could only be fitted in by making the bays unusually short, about two-thirds of the average for an English cathedral. If the width of the main vessels had been reduced by the same proportion the chapel would have become almost unusable; hence the cathedral-like clear span of c. 11m.

The high ambition of St George's is evident in the choice of sources for the elevations: the Gloucester choir [*154*] and the Canterbury nave [*157*]. From Gloucester come the tall clearstorey and the all-over panelling treatment culminating in tripartite east and west windows. Canterbury's main contribution is the pier treatment which entails bold responds and arcade arches of asymmetrical section. The piers, of more complex section than at Canterbury, are very narrow on the longitudinal axis, with the result that one has an almost unimpeded view from the main vessel towards the other main Canterbury borrowing, the three-tier aisle windows [cf. *56*]. Like the main arcades and nearly all the other windows in the chapel, these incorporate four-centred arches of the extremely flattened form which had been gradually gaining ground from c. 1400. One of the most popular uses for these very obtuse arches was in the terminal walls of parish churches and secular buildings, where they allowed the maximum extension of glazing under low-pitched wooden roofs. It is perhaps not too fanciful to see the uniquely shallow vaults over the central vessels at St George's as the architects' answer to the challenge posed by the carpenters. The architect who began the chapel, Henry Janyns, had as a young man been second in command at Eton College Chapel, the only earlier 15th-century building of large scale designed to receive such a flat vault. The Eton vault remained unbuilt, so the inclusion of this piece of virtuoso construction at St George's seems to be a clear-cut instance of Edward IV's outdoing the patronage of his ousted rival. Although the square aisle bays are covered by fan vaults, the very short bays of the main vessel precluded the use of the same form over the central span. Like the elevations, the high vault can be understood to some extent as an amalgam of Canterbury and Gloucester: the shape of the conoids and the use of the central area to display flat patterning are borrowed from the former, the tunnel vault with penetrations from the latter. The central area is decorated with a pattern of stars and triangles based on the vault in the porch to the St George's precinct (c. 1350–53), one of the most important precursors of fully developed fan vaulting. The perfection of St George's owes much to its creators' ability to draw on more than a century's accumulated experience of Perpendicular design by the royal works organization.

A still more impressive testimony to the central place that the great church tradition retained in late medieval English culture is the chapel which Henry VII built onto the east end of Westminster Abbey *c.* 1503–9 [*163–165*]. The 15th century had seen considerable numbers of elaborately decorated single-room Lady Chapels added to older great churches, but the Westminster chapel transcended the limitations of the genre because it was intended to serve as a Tudor mausoleum centred on the relics of the canonized Henry VI. Parity with St Edward the Confessor's shrine chapel was established by making the main vessel exactly as wide and long as that of the eastern arm of Henry III's church and by building an apse and radiating chapels echoing the earlier chevet. Even the floor level matches that of the Confessor's chapel. However, Henry VI was never formally canonized and his shrine remained unbuilt. Since Henry VII's tomb stands in the apse, where the shrine should have been, the chapel is today named after its builder. Originally the intention was that Henry VI and Henry VII should lie in the Lady Chapel of St George's, Windsor, but when that plan was abandoned it seems to have become imperative that the Westminster chapel should eclipse St George's. In terms of overall size this was clearly impossible, although Westminster is higher. Externally, however, Westminster's triumph is complete, for it is by far the most richly treated church exterior in England. Nevertheless, the extraordinary idea of replacing normal aisle windows by bay windows was almost certainly inspired by the transepts and transeptal chapels at St George's [*161*], whose polygonal form follows that of the bay windows which project from the sides of English late medieval great halls. The faceted form of the Westminster bays comes from Henry VII's palace buildings of the 1490s at Richmond and Windsor, the latter designed by Robert Janyns, the son of Henry Janyns and the strongest of three candidates for authorship of the chapel. Between the bays are not ordinary buttresses but another borrowing from secular architecture, octagonal turrets, their upper sections originally sanctified by statues of Apostles and prophets. The contrast with the heraldic beasts perching on the pinnacles of Edward IV's temple of chivalry may well have been intentional. The turrets end in onion cupolas probably conceived as superior versions of the lead-covered domelets at St George's, although their ribbing and crocketing show an awareness of Low Countries or French examples.

The interior is as self-consciously a *tour-de-force* as the exterior. The basic scheme of the elevation derives from Windsor, but everything else is treated with the small-scale delicacy and richness normally confined to the most ambitious chantry chapels [*166*]. The resemblance suggests that Henry VII's Chapel was intended to surpass all existing funerary chapels, thereby giving palpable expression to the distance between the new Tudor dynasty and the

163–165 Henry VII's Chapel, Westminster Abbey, London, c. 1503–9. *Above:* high vault. The openwork structure of the outer parts of the vault was probably intended to rival the complex types of timber roof developed in late medieval England. *Below left:* south side. As in most Perpendicular buildings, the rectilinear emphasis of the elevations is enhanced by the use of inconspicuous low-pitched roofs. *Below right:* the constructional technique of the high vault.

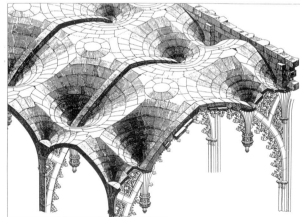

kind of overmighty subject who had several times usurped the English throne since 1399. After all, Henry VII was himself only the most successful of these usurpers. The image-lined 'triforium' may derive from the Wells choir [151], but it enhances the chantry aspect of the chapel as much as the great church aspect. The climax of the interior is unquestionably the vault [163, 165]. Technically it is a unique achievement: the only large-scale fan vault to use the ashlar shell technique of the Gloucester cloister [155]. Small fan vaults incorporating pendants were being built in England from the late 14th century, but the only earlier large pendant vaults were conventional rib vaults. The finest of these is in the Divinity School, Oxford (c. 1480) and will have been known to Robert Janyns since Oxford was his home town. But Westminster outdoes Oxford in concealing the greater part of the transverse arches which form the structural skeleton of the vault; and although the pendants are structurally like those at Oxford in being simply extra-large arch stones, they hang down much further. The ashlar shells between the transverse arches are no more than 9cm thick, excluding the surface tracery. The tracery is one of the most brilliant strokes in the design, for its uncommonly bold projection converts the intervening masonry into deep shadows which make one forget that the vault is a solid structure and not some kind of petrified spider's web. It is hard to see where the English great church tradition could have gone from here. The dismantling of the medieval order by Henry VII's son ensured that it went nowhere.

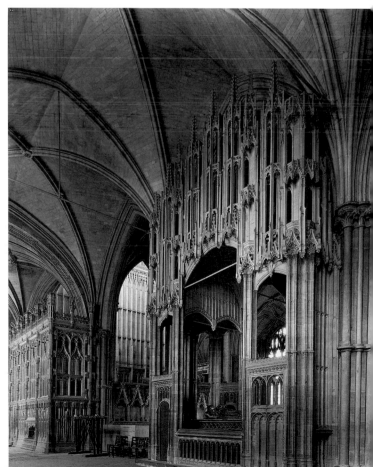

166 Winchester Cathedral, south aisle of the early 13th-century eastern chapel complex ('retrochoir') looking north-west, with the chantry chapels of Bishop Beaufort, c. 1447 (foreground) and Bishop Fox, c. 1513–18. The English late medieval practice of constructing private funerary chapels within the main spaces of great churches contrasts with the Continental usage of building out extensions from side aisles [64, 195].

Central Europe

The enormous production of church buildings in Central Europe during the late Middle Ages was fuelled chiefly by the competitive civic pride of the region's burgeoning towns, and as a result the main focus of creative effort was the urban parish church rather than the cathedral or monastic church. It seems legitimate to associate the matter-of-fact directness of the normative type, the hall church [*112*], with the practical tenor of town life, although increasingly often during the 14th century the hall format was adopted by major ecclesiastical corporations whose counterparts elsewhere in Northern Europe would automatically have built great churches. Austerely detailed basilicas in the Freiburg-im-Breisgau mould [*113*] continued to find favour, especially with the friars, and, like hall churches, they could be executed on the largest scale. The hall choirs of a few exceptionally ambitious parish churches incorporated some of the trappings of great church Gothic. Important examples are the radiating chapels at Schwäbisch Gmünd in Swabia (begun 1351), based on the chapels added from *c.* 1300 to the chevet of Notre-Dame in Paris, and the external elevations of the choir of St Sebald at Nuremberg (begun 1361), which incorporate traceried gables and image-lined buttresses worthy of any Rayonnant cathedral.

The one 14th-century church in Central Europe which adopted the French great church system more or less complete is Prague Cathedral [*167–171*]. This stylistic allegiance can be ascribed without hesitation to the patrons, the Luxemburg dynasty of Bohemian kings, allies of the French royal house in family, politics and culture. Under King John (1310–46) and his son, the Emperor Charles IV (1346–78), Prague was transformed into a Central European Paris, complete with a university, the first in the Empire north of the Alps. Its centrepiece was the cathedral which, like Henry III's Westminster Abbey, stood beside the main royal palace and combined the functions of Reims (coronation church), St-Denis (royal mausoleum) and the Sainte-Chapelle (relic cult glorifying the monarchy). Prague was less directly the personal creation of the ruler than Westminster only in the sense that the administration of the works remained in clerical hands, for Charles IV spared no effort to ensure that the new cathedral would be an effective symbol of the enhanced power and prestige of Bohemia. In 1341, when Charles was already co-regent, a tenth of the very large royal revenues from the Bohemian silver mines was granted to the chapter specifically to meet the costs of building; in 1344 Charles personally negotiated with the pope the carving out of an archdiocese of Prague from that of Mainz; in 1355 he acquired relics of the cathedral's patron, St Vitus; and by 1358 he had remade the shrine for the relics of St Wenceslas – like Edward the Confessor, a canonized representative of the previous indigenous dynasty. The clearest indication of Charles's interest in the building itself is that while engaged in discussions with the pope at Avignon, he recruited the architect Matthew of Arras. Matthew died in 1352 when the ambulatory and radiating chapels

167 Prague Cathedral, choir looking north-east, 1344–85. The heavy sill under the triforium breaks forward from the wall and thereby draws attention to the bay-defining vault shafts, but its horizontality also complements the bay softening aspect of the high tunnel vault.

were complete and the straight bays had been begun. His work is in an elegant Rayonnant manner strongly influenced by the late 13th-century parts of Narbonne. The pivotal position of Prague in the history of German Late Gothic is due not to Matthew but to Peter Parler, who took over in 1356 at the extraordinarily young age of twenty-three. Parler completed the sacristy on the north side of the choir in 1362 [*170, 172f*], the south transept porch in 1368 [*171*], the arcade level of the choir by 1370 and the upper levels by 1385 [*167*]. Work on the great tower west of the south transept continued until *c.* 1420, when the Hussite revolution halted church building throughout Bohemia. The nave, whose foundation stone was laid in 1392, remained unbuilt until the early 20th century.

The acceptability of the youthful Parler in Prague had no doubt much to do with his being a member of a well-established family of architects active in the Rhineland and Swabia. His father Heinrich was probably architect of the choir of Schwäbisch Gmünd. His first work at Prague, the sacristy, shows him to have been abreast of the most advanced developments in German architecture. Its two square bays are covered by vaults from which are suspended, with the aid of concealed ironwork, open conoids of ribs not unlike the spokes of an umbrella [*170, 172f*]. There can be little doubt that the main inspiration for these pendant vaults was the larger octagonal vaults

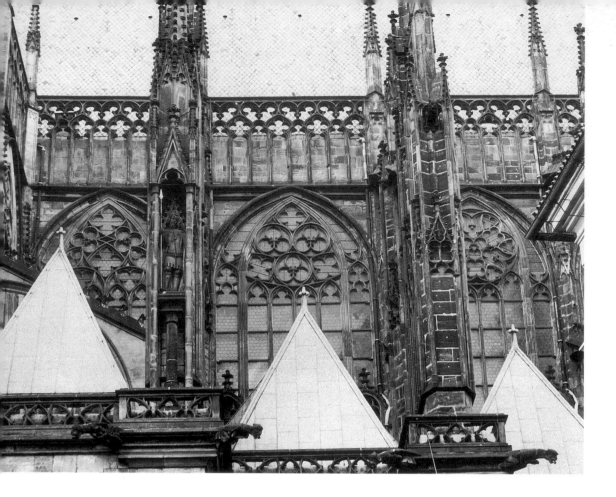

168, 169 Prague Cathedral. *Above:* south clearstorey of the choir, begun 1374. *Left:* upper part of the south transept façade, begun *c.* 1371 and abandoned incomplete *c.* 1420 (window tracery early 20th-century).

170, 171 Prague Cathedral. *Above left:* vault over the west bay of the sacristy, complete by 1362. *Above right:* vault of the south transept porch, complete by 1368.

which, until their failure and replacement in the mid-16th century, covered the two-bay chapel of St Catherine on the south side of Strasbourg Cathedral (begun *c.* 1338) [*172e*]. It is almost certain that the Strasbourg pendants anticipated Prague's omission of webs, but the possibility exists that they resembled the considerable numbers of early 13th-century Rhenish vaults with small pendants, all of which include webs. The earliest German rib vaults without webs are those in the west tower at Freiburg Minster and the 'Tonsur' chapel in the cloister at Magdeburg Cathedral, both of *c.* 1310–30. Similar but smaller vaults had been used slightly earlier in England, in the vestibule to the sacristy of St Augustine's, Bristol (begun 1298) and in the Easter Sepulchre at Lincoln Cathedral (*c.* 1290–1300). If this were the only correspondence between German and English vault design of the late 13th and early 14th centuries it could be dismissed as coincidence, but in fact there are many German vaults besides those of the Prague sacristy which can readily be understood as variations on earlier English designs.

The plan of the ribs in the centre of the vault over the eastern sacristy bay at Prague is a four-point star. This design and the eight-point stars of the Strasbourg vaults were among the more spectacular manifestations of a long-standing and widespread Continental interest in the stellar vaults used in English circular and polygonal chapter houses from the late 12th century onwards. One of the earliest signs of this interest is a plan of *c.* 1230 in the 'sketchbook' of Villard de Honnecourt showing a square chapter house covered by a simplified version of the vaulting scheme exemplified by the mid-13th-century chapter house at Westminster [*172a,b*]. Some of the material in the Villard sketchbook suggests close connections with the Cistercians, whose international and centralized organization provided ideal channels for transmitting information about English chapter houses to the Continent. It is likely that this is what actually happened, for the revival of interest in the centrally planned chapter house at the end of the 12th century took place under the auspices of the Cistercians of south-west England and Wales, and some of the earliest Central European star vaults are found in Cistercian chapter houses or strongly Cistercian-influenced buildings. Unlike the English designers, who admired the proto-fan vault character which the profusion of ribs in chapter houses gives to the central conoid, the Central Europeans found various ways of emphasizing the autonomy of the constituent Y shapes or triradials, a formation used in the Rhineland from *c.* 1220 onwards. The most favoured way of doing this, the omission of radial ribs linking angles and centre, is anticipated in the Villard plan. The triradials in the triangular corner compartments of the east sacristy vault at Prague have no English antecedents and register to some extent as autonomous elements by virtue of their exclusion from the central pendant-containing diamond shape.

Peter Parler was evidently intrigued by the fact that star vaults could be built with or without a central pier, for his sacristy vaults appear to have been conceived as a way of combining the two types. The skeletal pendants correspond to the configuration of ribs in the solid conoids over central piers, while at the same time allowing a view of the central section of the vault, on whose surface there are conventional ribs mirroring the plan of those in the pendant [*170*]. Perhaps Parler knew of the two chapels at the west end of Lincoln Cathedral, the southern one with a single-span vault identical to that of the west bay of the Prague sacristy except that it lacks the pendant, the other with a central pier carrying a vault of the same plan [*172 o,n*]. It is more probable that he had seen the crossing vault of Our Lady at Trier (begun *c.* 1227) whose plan, like that of the south chapel at Lincoln, resembles four bays of quadripartite vaulting.

Parler's slightly later vault over the south transept porch at Prague can be seen, when viewed as in *171*, to combine the mirroring of pendant ribs in surface ribs, which occurs in the west sacristy bay, with kite shapes like those which make up the four-point star in the east bay. Whether deliberately or not, the ultimate origin of Parler's vaults in chapter houses is evoked by the presence of a pier below the skeletal rib conoid and by the half-polygonal form of the conoid itself. Viewed longitudinally, the south porch vault takes on the aspect of an aisle divided into triangular bays whose centres are displaced alternately to left and right so as to generate a vista of asymmetrical, overlapping conoids [*172j*]. These so-called jumping vaults had already appeared around 1310–40 in north Germany and Swabia as by-products of building rectangular rooms covered by a series of star vaults carried on piers [*172h,i*], so it is likely that Parler's immediate source of inspiration was there rather than in the English chapter houses. At Prague too much of the lower levels of the choir had been completed by Matthew of Arras to allow the

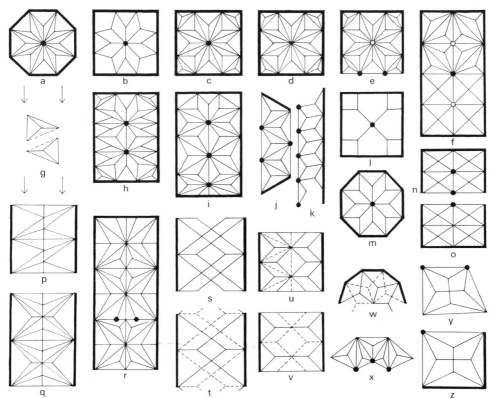

172 Diagrammatic plans of Central European and English Gothic vaults (not to scale; open circles indicate pendants, black circles indicate piers): (**a**) English chapter house of Westminster Abbey type [cf. *134*]; (**b**) chapter house scheme from the 'sketchbook' of Villard de Honnecourt; (**c**) Eberbach, chapter house; (**d**) Burgos Cathedral, chapter house; (**e**) Strasbourg Cathedral, one bay of St Catherine's chapel; (**f**) Prague Cathedral, sacristy [cf. *170*]; (**g**) two triradials; (**h**) Lübeck, St Mary, Briefkapelle; (**i**) Maulbronn, chapter house; (**j**) Prague Cathedral, south transept porch vault [cf. *171*]; (**k**) Zvíkov Castle, cloister; (**l**) Vyšší Brod, chapter house; (**m**) Kouřim, St Stephen, crypt; (**n**) Lincoln Cathedral, north nave chapel; (**o**) Lincoln Cathedral, south nave chapel; (**p**) Lincoln Cathedral, choir, main vessel [cf. *123*]; (**q**) Lincoln Cathedral, nave, main vessel [cf. *124*]; (**r**) St Stephen's Chapel, Westminster Palace, lower chapel; (**s**) Prague Cathedral, choir, main vessel [cf. *167*]; (**t**) Prague Cathedral, choir, main vessel, showing intersecting triradials; (**u**) Prague, Charles Bridge, Old Town Tower, entrance hall, showing small triradials; (**v**) Prague, Charles Bridge, Old Town Tower, entrance hall, showing intersecting triradials; (**w**) Prague Cathedral, choir, apse, showing intersecting triradials [cf. *167*]; (**x**) Kolín, part of the ambulatory; (**y**) Kutná Hora, south-east ambulatory bay; (**z**) 's-Hertogenbosch, one bay of the south transept porch.

introduction of jumping vaults such as occur in the ambulatory of the basilican choir built by Parler *c.* 1360–78 at Kolín, east of Prague [*172x*].

The high vault in the choir at Prague [*167*] resembles the vaults so far discussed in being a complete synthesis of English and German elements. It can hardly be doubted that the basic concept of a tunnel vault with low penetrations and decorative surface ribs was taken over from recent south-western English vaults like Wells [*151*], for the only earlier Continental vaults of this kind are in the 13th-century hall churches and aisleless churches of Anjou, a regional 'vernacular' tradition which appears never to have influenced great church architecture. Moreover the Prague vault is the first outside England to imitate the curious Wells trick of splitting foliage bosses to reveal rib junctions. For the pattern applied to the surface of the tunnel the main source appears to be Parler's own slightly earlier vault in the Old Town Tower of the Charles Bridge at Prague [*172u*]. This is a pointed tunnel without penetrations whose constituent curved planes are both overlaid by a pattern of ribs almost identical to the plan of the south transept porch [*172j*] except that bounding triangles are omitted so as to leave only triradials. The omission of bounding triangles was fairly common in Central Europe by this date, and the possible sources of the feature include a number of late 13th-century Bohemian vaults [*172k*]. As in the cathedral porch, the bridge tower vault has no complete transverse ribs but, unlike the porch, it is symmetrical about its longitudinal axis. What was wholly new was its capacity to be read as a series of intersecting triradials [*172v*], an aspect of which Parler was undoubtedly aware, for in the high vault of the cathedral intersecting triradials are made even more prominent [*172t*]. This is done partly by allowing them to extend across the full width of the central vessel and partly by eliminating the alternative reading of them as a series of small self-contained triradials. The avoidance of complete transverse ribs and the way in which each triradial straddles two adjacent bays are complementary devices for reinforcing the longitudinal character of the tunnel. The continuous sequence of alternately large and small diamond shapes at the vault crown makes this the prototype of all the innumerable 'net vaults' to be raised over Central European churches during the next century and a half [*174*]. Whereas the structurally more daring skeletal vaults of the sacristy and porch could only be realized on a small scale, the high vault was both imitable and capable of any number of variations. The apsidal part of the vault has a very ingenious variation on the intersecting triradial theme whose only drawback is that it results in penetrations which obstruct the heads of the clearstorey windows [*167, 172w*].

The main elevations at Prague are a version of the French Rayonnant formula whose strong lines function as a kind of showcase for the display of a series of brilliantly original decorative set pieces [*167*]. Of necessity, the arcade storey had to be completed in general accordance with Matthew of Arras's design, although in the west bays, which are entirely Parler's work, the high vault responds are thickened. Comparison of the upper storeys with those of Cologne [*84*], which Parler undoubtedly knew, shows that he was prepared to make some fairly radical departures from Rayonnant precedent for the sake of ensuring that the elevations complemented the high tunnel vault in emphasizing the unity of the choir as a longitudinal space. The main devices which promote this reading are the heavy horizontals of the triforium parapet and the strange angled projections of the clearstorey sills, which almost cut through the western high vault responds and which actually do sever most of the thin responds inherited from Matthew's arcades. The partial cutting was no doubt the effect preferred by Parler, but the complete cutting must have been acceptable to him both for itself and because his father had used something very similar in the ambulatory at Schwäbisch Gmünd. At Prague the angled sill projections register as being a subordinate part of an even stranger feature, the angled clearstorey lights and triforium openings. The pretext for this angling was the positioning of the internal triforium passage and external clearstorey passage so hard up behind the high vault responds as to preclude a normal junction between the responds and the triforium arcade and clearstorey tracery. (Both passages were blocked in the 19th century because they were held to endanger the structural stability of the choir, and in the 20th century doors to a new walkway passing behind the buttresses were formed in the adjacent parts of the triforium windows.) The extra width of the triforium arcade openings next to the vault responds allows a good view from ground level not merely of the entrances to the triforium passage but of the celebrated sculptured busts which surmount them. Painted inscriptions formerly identified the busts as the family of Charles IV, the successive archbishops and clerical building administrators, and the two architects of the choir. The scheme as a whole is unique, although parallels for the use of busts above passage entrances are in the choirs of Sées [2] and St Augustine's, Bristol. In fact, the upper choir elevations seem to be as much indebted to south-western English sources as the high vault, for the only antecedents of the angled lights of the clearstorey are the similarly finialed entrances to the Wells clearstorey passage, especially those in the east wall where, in contrast to the side walls, the angling is not continued into the jambs [151]. Above the angled lights at Prague there is not solid masonry, as at Wells, but single glazed lights which serve to make the tracery heads uniform in width and height with those in the narrow apse windows. Possibly Parler knew the similar arrangement in the mid-13th-century Rayonnant choir of León [118]. The actual tracery patterns used at Prague reflect the influence of English flowing designs merely in a general way, for they are the most original Continental tracery of the 14th century. The only clearly identifiable borrowings are from Swabian sources, notably the windows of c. 1330–47 in the nave at Schwäbisch Gmünd (the strange 'melting' of one form into another in the internal and external parapets) and the east window of c. 1335 at Bebenhausen Abbey (the cusping of the large circle in the right-hand window in 168 which impinges on some of the forms it encloses).

There is some irony in Parler's indebtedness to English Gothic, for King John of Bohemia died fighting on the French side at Crécy in 1346, and Edward III had lent his support to Charles IV's main rival for the imperial crown, Louis of Bavaria. Nevertheless, from the viewpoint of the architect rather than the patron it would have been quite natural to take cognizance of the achievements of the most creative tradition of 14th-century cathedral Gothic, especially as Prague was a 'one-off' rather than the product of an established German tradition of great church architecture. Awareness of English Gothic in the Rhineland and Swabia went back to the late 13th century when the masons of Strasbourg Cathedral recorded their decision to adopt the craft organization of the English masons and when the windows and piers of the basically French-inspired abbey church of Wimpfen-im-Tal (begun 1269) were described in a contemporary source as being of an English pattern. German political horizons had long encompassed England, if only as a counterweight to France, and when Parler arrived in Prague in 1356 Edward III's victories over the French had raised English prestige in Europe to its highest level during the Middle Ages. Nevertheless, it has to be emphasized that Parler's borrowings from the Decorated style were integrated into a design which is not English either in its basic premises or its detailed handling, for in the late Middle Ages no single nation could exercise cultural leadership in Europe in the way that France had done during the 13th century. How Parler was able to learn about English Decorated is not known. A study tour during apprenticeship is possible, for these are documented in late medieval Germany, but it may be that some kind of agreement existed which enabled architectural information in the guise of drawings to circulate among the main cathedral lodges. Around 1350 the Strasbourg lodge obtained plans of the choirs of Notre-Dame in Paris and Orléans Cathedral, but it is not known how or by what route they came.

The influence of Parler's net vaults and complex tracery endured in Central Europe as long as Gothic architecture itself, and by around 1500 the Parler family had become known as the 'Junckherrn' (squires) of Prague and had acquired the mythical status of founders of German masonic practice. Yet the Prague choir did not start a spate of cathedral building. At Augsburg a grand new Rayonnant chevet begun after the bishop visited Prague in 1354 was finished off lamely in the late 14th century. At the minster of Freiburg-im-Breisgau, the main town in the Black Forest region, a cathedral-like choir was begun in 1354 by Peter Parler's brother Johann, but a quarrel between the town and the ruler of the surrounding area soon brought work to a standstill. Other institutions which might have been expected to build a great church were content with much simpler schemes. A case in point is Aachen Minster, where the new choir added after the formal designation of the church as the coronation place of future German kings in 1356 was essentially an enlarged version of the Sainte-Chapelle. That it was not a German Reims must have been partly due to the wish to preserve Charlemagne's venerable 9th-century Palatine Chapel, but it also reflects the lesser importance of the imperial office in the late Middle Ages compared to what it had been until 1250. On the relatively rare occasions when major church building was patronized by the territorial princes, the real rulers of late medieval Germany, the outcome was invariably a hall church.

The best of 15th-century Germany's very few great churches, the continuation of the Freiburg choir from 1471 by Hans Niesenberger,

173, 174 Freiburg-im-Breisgau Minster. *Above left:* ambulatory looking north-east, begun 1471. The town of Freiburg placed itself under Austrian protection as a counter to the hostility of the local princely family, the Zähringer; hence the designation of the two eastern radiating chapels as the emperor's. *Above right:* choir, consecrated 1513. As in the two eastern radiating chapels, the vault includes some relatively restrained examples of skeletal or 'flying' ribs.

provides an exemplar of many of the stylistic traits of the latest phase of German Gothic, although it was not a building of the seminal importance of Prague. As in the major hall churches, the emphasis is firmly on rich and complex vaulting. The central vessel has a net vault which must be numbered among the vast progeny of the high vault at Prague [*167*], although its close and even mesh of ribs is typical of late 15th- and 16th-century designs [*174*]. The ambulatory vault is quite different and exemplifies the restless, organic quality of much 15th-century German Gothic in its sprawling and irregular-looking rib patterns, its tangled and capital-less springings, its limited use of skeletal ribs and its overshot rib junctions suggestive of branches lashed together [*173*]. This last element is used inconspicuously in the high vault at Prague, but at Freiburg and the many other late 15th-century churches where it is echoed in the cusping of the window tracery it almost becomes the *leitmotiv* of the interior. The ultimate development of the idea, the naturalistic rendering of untrimmed branches, did not impinge on great church architecture as such, although it can be seen on fittings and ancillary structures, for example the nave pulpit and the chapel of St Lawrence at Strasbourg [*176*]. It is not at all clear what specific meanings, if any, were attached to this quasi-vegetal strain of Gothic.

Despite its cathedral scale and token triforium, the Freiburg choir has less in common with the Prague choir than with the rather simply treated two-hundred-year-old nave at Freiburg [*113*]. In fact, apart from the collegiate church of Kutná Hora in Bohemia, which Peter Parler or his son Johann began in 1388, and the Regensburg-inspired choir begun in 1405 at Passau Cathedral in Austria, there were no Central European sequels to Prague's modernized Rayonnant elevations. Even the biggest church building of late medieval Germany, the 42m-high nave of Ulm Minster, gives no sign that its designers could summon up any enthusiasm for what was by the late 14th century the unusual task of designing a basilica. Indeed, the bleak wall surfaces and tired detailing of Ulm serve to highlight the solid if unspectacular virtues of the Freiburg choir elevations. Ulm had been begun as a hall church, but its conversion to a basilica was already under way in 1392 when Ulrich von Ensingen arrived to begin work on the west tower, the finest Late Gothic steeple in Central Europe [*175*]. This truly prodigious structure was not merely an assertion of Ulm's leadership of the Swabian League of towns but a gesture of defiance in the face of the rout of the League's forces by the duke of Württemberg in 1388. The choice of a single tower rather than a pair is not surprising, for Germany had a tradition of single-tower façades which was already more than five hundred years old. In 1392 the only large German Gothic steeple which had reached completion was the axial west tower of Freiburg, and even the west front at Strasbourg was at that time intended to be finished with one central tower. Like most medieval steeples conceived on the grandest scale, the Ulm tower rose very slowly. After exactly a hundred years the bell-stage was completed, and nothing more was done until in 1885–90 the top storey and spire were built from drawings of 1477 by Matthäus Böblinger, Ulrich's fourth successor. The completed tower is essentially what drawings from Ulrich's time show he intended: a compilation of all the most ambitious features of the rival towers and façades completed or in progress in 1392. From the south transept tower and façade at Prague come the deep tracery-sheathed buttresses, the openwork staircases [*169*] and the triple porch (the last possibly via the south tower at St Stephen's, Vienna, begun soon after 1359). Strasbourg contributes the unglazed lancets screening the west window and the 'harpstring' tracery of the bell stage [*100*], whereas the pierced tracery spire is in the tradition inaugurated at Cologne [*110*] and Freiburg.

Ulrich von Ensingen's reputation was such that he became a prime example of that characteristic late medieval phenomenon, the architectural pluralist simultaneously responsible for several major projects and able to delegate day-to-day supervision to deputies. He began the small west tower

175 Ulm Minster from the south-west; tower, 1392–1492 (three lower storeys) and 1885–90. The flying buttresses on the nave were added for appearance's sake in the 19th century, around 400 years after the building of the high vault.

176 Strasbourg Cathedral, former chapel of St Lawrence, north of the north transept, by Jakob von Landshut, 1495–1505. The overhanging portal canopy is closely modelled on one of 1429 at the main parish church of Jakob's Bavarian home town, but the jagged quality of its intersecting arches is typical of German architecture *c.* 1500. The niche canopy to the left of the portal is one of several passages of the design where Gothic detailing gives way to imitations of tree branches.

of Our Lady at Esslingen in 1395, and the immense north-west tower at Strasbourg in 1402, and in 1414 he or his son provided designs for another north-west tower, that at Basle Minster. European admiration of German tower design is attested by the pierced tracery spires added from 1442 to the west towers of Burgos Cathedral in Castile by Juan de Colonia (Johann of Cologne), by the many detailed borrowings incorporated into the most ambitious towers built in the Low Countries [*185, 186*], and not least by the invitation issued to Hans Niesenberger to take charge of building the crossing tower of Milan Cathedral in 1482.

The Low Countries

If material prosperity had been the main prerequisite for the establishment of a flourishing tradition of great church architecture, the cities of Flanders ought to have assumed leadership in this field by the early 13th century. As it was, the burgesses of Ghent, Bruges and Ypres kept their capital at work in their industrial and commercial enterprises and showed no signs of being willing to sink a significant proportion of it into church building. As surprising as their want of ambition is the imaginative poverty which characterizes nearly all the few large church buildings put up in Flanders during the late Middle Ages, the very period when the region's painting and sculpture enjoyed a European reputation. The absence of bishops' sees other than Tournai in the extreme south may have deprived Flanders of the most obvious kind of leadership in great church architecture, but this cannot be the whole explanation for the low status of the genre within Flemish mercantile culture, since the only cathedral-like schemes embarked on in Flanders during the 13th century, the choirs of St Salvator, Bruges and St John, Ghent, are simplified versions of Tournai's choir. Moreover, the 14th century saw the emergence of the Low Countries' principal tradition of great church design in Brabant, where there were no cathedrals at all during the Middle Ages. The main circumstances favourable to the rise of Brabant Gothic were the region's rapid economic growth and the lateness of that development, which meant that in 1300 most of the large towns had still not been able to afford to replace their comparatively small Romanesque churches. Of the few ambitious churches begun before 1300 only Ste-Gudule in Brussels can be classed without hesitation as a great church, but the coarse and hybrid design of its slowly built choir (c. 1226–73) ensured that it was ignored once Brabant as a whole became enthused for great church building. Inevitably, the renewal of Brabant Gothic would be led by architects recruited from outside.

One of the first signs of this renewal was the start of work in 1321 on the choir of St Sulpicius at Diest. The first architect was the otherwise unknown Peter of Savoy, but the only part of the choir universally accepted as being by him is the ground plan of the chevet. The layout of the radiating chapels has been compared to St-Père-sous-Vézelay in Burgundy, but a far more remarkable connection is their reproduction of the strange little rooms (sacristies?) tucked in between the radiating chapels at Narbonne Cathedral. How much of the existing superstructure was envisaged by Peter is unknown, but there is at least a possibility that the capital-less cylindrical piers and the 'dying in' arch mouldings were part of the original design, for they are strikingly similar to the main arcades of Narbonne [88]. The Diest chevet plan had no followers and the dying-in arcades attained only a local popularity in the Demer valley region.

The building which has traditionally been placed at the start of Brabant Late Gothic is the choir of St Rombout at Mechelen (Malines), begun in the

177 Mechelen, St Rombout, north side of the choir from the south aisle, possibly begun after a fire in 1342. The blind tracery cladding of the mid-15th-century apse (on the right) differs only in small details from that of the 14th-century bays.

1330s or 1340s and apparently designed by another Frenchman, Jean d'Oisy. So far as the chevet is concerned this interpretation is not justified, as there is clear evidence for its addition in the 15th century, but the rectangular part of the choir is almost certainly the oldest representative of the scheme which became standard in Brabant for nearly two centuries [177]. In part its success may have been due simply to its being first in the field, but one must not underestimate the appeal exerted by its carefully contrived blend of the familiar and the novel. Among the familiar features are the tall columnar piers – almost universal in the 13th-century Low Countries – and the narrow triforium and clearstorey reminiscent of the most important early 14th-century churches of the adjoining Meuse region, for example Notre-Dame at Huy, begun in 1311. The features which would have appeared novel in Brabant had all been current in French Rayonnant for a long time: the blind tracery cladding of wall surfaces, the omission of capitals from the vault responds, and the delicate tufts of foliage in two tiers on the main arcade capitals. The wiry feel to the tracery and the upper elevations generally is due to the use of the grey-white sandstone which abounds to the north and east of Brussels, for this has the advantage of taking fine detail but the disadvantage of being available only in very small pieces. The extraordinary longevity of the Mechelen scheme is illustrated by the choir of St Gummarus in nearby Lier, completed in 1515 [179]. Virtually all that has changed is the tracery.

Inter-civic hostility may explain why the Mechelen scheme was not adopted for the choir begun in 1352 at Our Lady in Antwerp. Work on the choir was suspended during the war with Flanders (1356–78), so it is not clear how far the central vessel conforms to the original intentions. If the continuously moulded main arcades were designed in 1352 they must be regarded as the source of those at St John in 's-Hertogenbosch (begun *c*. 1370), which is a far more impressive church, despite being built by a much smaller and less wealthy community. Apart from its continuous arcade mouldings, 's-Hertogenbosch is based on the choir of Mechelen. Still more polished than 's-Hertogenbosch is its close copy, the choir of St Peter at Louvain, begun by 1409–10 [*178*]. Admittedly the height is reduced from the exceptional 29m of 's-Hertogenbosch to the 24m usual in the major Brabant churches, and the exterior lacks some of the richness of the earlier building, but these reductions are more than compensated for by the increased number of lights in the clearstorey windows and by the introduction of upright panels into the arcade spandrels. Both changes enhance the splendid vertical élan achieved at 's-Hertogenbosch by combining the capital-less vault responds of Mechelen with the similarly treated main arcades of Antwerp. The drily repetitive quality of the tracery in these buildings is mitigated at Louvain by alternating the small-scale blind tracery forms as well as the elaborate tracery patterns in the clearstorey. The latter are among the earliest examples of flowing tracery in the Low Countries, and their curvilinear elements are mostly still confined within small circles, as in the earliest French Flamboyant tracery. Only in the reproduction of the Louvain elevation at

178 Louvain, St Peter, north side of the choir, begun before 1409–10, dedicated 1441. The Crucifixion group of *c*. 1490 is the only late medieval example in the Low Countries still *in situ* above a contemporary choir screen.

179 Lier, St Gummarus, transept and choir looking north-east: transept begun 1460; north window, *c.* 1533; choir, 1477–1515, by Herman and Domien de Waghemakere; choir screen, 1535–40, by Frans Mynsheeren and Jan Wishaegen (pinnacle 19th-century).

180 Leiden, St Pancras, choir looking north-east, *c.* 1500 (wooden high vault reinstated in the 19th century).

Ste-Waudru in Mons, begun in 1450, were flowing tracery patterns allowed to invade the arcade spandrels and the triforium.

Mons lies in Hainault and exemplifies the exportation of Brabant Gothic throughout the southern Low Countries. Most of the customers for this commodity were towns on or near the coast of what is now southern Holland. The choir of Our Lady at Breda (completed *c.* 1410–20) is basically a reproduction of the Mechelen choir as it was in its original ambulatory-less state, but the formation of the crossing piers as four fat shafts derives from the 13th-century crossing of Ste-Gudule in Brussels and appears to be the earliest example of what became a standard feature of major Dutch churches. The bulky, pneumatic character of the few examples in Brabant makes a curious contrast with the brittle linearity of the upper elevations [*179*], whereas in Holland they eventually become an integral part of an austere aesthetic stemming from the dearth of freestone and the consequent reliance on brick. St Pancras in Leiden [*180*] typifies the great town churches of late medieval Holland in its use of brick for the basic carcass and imported stone for the dressings. In its omission of the Mechelen-Louvain kind of triforium, a feature very extravagant of dressed stone, Leiden conforms to a distinctively

Dutch type, of which the earliest example is Our Lady in Dordrecht (begun 1439). Dordrecht was designed by Evert van Spoerwater who, as the architect then in charge of Our Lady in Antwerp, was well placed to recognize the applicability in Holland of that church's two-storey elevation and tall clearstorey. By using exceptionally elongated proportions, the unknown Brabanter who designed Leiden achieved a spare elegance that does not suffer by comparison with the much richer designs from which it derived.

Low Countries architects were seldom called on to design churches more complex than the Mechelen–Louvain type, and on the few occasions when this did happen the results are not impressive. At the abbey church of St-Jacques in Liège (begun 1513) aggrandizement was attained by means of a naïve eclecticism which highlights the limited resources of the Gothic great church tradition in the Low Countries [181]. All too obviously, the aim was to incorporate the richest known versions of each element, irrespective of their capacity to form a coherent ensemble. The twin arches of the Leiden-type middle storey are rendered absurd by the use of a balustrade so high and elaborate as to leave visible only their topmost parts and by the introduction of blind arcading which would have made a perfectly adequate triforium on its own. The pierced 'frills' to the main arcade arches and the thick central mullions of the clearstorey are both commandeered from the repertory of special forms normally reserved for façades and portals. Even this pretentious fare has to be supplemented from non-indigenous sources: French Renaissance foliage scrolls and head medallions in the spandrels, and a German Late Gothic net vault rising from oddly broken-necked springers apparently resulting from a belated raising of the pitch.

181 Liège, St-Jacques, nave looking east, by Aert van Mulcken, begun 1513. The tracery, in the Brabant Florid style, illustrates the ascendancy gained by Brabant architectural traditions in other parts of the Low Countries.

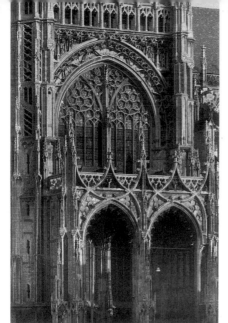
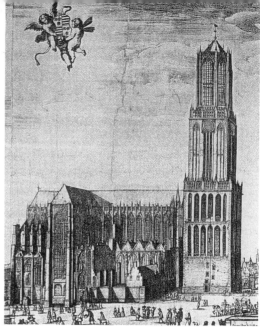

182 's-Hertogenbosch, St John, south transept façade, probably designed *c*. 1430–40, built by 1461. The tracery below the Y shape in the main window is 19th-century and does not exactly reproduce the original design. Pinnacles formerly bisected the two ogees above the arches of the porch, reinforcing their resemblance to the south transept parapet at Prague [*169*].

183 Utrecht Cathedral from the north: choir, 1265–*c*. 1360; transept, 1440–80; nave, 1490–1517 (destroyed in 1674); west tower, 1321–82. The exceptional triple aisles of the nave were built in rivalry with Our Lady at Antwerp and provided space for a very large number of privately founded altars.

Low Countries architects had shown intermittent interest in German Gothic for over a century before the start of work at Liège, but the single most important manifestation of this interest was the south transept façade of 's-Hertogenbosch [*182*], designed by an architect who must have had contacts with Strasbourg Cathedral and Ulm Minster during the period when both churches were under the direction of Ulrich von Ensingen. The south porch is a two-arched version of the triple porch at Ulm [*175*], and its extraordinary cresting of intersecting arches is an almost exact copy of the blind arches near the top of the north-west tower at Strasbourg. However, the pierced form of the 's-Hertogenbosch cresting and its use on a parapet show that the designer was aware that the source of the Strasbourg arches was the parapet on the south front of Prague Cathedral [*169*]. Building had ceased at Prague around 1420, so the likeliest means by which an architect would learn about the central work of German Late Gothic was via Parler's followers, of whom Ulrich von Ensingen was one. Ulrich's designs are full of Parlerian quotations, so one can safely assume that his drawing office at Strasbourg housed copies of designs for Prague like those which happen to have survived from the lodge of St Stephen's in Vienna. Access to the Strasbourg plan chest would also account for the close resemblance between the vaults in the porch at 's-Hertogenbosch and those in Peter or Johann Parler's work at Kutná Hora in Bohemia (begun 1388) [172y]. This four-point star pattern became the most commonly used decorative vault type in the late 15th-century Low Countries [180]. Another German feature apparently disseminated from 's-Hertogenbosch is the ungainly mullion-cum-buttress which runs right up to the apex of the great south window. It is possible that such a feature was intended in the tracery of the great south window at Prague, where it would have complemented the otherwise arbitrary-looking central pinnacle of the parapet [169], but small examples were actually executed on the Ulm tower and the almost equally Parlerian west tower of St Bartholomew at Frankfurt. Like the intersecting gables of the porch front and the four-point star vaults inside the porch, the thick central mullion of the south window at 's-Hertogenbosch became far commoner in the Low Countries than it had ever been in Germany [181]. Probably it was regarded as a supplement to the heavy Y shapes long used there to subdivide very large windows. Both features served to stabilize tracery built of the small stones yielded by most Brabant quarries.

The German sources of the south transept front at 's-Hertogenbosch have received little attention from Dutch scholars, who have generally favoured a late 15th-century dating. However, a dating in the 1430s is not only more appropriate stylistically but accords better with the documented building history of the church. If the façade does indeed date from c. 1430–40, there is a very good chance that it was the seminal work of the most original phase of Low Countries Gothic and the only one to influence the course of European architecture [192, 214, 215]. The term 'Flamboyant' applied to this style by Belgian and Dutch scholars is intended to convey the everyday sense of 'florid' or 'extravagant' rather than its original, technical meaning as a description for the flame-like forms of French Late Gothic tracery. In fact, late 15th- and early 16th-century Low Countries tracery is so unlike the French Flamboyant-derived patterns generally used in the early 15th century that it seems preferable to adopt the alternative term 'Florid Gothic'. The main characteristic of Florid tracery is its emphasis on small forms generated by the intersection of upright and inverted arches with one another and with straight lines – in other words, the scheme which is present in basic form on the parapet of the south porch at 's-Hertogenbosch. This design seems also to have sparked off the Florid craze for strangely shaped gables formed of inverted and richly crocketed arches [184, 186]. Unfortunately, the origin of the Florid style is one of the least well researched episodes in the whole history of Gothic architecture, but on present evidence it appears that it was invented by Andries Keldermans (fl. 1439–99), a member of the six-generation dynasty of architects and artificers who gradually came to dominate the architectural scene in the southern and central Low Countries during the period c. 1380–1530. Andries Keldermans's main surviving works are the west towers at Zierikzee on the Dutch coast (founded in 1454) and at

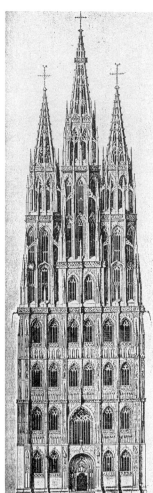

184 *Far left:* Antwerp, Our Lady, west front, begun 1422, the south tower at its present height by 1470, the uppermost square stage of the north tower complete by *c.* 1480, the octagon 1501–7 by Herman de Waghemakere, the spire 1508–18 by Domien de Waghemakere, Antoon Keldermans II and Rombout Keldermans. The octagon and spire are the only parts in the Florid style.

185 *Left:* Louvain, St Peter, design for the west front, begun 1507. The central spire would have stood *c.* 140m high.

St Rombout in Mechelen [*186*]. The undertaking of these huge projects signalled the emergence of Brabant as a first-class power in Late Gothic architecture.

The most obvious trait which distinguishes the Low Countries prodigy towers from their German counterparts is their far greater height relative to the main body of the church which they adorn [compare *186* and *175*]. The first of the series, the west tower at Utrecht Cathedral (1321–82), set the pattern in this respect and also in the shortness and structural openness of its octagonal top storey [contrast *183* and *110*]. In Brabant the earliest towered west front of the highest ambition is at Our Lady, Antwerp, begun 1422 [*184*], but its twin towers were only imitated once, at Ste-Gudule in Brussels (*c.* 1450–90). The well entrenched Romanesque and earlier Gothic preference for single towers received reaffirmation from what elsewhere in Europe would have been an unlikely source, the steeple of the Town Hall in Brussels (1444–54). The short building period of the Brussels steeple and the fact that it predates the completion of any major church tower in Brabant are sure indications that even in the part of the Low Countries with the most flourishing tradition of ecclesiastical architecture, churches still lagged behind secular civic buildings as expressions of communal pride. To be fair, most of the important Low Countries towns had by the mid-15th century secured the elevation of their main parish churches to collegiate rank – an expensive process, not least on account of the building and equipping of cathedral-like choirs suited to the performance of an elaborate liturgy. Nevertheless, it is generally true that the municipalities were prudent enough to finish their most expensive secular works before committing themselves to a major project of church tower building.

This was the case at Mechelen, where the west tower of St Rombout was begun in 1452 by the Brussels architect Wouter Coolman. The idea of dividing each free face of the tower into two bays was almost certainly taken from the Brussels Town Hall tower rather than from Antwerp, where the division of the towers is a logical and traditional way of indicating the presence of double aisles behind. It is unlikely that much else of the 1452 scheme was retained when Andries Keldermans took over in 1468, for above Coolman's conservatively treated portal storey the detailing suddenly switches to the full-blooded Florid Gothic used in the rest of the tower and in the drawing of 1550 which preserves the design of the largely unexecuted spire [186]. There is no means of ascertaining exactly how far work had progressed when Andries died c. 1500 or how much of the design shown in the drawing was by him rather than by his son and grandsons – Antoon I, Antoon II and Rombout II – who succeeded him as architect to Mechelen and who continued working in his style. Construction of the spire probably began c. 1513, but in 1520 it was stopped and never resumed – a great misfortune since this ranks as one of the most beautiful of all medieval spire designs. Its originality resides in its manner of effecting a transition from the square plan of the tower to the basic octagonal plan of the spire. Instead of the usual method of installing substantial pinnacles in front of the diagonal faces of the octagon, two walls of openwork tracery project from each angle of the octagon and line up with the corner and face buttresses of the tower. In plan these tracery walls make an eight-point star. As at Freiburg and Strasbourg, the boundary between tower and spire is marked by a boldly projecting parapet which continues around the tower buttresses. At Antwerp [184] there is a similar parapet, but vertical continuity between tower and octagon is achieved by the simpler method invented at the Brussels Town Hall, namely

186 Mechelen, St Rombout, design for the west tower. The nave vault is level with the tops of the lowest windows. This an idealized rendering in that it shows the lowest storey not as actually built but in the same Florid Gothic style as the rest of the tower. The total height would have been c. 168m; compare Ulm (161m), Strasbourg (142m), St Stephen in Vienna (136m), St Martin in Landshut (127m), Antwerp and Salisbury (c. 123m) and Utrecht (112m).

the rotation of the octagon so that its angles appear above the face buttresses of the tower. Parallels for the star plan of the Mechelen spire can be found in many Late Gothic canopy designs including the 12m-high tabernacle for the sacrament at Louvain (1450), but it required a stroke of genius to see in this motif the solution to the aesthetic problems posed by the deep buttresses inherited from Wouter Coolman's designs.

If the Mechelen spire had ever been built it would have completed a process of transition barely begun in the upper parts of the tower, that is the progressive reduction of the depth of the buttresses and the consequent gain in prominence for the windows. In the lowest stage of the spire, windows are for the first time on an equal footing with buttresses and the upper part of the topmost stage is free from buttresses altogether. Windows, and indeed arches generally, incorporate a whole series of inventive variations on the inverted and intersecting arches of the 's-Hertogenbosch porch, but here they attain an almost Rococo lightness and capriciousness. One motif which seems to derive not from full-scale architecture but from the fictive architecture of panel painting is the strange 'round-topped ogee', later taken up by French architects [193]. To all appearances, its inventor was Rogier van der Weyden, the leading painter of mid-15th-century Brabant. Such a borrowing is indicative of the relative status of painting and architecture in the Low Countries. In the longer established traditions of Gothic great church architecture in France, England and Germany influences from other art forms had virtually ended with the early 13th-century injection of motifs derived from goldsmiths' work.

The openness of Brabant's late medieval architecture to other art forms encompasses not only its sources but its practitioners. The west front of St Peter's, Louvain (begun 1507), the most ambitious façade undertaken anywhere in the late Middle Ages, was designed by Joos Metsys, whose main work was as a smith and clockmaker [185]. It would be tempting to ascribe the bizarre three-tower format of this façade to its author's relative inexperience in architecture, but there is good evidence to suggest that it was stipulated by the patron, the town council. Despite obvious debts to Cologne [110] and the later parts of Strasbourg, the new building was conceived primarily as an improved version of the Romanesque and Gothic westwork which it replaced. This large rectangular mass topped by three turrets was clearly seen as a symbol of Louvain's civic identity: it had long been portrayed on the town seal and on coins minted at Louvain, and it had even been imitated in the end façades of the magnificent Town Hall built in 1448–63. Apparently the three-tower scheme for the new west front of St Peter's was decided on in the 1450s while the architect was the same as for the Town Hall, a circumstance which would help explain why the lower halves of both buildings consist of four similarly treated storeys.

It is quite certain, however, that Metsys was not merely the executant of a 50-year-old design, for his detailing is Florid Gothic in style. Moreover his drawings were used as the basis for the unique stone model of the spires begun in 1525 and still preserved. Apart from 15th-century German craft regulations requiring that masons be able to model in clay, there is no other evidence for the use of models in Northern Gothic architecture. In Italy, the use of wooden models is documented from the late 14th century (see p. 265), so it is possible that the Louvain model reflects the influence of Italian practice. Or it may have been merely an exceptionally thorough way of ensuring compliance with the declared wish of the town council that Metsys's design would be adhered to after his death. Future architects would of course have been able to work from Metsys's drawings but a model would have made it far easier for laymen to judge whether work was proceeding to the original designs. It must also have served to foster enthusiasm and generate funds for the project, functions fulfilled on other occasions by highly finished drawings. In 1481–2 a coloured drawing of an earlier scheme for the Louvain west front had been mounted on a panel and displayed in the church. It is difficult to share the Louvain councillors' admiration of their monster westwork or to regret that most of what was built fell down in the late 16th century. The lack of continuity between the monotonously grid-like substructure and the drily spiky spires is reminiscent of those early 20th-century American skyscrapers whose blank and interminable elevations are intended to be redeemed by a crowning dollop of conventional architecture.

The Louvain front is only one of the largest of many projects which were being vigorously prosecuted in the southern Low Countries at a time when most parts of Northern Europe were experiencing a sharp decline in church building. In 1520 work began at Antwerp on an east end four times the area of the late 14th-century choir and apparently intended to be the first phase of a rebuilding of everything except the newly completed north-west tower. The inspiration behind this megalomaniac scheme was no doubt the wish that Antwerp should possess a church commensurate with its status as the richest city in Northern Europe, and it is possible that there was also a desire to rival the immense cathedrals under construction in the other main part of the Habsburg Empire, namely Spain. However in 1533 fire gutted the existing church, and by the time repairs had been completed interest in the new choir had evaporated. The flavour of the designs is probably preserved in the ultra-enriched façades of the Ghent Town Hall, under construction at the same time and by the same architects, Rombout Keldermans (son of Antoon I) and Domien de Waghemakere. Within the sphere of great church architecture, the most impressive surviving examples of this final and most exuberant phase of Florid Gothic are fittings like choir screens and tabernacles for the sacrament. When the screen at Lier [179] was begun in 1535, patrons of church furnishings had a choice of styles between Florid Gothic and Renaissance, but until the outbreak of sectarian strife in the 1560s brought religious art production to a sudden halt, Gothic remained entrenched as the only style appropriate for use in great church architecture.

France

Considering how severely France suffered during the Hundred Years War with England (1339–1453), it is remarkable that so many cathedral and monastic chapters felt able to continue with churches that had been left incomplete when the 13th-century building boom receded. A notorious case is that of the monks at St-Ouen at Rouen, who were so intent on finishing their church that they refused to contribute towards the defence of the city against the besieging English forces. But even in Rouen, where the English occupation of 1419–49 brought relative prosperity, rapid rates of building were only possible in the last third of the century, a period which saw the economy of France as a whole make a dramatic recovery. The building of most of St-Ouen's nave [*187*] in a single campaign from 1469 to *c.* 1500 was part of a general quickening of urban church building activity at all levels. Paris in particular was endowed with considerable numbers of parish churches, the most ambitious of which were to play a part in the development of great church architecture after *c.* 1500.

No such influences are apparent in the nave of St-Ouen where, as in so many other 15th-century continuations of earlier great churches, the initial impression is of a Rayonnant design modified only by the introduction of flowing tracery. It was obviously imperative that harmony be achieved with the exceptionally splendid choir of 1316–39, but this did not deter the architect from making some comparatively inconspicuous concessions to what can be regarded as the central principle of French Late Gothic or Flamboyant architecture, namely the fragmentation of the Rayonnant system through the contrary yet complementary processes of elision and disjunction. Thus the lesser mouldings of the arcade arches are made continuous with the pier shafts, while towards the aisles, where visual continuity with the eastern parts was less important, some shafts are arbitrarily replaced by paired diagonal buttresses. Precedents for the continuous arcade mouldings and even for the internal buttresses can be found in late 13th- and early 14th-century architecture [*35, 86*], although only at St-Urbain in Troyes had the use of such motifs amounted to a concerted assault on the systematic character of Rayonnant. It must be significant that the widespread move away from the certainties of Rayonnant coincided with the introduction of English-inspired flowing tracery patterns during the last decades of the 14th century. To architects accustomed to designing tracery consisting of distinct and easily readable shapes, the charm of mouchettes and soufflets which seem to swell suddenly out of nowhere and wriggle around of their own accord must have resided in their very capriciousness and irrationality, and it was perfectly natural that architects would begin to explore ways of investing the other parts of their designs with the same qualities. Nevertheless, it would be misleading to suggest that the early development of the Flamboyant style was anything other than a fitful affair. A detailed history of the subject has yet to be written,

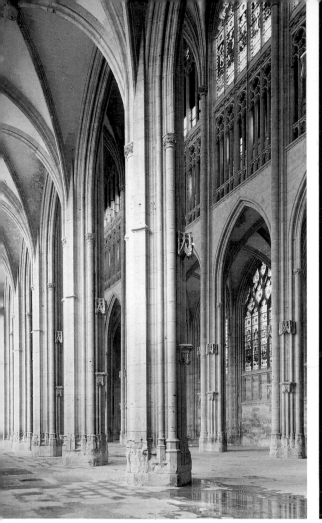

187 Rouen, St-Ouen, nave looking north-west, begun 1469. (The triforium and parts of the clearstorey are shown here blocked and with much of their glazing removed for restoration.)

188 Nantes Cathedral, nave looking north-east, begun 1435.

but it is clear that some important late 14th-century French architects rejected flowing tracery and that the great churches were in general less fertile ground for innovation than the palaces built by the crown and the royal dukes. Proximity to England may possibly account for the main exception to this generalization, the work of *c.* 1390–1400 on the screen added from *c.* 1370 to the upper part of the west front of Rouen Cathedral, although it must be admitted that the tracery forms used here are by no means the most English-looking to be found in France at this period.

The only important example of patronage of great church architecture by a late medieval French ruler was also the only comprehensive rebuilding scheme embarked on at any French cathedral during the early 15th century. Nantes Cathedral, begun in 1435, owed its origin to Jean V, duke of Brittany, by whom it was conceived as an ornament to his chief city and hence an adjunct to his policy of asserting Breton independence from the French crown [*188*]. Nantes is thus in the same tradition of 'political' great churches as Westminster and Prague, and like those churches it was adversely affected by the vagaries of its patrons' fortunes. The nave, the only part ever brought to completion, took over two centuries to build, but the temptation to modernize the original designs was resisted in the interests of overall consistency. The most distinctive traits are the almost oppressive bulk of the piers and responds and their relentless subdivision into filletted roll mouldings separated by deep hollows. The clash contrived in St-Ouen's nave arcades between the partly continuous mouldings and the intrusive buttresses has its counterpart here in the contrast between the omission of capitals from the arcades and the extreme elaboration of the pier bases, with their major and minor elements and a sloping plinth modelled on external portal architecture [*96*]. Bases of this type, which demanded high skill both in design and execution, seem to have been regarded almost as a hallmark of great church architecture in the 15th and early 16th centuries [*187, 220*]. The upper storeys at Nantes exhibit the same stylistic traits as the arcades. The clearstorey windows have deep and richly moulded embrasures separated from the high vault and its responds by considerable areas of plain walling, and there is no linkage with the three wide arches of the unlit triforium, which are also deeply moulded. As in virtually all 15th-century French Flamboyant churches, the use of plain quadripartite vaulting incorporating very heavy transverse arches secures the traditional primacy of the bay divisions. In fact the nave as a whole can stand as a paradigm of the mid- and later 15th-century great church in France, although its slow rate of building and the remoteness of Nantes from the main centres of cathedral architecture ensured that it was not influential.

By far the most productive French cathedral architect working around 1500 was Martin Chambiges, for whose services the chapters of Beauvais and Troyes found themselves competing during the first two decades of the 16th century. The distinctive qualities of Chambiges's prestigious art can best be savoured in the transepts at Beauvais [*189, 191*], although the exigencies of building onto the 13th-century choir and east transept aisles resulted in certain eccentric features such as the unequal supports, the sexpartite vault and the miniature Wells-type struts which strengthen the clearstorey windows against the longitudinal thrusts exerted by the sexpartite vault and east and west crossing arches. Because the nave was never built, Chambiges had no opportunity to implement the regular bay design of which the transept bays are an imperfect reflection, but some impression of its effect can be gained from the simpler and much smaller choir of St-Etienne in Beauvais, almost certainly a Chambiges design [*190*]. The Beauvais Cathedral system thus reconstituted can be recognized as one of the most impressive applications of the Flamboyant technique of combining elisions and disjunctions. The single most important instance of elision is the

189 Beauvais Cathedral, east side of the south transept, probably designed *c*. 1500, built from *c*. 1520. (The windows are shown blocked during restoration work.)

190 Beauvais, St-Etienne, south side of the choir, probably begun 1502, the high vaults inscribed with the date 1545.

Bourges-inspired arrangement whereby the high vault responds are treated not as distinct elements but as segments of piers continuous with those in the main arcades, although the most eye-catching application of the concept is to the supports themselves, which give the impression of a High Gothic pier whose shafts have melted and become fused with the core. Piers formed of continuous undulations can be seen in the Early Gothic ambulatory at Noyon and in the main arcades of the southern French cathedral of Rodez (begun 1277), where the undulations are comparatively shallow, as here. The main arcades at Rodez, like those in the stylistically closely related choir of Narbonne [*88*], foreshadow one of the most striking effects at Beauvais, the way in which the finely moulded ribs and arcade arches spring suddenly from out of the smooth surfaces of the piers. Although the effect itself is classifiable as a disjunction, its realization depended on an elision, namely the omission of capitals. Chambiges's knowledge of Rodez and Narbonne may have been acquired at first hand but it is more likely that it was transmitted via a group of Flamboyant churches which, though not great churches, were innovatory and of high quality. The series starts with two Loire valley churches rebuilt under royal patronage after their destruction by the English in 1428 (Cléry and St-Aignan at Orléans) and continues in the late 15th century in Chambiges's native Paris (St-Merry, St-Etienne-du-Mont, St-Gervais). All these churches resemble Beauvais in having arch mouldings consisting of narrow filleted projections separated by broad and deep hollows, and all anticipate in some measure the Beauvais disjunction between squashy-looking piers and responds and sharply linear arched elements, including tracery. Thus Chambiges was heir to a tradition of Gothic which instead of aiming to create the illusion of an integrated and self-consistent system was concerned primarily with the generation of dramatic sculptural contrasts. Presumably this aspect of Chambiges's transepts was as much appreciated by the chapter at Beauvais as the high masonry-to-void ratio on which its realization depended, a ratio doubtless intended to provide reassurance that there would be no sequel to the collapse of the choir in 1284.

In most regions of Europe, Late Gothic styles displaced or transformed earlier traditions, and except when the presence of older work demanded compromise, these styles were exploited with all the unselfconscious enthusiasm which was the normal later medieval response towards modernity in the visual arts. In 15th- and early 16th-century France, however, no-one can have been unaware that those times were much less productive of great church architecture than the 13th century, and it may be that a sense of inferiority to a past Golden Age was responsible for the widespread reluctance to challenge the basic premises of Rayonnant architecture. This confinement of innovation to matters of detail affected not just continuations to earlier main vessels, like the nave of St-Ouen at Rouen, but also façades, whose impact on the internal unity of a church was slight and which for this reason 12th- and 13th-century architects had not hesitated to revise whenever the opportunity arose. In fact, great church façades are the field in which Flamboyant architects consistently failed to achieve a convincing accommodation between their 13th-century inheritance and the dictates of the Flamboyant style. As was noted in the previous chapter, the residually Romanesque conventions perpetuated in French High Gothic and Rayonnant façade design were abandoned in other countries once it had become apparent that they were incompatible with the Rayonnant principle of integration which governed interior elevations. The irreducible distinctness of rose windows and deep sculptured portals gave no scope for Flamboyant elisions but all too much scope for disjunctions.

Even so skilled a designer as Martin Chambiges did not achieve formal coherence in his transept façades at Beauvais [191]. The extreme tallness of the main vessels prompted him to introduce two elements normally and logically regarded as alternatives rather than complements: a tall window incorporating a rose, in the manner of St-Nicaise in Reims [94], and a triforium gallery like those on the transepts of Notre-Dame in Paris [95]. On the south transept front a gratuitously high balustrade to the triforium gallery prevents one from reading the two levels as a single transomed

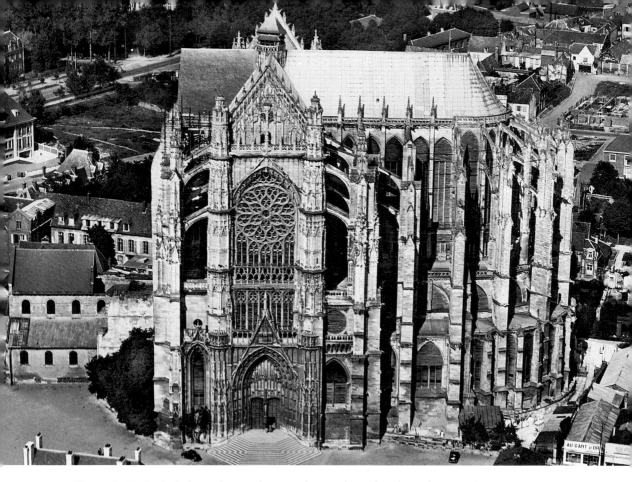

191 Beauvais Cathedral, from the south: nave, late 10th- and early 11th-centuries; transepts, 1500–1550s; choir, c. 1225–60 and c. 1284–1338. The nave exemplifies the modest architecture and early date of the churches which were superseded by the major Gothic churches of the Ile-de-France. The choir is the tallest in Gothic architecture; its upper parts collapsed in 1284, and the original three rectangular bays were rebuilt as six.

window and also accentuates the stunted proportions of the lights in the upper level. The turrets flanking the central section of the façade display the same uncoordinated quality as the windows. Following the mid-15th-century west front at Tours Cathedral, Chambiges has sheathed them in gabled niches separated into distinct tiers by heavy horizontal mouldings. The latter correspond only twice to major horizontals in the central section, those at the top of the portal arch and at the base of the gable. The very prominent horizontals above the curious bare patches where the turrets suddenly shed their arched cladding correspond to nothing at all, and the next horizontals continue the line of the 'handrail' to the Brobdingnagian balustrade rather than the far more important horizontal at its base. In coinciding with the springing of the window arch the penultimate major horizontal misses both the springing of the upper semicircle of the rose and the horizontals in its tracery. The result is to heighten the disquieting effect already conveyed by the sagging line of two-light 'windows' under the rose, namely that the rose itself is slipping downwards.

Since few if any early 16th-century French architects were better able than Chambiges to organize a major façade, the faltering composition of the Beauvais frontispiece would probably not have registered with many contemporary observers. Moreover, the expectations of patrons are likely to have been conditioned to some extent by the combination of rich detailing and extreme informality of composition which characterizes the ambitious secular buildings put up in such great numbers in late medieval France. Probably it was enough that the Beauvais front was splendid in its general effect and exquisite in its detailing. Like all the leading late 15th- and early 16th-century French architects, Chambiges was a past master of tabernacle design [192, 194], but rather more than most, he was receptive to the novel forms of Brabant Florid Gothic. Indeed the façade owes much of its liveliness to large and small versions of the fanciful gable and arch forms popularized by the Keldermans family [186]. Among the more prominent are the concave-sided gablets on the flying buttress piers and the 'round-headed ogees' on the balustrade below the rose. Chambiges would not have needed to visit Brabant in order to familiarize himself with these forms, since they had been brought to France by the considerable number of Low Countries architects who found work there, and also by the importation of Brussels- and Antwerp-made wooden altarpieces incorporating miniaturized versions of Florid tabernacle work. The tracery of the Beauvais façade is far less inventive, the rose being of a type which was more or less standard throughout the period c. 1450–1550. The composition of such roses from small repetitive units made them far easier to design than flowing tracery for large windows of upright format.

In the early 16th century the Beauvais south transept façade was extreme neither in its richness nor in its shaky organization. At Senlis Chambiges's son Pierre built a façade which must be counted among the wildest creations of late medieval architecture [193]. The key to understanding it is surely the familiar competitive urge, which here takes the form of outdoing all the most arbitrary and exotic features of Beauvais. Thus the round-topped ogee which Martin Chambiges used in nothing larger than a balustrade is used by Pierre for the single most prominent arch of the façade, that of the portal gable. The two-light windows below the rose are here not only absurdly squat but almost invisible behind an open arcade which is itself disrupted by the intrusion of the arch-like top of the portal gable. The Beauvais motif of obscuring the turrets by pinnacles flanking the portal is carried to the point where the turrets appear amorphous. The most perverse feature of all is the series of short vertical bars hanging down from the arch of the portal. Comparison with Beauvais shows that they are enlargements of the bars in the same position and above the rose, but whereas at Beauvais these bars are part of a conceit – that the uprights in the panelled spandrels have somehow slipped and broken through the arches – at Senlis there is nothing in the spandrels above the portal to advertise their alignment with the uprights in

192 Beauvais Cathedral, south transept portal, c. 1500–1510.

193 Senlis Cathedral, south transept façade, 1521–34. The fleur-de-lys balustrade below the rose and the royal arms over the portal acknowledge subventions from Louis XII and Francis I towards the reconstruction of the cathedral after a serious fire in 1504.

the gallery under the rose. An already mannered feature has become incomprehensible except to those who know its parentage. It is entirely in keeping with his craving for novelty at all costs that Pierre Chambiges included more Brabant Florid motifs than his father had done at Beauvais. These include the mullion-cum-pinnacle slicing through the tympanum tracery and the intermittent cusping of the open arcade over the portal. Perhaps the least expected thing about this tasteless farrago is that its oddest ingredient was included for symbolic reasons. The detailing of the pair of corkscrew shafts beside the portal comes from two piers in the late 15th-century ambulatory of St-Séverin in Paris, but their placing makes them clear allusions to the brazen columns at the entrance to Solomon's Temple.

Like all late medieval French cathedral architects, the Chambiges were not so much participants in a well-defined tradition of great church design as individuals feeling their own way towards solving the fundamentally insoluble problem of how to reconcile Late Gothic enthusiasm for complex ornamental effects with the constricting conventions inherited from the 13th century. Not surprisingly, very few designers managed to avoid being either over-respectful of these conventions or over-anxious to demonstrate their independence of them. An obvious escape route from this impasse, the revival of archaic and regional forms displaced in the 13th century, was widely resorted to only at the less ambitious levels of church architecture.

194 Albi Cathedral, choir enclosure looking north-west, *c.* 1500. Albi has the best preserved of the many choir enclosures erected in French cathedrals during the late Middle Ages. Exceptionally, the stall canopies are of stone rather than wood. In the background is the late 13th- and 14th-century single-span nave. The cellular lateral chapels originally rose the full height of the nave but were later subdivided.

Even more than in other countries, high ambition and wholeheartedly Late Gothic character tended to be combined convincingly only in such peripheral parts of great churches as single towers, porches, side chapels and fittings [*194*]. Nevertheless, these ancillary structures did make at least one important contribution to great church design, for it was their influence which finally broke down the French insistence on using only plain quadripartite vaults over aisles and main vessels. Yet even the most complex decorative vaults found in late medieval France – pendant vaults – emphasize the centre of each vault compartment and thereby perpetuate the French tradition of firmly demarcated bays. Pendant vaults belong almost as much to Renaissance as to Gothic architecture, for by the time that they achieved general currency around 1520 it had become normal to decorate them with ornament 'à l'Antique', an association which probably led most contemporaries to think of the two elements as integral parts of the same modern idiom, notwithstanding their totally different origins. In a vault like that over the chapel of Notre-Dame-des-Joies at Noyon [*195*], the Renaissance components are no more than an alternative to Late Gothic foliage ornament.

A more even-handed synthesis was attempted in the only great church to be begun from scratch in early 16th-century France, the Parisian parish

195 Noyon Cathedral, chapel of Notre-Dame-des-Joies, probably begun shortly after 1528. The image niches were restored in the early 20th century.

196 Paris, St-Eustache, north transept and choir seen from the outer north aisle of the nave, begun 1532.

church of St-Eustache [*196*]. The overall design here is still unequivocally Gothic and invites comparison with some of the grandest products of the heroic age of French cathedral building: Notre-Dame in Paris for the plan, Beauvais Cathedral for the low peripheral chapels, Amiens for the proportioning of the main interior elevations, and St-Denis for the glazed triforium. Inevitably in a building whose vessels are so narrow the detailing cannot be correctly Classical; and though there is no sign that the unknown designer was anxious to be correct, the seriousness of his allegiance to the new manner is evident from the fact that the square-plan cores of his piers show one of the very earliest examples in France of the three main Classical Orders used in their proper sequence. The pier plan as a whole may have been consciously derived from Romanesque prototypes, since the Corinthian columns under the diagonal ribs are remarkably like those in the same position at St-Lazare at Autun and St-Trophîme at Arles, two of the most Roman of French Romanesque churches. No doubt from a Classical stand-point St-Eustache is a freakish hybrid, but it has to be remembered that the only Italian Renaissance churches actually completed when St-Eustache was begun in 1532 would have appeared too modest in scale or too rudimentary in conception to be considered as alternatives to the Gothic cathedral.

Italy

Italy's contribution to Gothic great church architecture was not commensurate with its wealth and importance during the Middle Ages. To some extent this was due to the cool reception accorded to the Gothic style by the Italians, but a more fundamental factor was that very few of the numerous churches built in Italy during the Gothic period were great churches. At the root of both these divergences from the Northern European pattern lay Italy's unique inheritance from pre-medieval times. The sense of being the spiritual heirs of the ancient Romans must provide most of the explanation for the general reluctance to abandon completely the concepts embodied in the basilican church type invented in the early 4th century [7]; and there can be little doubt that atavistic feelings of fear and disdain towards the barbarian West were a contributory factor in the Italians' generally grudging response to what was clearly recognizable as a French style. A Roman legacy which hindered the formation of a tradition of great church architecture in any style was the large number of towns in northern and central Italy. After the barbarian invasions of the 5th and 6th centuries the towns shrank to a fraction of their former size, yet the great majority were still in being when steady expansion began again in the late 10th century. Since virtually all towns of any consequence had had a bishop from the 4th century, most Italian dioceses were small (and consequently poor) by comparison with the huge territorial dioceses centred on the far fewer important Northern European towns which had managed to continue functioning after the collapse of the Roman Empire. In this situation it was inevitable that responsibility for cathedral fabrics would pass from bishops and chapters to the city governments who were the leading powers in medieval Italy. However, it was normally only the municipalities of the very greatest cities who were able to build cathedrals which measure up to the most ambitious churches of Northern Europe. The fierce rivalries existing between these cities are probably sufficient explanation for the absence of any consensus about the form appropriate to an Italian great church.

Alongside racial, political and economic factors there is one other cultural difference which helps explain Italy's failure to generate a tradition of great church architecture comparable to that of Northern Europe: the low prestige of architecture relative to the figural arts, particularly painting. To some extent this may have been another consequence of Italian fidelity to the basilica, in which the architect's contribution inevitably appeared less distinctive and memorable than that of the painter who not only enriched but transformed the unarticulated wall surfaces making up most of the interior elevations. When architecture could be regarded as little more than a support for paintings, it is unlikely that anyone thought it odd that painters should assume the role of architect, and it is equally unsurprising that the buildings designed by painter-architects [1] owed as little to Northern Gothic concepts as did the tradition of monumental fresco painting which emerged

197 Siena Cathedral, from the south-west: lower storey of the west front, 1284–97 by Giovanni Pisano; upper storey and nave clearstorey, c. 1369–77; nave and transepts, c. 1220–60 (marble facing, 17th-century); dome, finished c. 1260 (lantern, 17th-century); bell tower, late 12th- or early 13th-century. The disparity between the steep gables of the west front and the low pitch of the nave roofs recurs in other Italian Gothic churches.

in central Italy during the late 13th century. Although Italian sculptors were receptive to the more obviously relevant achievements of Northerners in their field, the buildings which they designed [197] are not markedly closer to Northern ideas than those designed by painters. Despite the occasional disaster due to inadequate technical knowledge, the practice of architecture by figural artists continued into the Renaissance period, when it spread beyond Italy.

As in other parts of Europe, it was the Cistercians who introduced the elements of Gothic architecture into Italy. In their two most important early 13th-century churches, those at Casamari (begun 1203) and its Tuscan daughter house S. Galgano (begun 1218), the Burgundian Romanesque scheme exemplified by Pontigny [14] was effectively Gothicized by substituting ribs for the pointed-arched groins of the vaults. This was not a purely Italian development, for exactly the same revision had achieved a wide diffusion in later 12th-century French Cistercian churches, probably

198 Siena Cathedral, interior looking east, mostly *c.* 1220–60 (choir replaced from 1316 and nave clearstorey and vault rebuilt from *c.* 1369).

because it was viewed as a modernization which did not challenge the ascetic traditions of the order. S. Galgano seems to have exerted important influences on the cathedral of nearby Siena, the only great church built in Italy during the first half of the 13th century [*198*]. The Siena bay design is not a straightforward copy of that at S. Galgano, but there is no other obvious source in Tuscany for its combination of Romanesque four-shaft piers with Gothic crocket capitals, for its lack of angled members to receive the diagonal ribs, or for the keeled profile of the latter. The consistent use of round arches, the tallness of the main arcades and the lowness of the original clearstorey (replaced when the vaults were rebuilt higher from *c.* 1369) can readily be understood as criticisms of the S. Galgano scheme made by a designer whose loyalties still lay partly with the traditional basilica form. In Tuscany by far the most impressive basilica was the huge Romanesque cathedral of Siena's pro-imperial and anti-Florentine ally, Pisa, and it seems reasonable to view the imitation of Pisa Cathedral's zebra-striped marble cladding as a demonstration of solidarity at a time when the bitter struggle between the emperor and the pope was fast approaching its final crisis in 1240.

Apart from its striped livery, which overpowers the three-dimensional articulation of the bay design, the most memorable feature of Siena is its unique hexagonal crossing. The symbolic allusion is fairly certainly to the centralized plan of the Roman Pantheon converted in 609 into a church dedicated to the Virgin and all Martyrs, for Siena Cathedral is dedicated to the Virgin and four other patron saints, some of them martyrs. Less evident is the reasoning behind the choice of the hexagon, whose four non–axial sides relate very awkwardly to the aisle-high transepts. An octagon would have been the obvious choice for this first Italian crossing to exceed the width of the main east–west vessel.

Although Siena is only marginally a Gothic building, in Tuscan eyes it probably seemed very novel when work began some time around 1220. Nevertheless, Siena had no immediate sequels, for in 13th-century Italy the cathedrals were left behind in the rush to build churches for the mendicant orders. Many Franciscan and Dominican churches were very large, so large in fact that a high proportion of the populace of any town could assemble in them to hear preaching. Nevertheless, out of respect for their founders the friars strove to keep their architecture simpler than that of the great churches. The appearance of elementary Gothic forms in mendicant churches should not be seen as the inevitable response to a more advanced style, for medieval Italy could often remain remarkably impervious to outside influences. It is likely that for the Franciscans at least Gothic acquired something of the character of an official style after its use at the 'headquarters' church of S. Francesco at Assisi (1228–c. 1239), one of the very few Italian 13th-century buildings which bespeak direct contacts with France. Because the mid- and late 13th-century mendicants' churches were sited in the towns which so dominated Italian life, they were far better able to perform their involuntary role of 'missionaries of Gothic' than the rurally sited Cistercian churches of the late 12th and early 13th centuries; yet by comparison with Cistercian churches, those of the mendicants were far less distinctive. In part this stems from the fact that the friars were not cloistered monks but evangelizers of the towns; their churches were not their spiritual homes in quite the way they were for the Cistercians or other monks. Another factor which made for diversity was the generous financial support for building given by the governments of the host towns, who would naturally tend to favour local architectural usage.

The lack of uniformity in 13th-century Italian mendicant architecture is well illustrated by the highly contrasting churches of the Florentine Dominicans and Franciscans, S. Maria Novella and S. Croce [*199, 200*]. S. Maria Novella was perhaps conceived as a modernized and marble-less version of the nave of Siena Cathedral in which all arches are made pointed and shafts rather than dosserets receive the diagonal vault ribs; the oculi in the clearstorey may reproduce what existed at Siena before its heightening. Alongside the limpid grace and poise of S. Maria Novella, S. Croce appears less perfectly resolved but more robust. The wide timber-roofed central vessel, the corbelled-out walkway above the main arcade, and perhaps also the octagonal columns, derive from the cathedral in the papal city of Orvieto, begun in 1290, only a year or so earlier than S. Croce, as a free adaptation of the great Early Christian basilica of S. Maria Maggiore in Rome. Like S. Maria Novella, S. Croce is more Gothic than its model, which has semicircular main arcades and bare upper walls devoid of any kind of vertical articulation. The long-standing attribution of S. Croce to the Florence-born but widely travelled sculptor Arnolfo di Cambio has recently received corroboration from archaeological investigation of Arnolfo's only

199 Florence, S. Maria Novella, interior looking east, begun by 1269. The painted stripes (recently restored) recall Siena Cathedral's marble-clad interior [198], but here they may have been an allusion to the Dominicans' black-and-white habit.

200 Florence, S. Croce, nave looking south-east, designed c. 1292. Extensive schemes of figural and decorative painting were obliterated in the 16th century. Until then the general Italian tendency to give monumental wall painting priority over architectural values was exemplified by a fresco of the Triumph of Death by Andrea Orcagna which spread across three bays of the south nave aisle wall.

major documented architectural work, the 1294 scheme for rebuilding Florence Cathedral. This has shown that Arnolfo planned a nave virtually identical in its dimensions to that at S. Croce, and the probability is that it was a similar lightweight, unvaulted structure. In Northern Europe such an important building would never have been modelled on a 'mere' mendicant church, but it seems that in Italy half a century's municipal patronage of the friars had to some extent blurred what was elsewhere a jealously maintained hierarchical distinction. In fact Arnolfo's cathedral would have successfully asserted its pre-eminence over the other churches of Florence partly through its elaborately tabernacled west front (destroyed in the 16th century), but even more through its extraordinary domed and centralized east end, a smaller version of the existing east end built between 1377 and 1436.

The inspiration behind the eastern parts of Florence Cathedral must have been primarily symbolic and only secondarily architectural. The central element, the wide octagonal crossing sheltering the choir and high altar dedicated to the Virgin, was conceived as a grander version of the Siena crossing, performing the same function of evoking and rivalling the christianized Roman Pantheon, S. Maria Rotunda. The Pantheon had already influenced the architecture of the most Roman of all Italian Romanesque buildings, the baptistery built beside Florence Cathedral during the rule of the fervently pro-papal Countess Matilda of Tuscany (1046–1115); and since the baptistery ranked as the main civic church of Florence before the completion of the cathedral, it was only natural that the crossing of Arnolfo's great church should resemble the city's earlier emulation of the Pantheon more than it does the Pantheon itself [203]. No-one would have thought the evocation of the circular S. Maria Rotunda was impaired by the adoption of the baptistery's octagonal plan, for in such relationships the essential concept counted for more than the exact form taken by the architecture. There is, however, one very important Classical architectural idea faithfully transmitted from the Pantheon *via* the baptistery, namely the treatment of the crossing space as a single unsubdivided unit. Siena's crossing has shafts in the angles indicating that it was conceived as the aggregate of six triangular bays, whereas at Florence the octagon consists primarily of smooth, completely unarticulated surfaces. The stark contrast in Arnolfo's designs between the serenity of the masonry-vaulted octagonal sanctuary and the longitudinal movement implicit in the wooden-roofed, multi-bay nave embodies a symbolic distinction appropriate to the differing functions of the two parts. As in the ancient world, the dome signifies heaven and eternity, while the much more Gothic nave, being the vestibule to the sanctuary and the part most accessible to the laity, registers as a modern structure and a symbol of earthly, temporal progression. This meaning is conveyed by the existing cathedral, although since the nave is vaulted [202] the contrast with the octagon is less than Arnolfo intended.

The treatment of the three limbs radiating out of the north, east and south sides of the octagon as part-octagonal apses may have been influenced by centralized Early Christian and Byzantine churches such as S. Lorenzo in Milan, S. Vitale in Ravenna or Hagia Sophia in Constantinople, but once again the initial impulse must have been iconographic more than aesthetic, for the church with apsidally ended transepts which would have been most familiar to Florentines was Pisa Cathedral. Pisa's transepts in their final, elongated form are quite unlike Florence's, but they derive either from the church of the Nativity in Bethlehem or from St Mary in the Blachernai in Constantinople, both of them 6th-century buildings and both no doubt familiar to the many Pisans involved in trade with the Levant and Byzantium. Arnolfo's cathedral thus seems to have been specifically designed to outshine the churches dedicated to the Virgin in the two cities which vied with Florence for pre-eminence in Tuscany. After its long-delayed incarnation during the late 14th and early 15th centuries, it became the prototype of all the innumerable centralized and quasi-centralized churches built from Renaissance times onwards.

Probably on account of the political crises which racked Florence at the start of the 14th century, the cathedral works were abandoned after only the

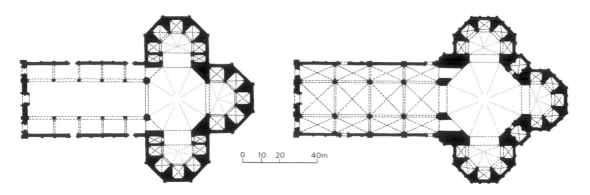

201 Florence Cathedral, plans of the 1294 scheme (left) and the enlarged scheme adopted by 1368.

west parts of the aisle walls had reached their full height. Nevertheless, the mere possibility that Florence would be able to boast the finest church in Tuscany had become by 1316 sufficient to spur the Sienese into replacing the short choir of their 13th-century cathedral with another more than twice as long [198]. Yet even before the Siena choir was finished, it had been decided to open out an enormous new nave to the south of the crossing and to turn the existing nave and half-built choir into transepts. Designs were drawn up by the goldsmith and bellfounder Lando di Pietro, but the *capomaestro* or executant architect was the sculptor Giovanni d'Agostino. Construction began in 1339 and progress was so rapid that when the Black Death intervened ten years later, the nave was more than half way towards completion. Unfortunately, the tall and slender main arcades had begun to tilt inwards in response to lateral thrusts from the aisle vaults, apparently because the designers had failed to use the standard Northern device for overcoming this problem: temporary tie beams linking the arcades to the outer walls until the building of the clearstorey provided a loading strong enough to enable the arcades to resist aisle vault thrusts [cf. *133*]. The Black Death was very nearly the *coup de grâce* to Siena's ailing economy, and after reports of 1356 and 1357 had condemned the tottering structure, all hope of completion was abandoned. With this spectacle of ignominious failure before them, it is small wonder that later patrons of great church architecture in Italy displayed an almost paranoiac anxiety about structural stability.

In 1337 a similar fiasco was averted in Florence when it was discovered that the walls of the great campanile begun three years earlier had only half the thickness necessary. The culprit in this case was none other than Giotto, who had been appointed *capomaestro* on the strength of his publicly acknow-ledged status as the greatest painter of his day. Giotto's design [1] easily excelled its simple and comparatively small precursors within the distincti-vely Italian genre of tall detached bell towers, but it showed no concern with lessening the traditionally self-contained character of the successive storeys or with finding a convincing relationship between these and the exotic, Strasbourg- or Freiburg-inspired lantern and spire. Giotto's successor, the goldsmith and sculptor Andrea Pisano, introduced into the second major storey pairs of shallow buttresses which would have eventually linked up to the angles of an octagonal lantern. Yet even this tentative approach towards Northern Gothic aesthetics seems to have been disliked, for in 1343 Andrea was sacked for over-elaborating the design. The three upper storeys completed by Francesco Talenti in 1359 mark a reversion to the flatness and the additive quality of Giotto's design, and in this they typify the more decorative kinds of central Italian Gothic [203].

In 1357, while the Sienese were resigning themselves to abandoning their half-built nave, the Florentines mounted a splendid ceremony to mark the resumption of work on their still inchoate cathedral. An enormous quantity of records charts the progress of the building and also sheds some light on the complex creative processes behind the formulation of the design, processes arising from the 'democratic' constitution of the commune which was paying for the work. In 1355, to enable non-expert citizenry to assess the merits of the design more easily than if they were relying on a drawing, Talenti was paid for a scale model, one of the earliest documented examples of what long remained a distinctively Italian type of visual aid. Some of the later models of the cathedral were made of terracotta so that they could stand out of doors, but Talenti's was of wood. Its specific purpose was to show the form of the chapels to be built on the foundations of Arnolfo's east end as well as a proposal for reconciling the narrow bays in the parts of the aisle walls built by Arnolfo with the three much longer bays which were now to constitute the nave. The panel convened to consider these matters was only the first in a succession of committees appointed during the late 14th and early 15th centuries, all of which exerted varying degrees of control over the design. Neither Talenti nor any of his successors was ever free to implement a major design decision without first obtaining the ratification of whatever committee was dominant at the time. Moreover the initiation of designs was not Talenti's exclusive province, as it would have been in a comparable Northern European project. Already by 1357 he had two major rivals, Andrea Orcagna, the most distinguished figural artist in mid-14th-century Florence, and Giovanni di Lapo Ghini, a specialist in vault construction. Both men were eventually to make important contributions to the design. Ghini was appointed joint *capomaestro* in 1363 and became sole occupant of that post during Talenti's temporary dismissal in 1364–6. Orcagna was active from 1357 in proposing alternative design solutions to Talenti's, but his main chance came later when he emerged as the leading light in a commission of painters which in 1366 succeeded in seizing control of the design. A model based on a scheme drawn up by the painters was made and voted on in a series of referendums by several hundred leading citizens. The result was an endorsement of the Orcagna faction's proposals that the dome be carried on a drum rising clear of the four arms of the church (the original arrangement at Siena) and that the internal width of the octagon be made equal to the width of the nave including the thickness of the aisle walls. Talenti and Ghini were opposed to this enlargement of the octagon but the most they could salvage was agreement that the heightening of the drum necessitated more massive piers between the crossing and the nave than those planned *c*. 1357. Once again, amateur architects had demonstrated their lack of expertise in the structural domain.

The lengthening of the nave to its present four-bay form seems a natural concomitant of enlarging the octagon [*201* right], although a fresco of the Church Triumphant in S. Maria Novella, which Andrea Bonaiuti, a member of the painters' committee, began in December 1365, shows a four-bay nave joined to the lower and narrower octagon planned by Arnolfo and endorsed by Ghini and Talenti. Bonaiuti's fresco may simply embody his own personal preferences among the various options under consideration in 1365, but if it records what was at some stage the official design, it raises the unanswerable question of whether the disputes arose from the commitment of the main protagonists to fundamentally opposed visions of the building or whether they were merely so much egotistical bickering about this or that favourite feature. By December 1368 the ferment had subsided, and it was resolved that all future *capomaestri* should swear to adhere to the painters' design, presumably modified to include the thicker piers between the octagon and nave which had been insisted on by Ghini and Talenti. That still left the constructional problem of raising the widest dome designed in the West since Roman times, but as early as 1371 Ghini had designed a special centering for which he received a handsome reward. The splendid achievement of Filippo Brunelleschi in constructing the dome from 1420 without recourse to any kind of centering does not need to be boosted by invoking the hoary myth that the builders of the octagon had no idea how to vault it.

The nave whose birth entailed such mountainous heaving on the part of so many is really not much more than an assemblage of elements culled from earlier Florentine churches. No doubt the leading citizens of Florence would have seen this as an appropriate expression of civic self-esteem. After all, Florentine painters and sculptors were in demand throughout Italy and beyond, the Tuscan language was rapidly gaining acceptance as the standard literary form of Italian, and alongside Venice, Florence was the greatest economic power in Europe. The square bays of the nave, its quadripartite vaults and its low clearstorey lit by oculi all come from no farther afield than S. Maria Novella [*199*], the piers are enlarged replicas of those in the church of Orsanmichele (begun 1337), and the corbelled walkway which so brusquely cuts across the vertical articulation is an obvious borrowing from S. Croce [*200*]. The records suggest that this last feature was conceived as a kind of ligature drawing together the otherwise hardly related elevations of the nave

202 Florence Cathedral, interior looking south-east: nave, 1357–78; apses and lower walls of the octagon, 1377–1421; drum of the octagon and dome, 1420–36. The internal height of the nave is *c.* 43m, only 3m lower than Cologne [*84*].

and octagon. Only the thin entablatures over the capitals definitely derive from a non–Florentine source, namely the choir arcades at Siena. But though the nave of Florence has one of the most austere of all major Gothic interiors, by comparison with the eastern parts it seems positively festive. Apart from the angles formed by the meeting of the sides of the polygons, there is virtually nothing here to break the continuity of the immense plane surfaces of white plaster and grey stone. The absence of more expensive finishes all but proves that in the 14th century the interior was conceived as a receptacle for great cycles of wall paintings. Most medieval people would probably have found the present internal bleakness baffling both in itself and in relation to the richness of the exterior [*203*].

The external marble cladding of Florence Cathedral appears at first sight to embody a purely stylistic evolution: Talenti's busy and overloaded work on the Arnolfian west bays of the aisles, the more consistent but still close-meshed treatment of the long east bays, the boldly arcaded manner on the apses, and finally the severely rectilinear panelling on the drum of the dome. In fact the arcading and panelling go together in that they both derive from the analogous parts of the baptistery. The late 15th-century extension of the panelling onto the nave clearstorey in place of the denser decoration planned in the 14th century blurs the meaning originally intended, namely the distinction between the modern Gothic treatment accorded to the nave and the Antique style which emphasizes the affinity between the eastern parts and their ancient prototypes, especially the baptistery. This distinction had probably been part of Arnolfo's designs of 1294, and the same may be true of the series of exposed abutting walls on the apses, for these recall the buttressing on the early 4th-century Basilica of Constantine, a building Arnolfo would have known when working in Rome c. 1277–93. The want of comparable abutments on the nave probably caused the high vaults to crack in 1366, but instead of adding buttresses, obtrusive iron tie bars were inserted. That no problems of this kind ever affected Brunelleschi's dome must have seemed an additional recommendation to the many Renaissance and Baroque architects who chose to emulate the energetic effect imparted to the exterior by its Gothic ribbing and pointed profile in preference to the more earthbound quality of the low-set domes built by the Romans.

No such posterity can be claimed for Milan Cathedral, the most ambitious Italian church begun in the late 14th century [*204, 205*]. This was medieval Italy's nearest approximation to a Northern Gothic cathedral and as a consequence stood outside the main currents of Italian architecture during the 15th and early 16th centuries, when the bulk of the building was erected in close conformity to the original designs. Milan was only the most important of many north Italian cities where communal government had been succeeded in the 14th century by *signoria*, the more or less autocratic rule of a single family, and there can be little doubt that the main impulse to rebuild the cathedral came from the Visconti, lords of Milan from 1311. The Visconti's links with the cathedral were in fact extremely strong, for the family fortunes had been founded by a late 13th-century archbishop and the lords buried there included the donor of a new campanile in 1333 and his successor who was simultaneously archbishop and lord. It cannot have been fortuitous that the start of work on the new cathedral in 1386 came barely a year after the accession of the great Giangaleazzo Visconti, who, had he not died suddenly in 1402, would probably have succeeded in making himself king of Italy. Since the Visconti palace stood right beside the cathedral, it seems clear that Giangaleazzo was consciously imitating the ensembles of royal seat and great church to be seen in Paris, Prague and Westminster. Emulation specifically of the French royal family, to which his wife

203 Florence Cathedral, from the south. From right to left: church, 1294–1436; bell-tower, 1334–59; baptistery, late 11th-century and later.

belonged, was one of the main characteristics of his art patronage in other fields, so it is very likely that this cultural orientation also accounts for the exceptionally wholehearted Gothic qualities of the cathedral.

Giangaleazzo granted a quarry yielding all the marble and granite needed for the construction, and his views were canvassed at certain critical moments in the evolution of the design, yet immediate control over the works was vested in a council whose membership was drawn from the upper echelons of lay and ecclesiastical society in Milan. In the early stages at least, the works acted as a focus for the civic sentiment of the Milanese in a still more remarkable way – the digging of the foundations by gangs composed of tradesmen, professional men, priests and even nobles, all of whom worked and ate alongside the paid labourers. Inevitably, and just as in the better known instances of mass involvement in church building recorded in 11th- and early 12th-century France, such extreme enthusiasm proved short-lived. The most enduring testimony to the importance which the building of the cathedral assumed in the life of Milan was the modernization of the city's canal system and the alterations of the course of the Ticino river, both improvements made specifically to facilitate bringing Giangaleazzo's marble by barge from the quarry near Lake Maggiore, a distance of nearly 100km.

Milan Cathedral, like Florence, but unlike the Northern Gothic cathedrals whose appearance it emulates, seems at no stage to have been the conception of a single architect. In 1387, when the masonry first began to rise above foundation level, Simone da Orsenigo was appointed *ingegnere generale* or chief executant architect, but by 1388, if not earlier, some of the other

204 Milan Cathedral, interior looking north-east. The height is only fractionally less than the 48m of Beauvais, the highest Gothic cathedral.

ingegnere, who were nominally Simone's subordinates, were submitting alternative designs for particular parts of the building. In 1389, the situation was further complicated by the appointment of the Frenchman Nicolas de Bonaventure as chief architect jointly with Simone. Nicolas was dismissed after a year, and it is reasonable to suppose that he had clashed with his Italian colleagues over what would have appeared to him a highly unorthodox design, for the same pattern recurred on all the many subsequent occasions when Northern experts were brought in during the next twelve years. But though rival visions of the cathedral were in existence throughout the 1390s this does not mean, as has been suggested, that the individuals responsible for the design and construction of the lower parts of the building had no clear conception of the form they wished the superstructure to take. What was presumably the officially accepted design is preserved in sketches made in 1390 by Antonio di Vincenzo, architect of S. Petronio in Bologna [*206a*]. These show a church far removed from French 14th-century norms and, except in its preposterous height of 67m, essentially similar to that which was actually built. For this reason it will be as well to consider the design of the existing cathedral before turning to the disputes by which the project was beset during the 1390s.

The plan of Milan could almost be that of a major French High Gothic cathedral, except that there are no towers on the west front and the chevet lacks radiating chapels. Its five-part section, like its 'split' piers, can be seen as an adaptation of Bourges, although the differences in height between the vessels are proportionately less. Influence from the nave of the Early Christian cathedral of Milan (S. Tecla) is also likely since this had five vessels which would probably have been staggered in height, as in the major

Roman basilicas [7]. According to a statement made in 1402 by Simone da Orsenigo, the original intention had been to have cellular lateral chapels instead of outer aisles, a scheme reminiscent of recent churches in neighbouring Lombard cities, notably S. Maria del Carmine in Pavia (begun *c.* 1370). Conformity to local tradition is most importantly evident in the abutment of the vault of the main vessels. This has wall ribs of the same height and pitch as the vaults in the square aisle bays, with the result that the lateral ridges slope very steeply. Structurally, though not visually, the effect is akin to a tunnel vault, and the huge lateral thrust exerted by such a covering is countered by two devices of ultimately Roman origin which were common in Lombard Romanesque architecture: exposed abutting walls and an upward extension of the high walls which increases the vertical thrusts. Both features had ceased to be used in France during the 12th century [cf. *22, 10*]. The smallness of all the windows save those in the apse is a very common feature of Italian medieval churches, but its combination with deeply coloured glass gives Milan one of the most stygian of all Gothic interiors. The only major ornamental accents are the extraordinary capitals consisting of rings of niched figures. Nothing else in the design reveals quite so pointedly Italian indifference to Gothic aesthetic principles, for the effect of these horizontal-stressing, splint-like bands is to destroy all sense of continuity between the many-shafted piers and the identically profiled responds of the high vault. It is possible that the source of their enriched figures, and hence of their height, was the circuits of small images which were by this date a regular feature of bishops' croziers, in which case the aim might have been to endow the architecture with appropriately episcopal resonances.

In contrast to the general reticence of the interior, the external elevations are given over to rich tracery panelling and openwork [*205*]. The concept is ultimately a Rayonnant one [cf. *100, 110*], though here it is far more systematically applied than on any earlier Northern cathedral exterior. Even the buttresses, of the vertically continuous pilaster-like form traditional in Italy from the early Middle Ages, are worked into this system. The outstanding individual feature of the exterior is the trio of huge apse windows, whose elegant flowing tracery so far transcends the general ham-handedness of Italian Gothic detailing that it has to be attributed to one or other of the foreign architects brought to Milan in the 1390s. The needle-like pinnacles, frilly parapets and cusp-encrusted flying buttresses were mostly executed from the 17th century onwards, but they conform closely to the designs made *c.* 1390–1400. The oddest feature of the exterior is the upward continuation of the clearstorey wall which masquerades as the clearstorey itself. What one readily accepts as windows lighting the main vessels are in fact only lighting and ventilation for the space between the vault and the outer roofing. Even the flying buttresses are primarily decorative, for the real work of abutment is done by the exposed abutting walls which, like the true clearstorey windows, are invisible from ground level.

The periodic summoning of Northern architects to Milan is a sure sign that the administrative council was racked by doubts as to whether their team of locally recruited architects was capable on its own of building a great cathedral in the Northern manner. Since a project of this kind had never before been attempted in Italy, such doubts were probably legitimate, but the main consequence of importing Northerners was to spark off acrimonious wrangles between them and the Italian architects. Conflict was inevitable, for the two groups had inherited very different assumptions not only about architectural practice but also about the status of the practitioners. Whereas Northern master masons were accustomed to the exercise of complete and unchallenged control over the design and execution of 'their' buildings once agreement had been reached with the patron, the documentary evidence for major Italian churches like Milan and Florence reveals chief architects to have been far less powerful and authoritative figures. A Northern cathedral architect would have found it anomalous, not to say intolerable, that his designs should have to compete for acceptance by the patron with those of men who at home would have had no say in the design process. From the point of view of the Milanese architects, it must have been no less galling that the council should have demonstrated its lack of confidence to the extent of bringing in outsiders. Yet the Milanese possessed a clear advantage of numbers, since only a single Northern architect was normally present at any one time, and the competitive situation to which they were accustomed seems to have given them the edge in polemic over their Northern rivals.

All the Northerners whose opinions on the subject were recorded agreed that the structural design of Milan Cathedral was flawed. In particular, they criticized the buttresses of the outer walls as being too shallow to resist the thrusts from the aisle vaults; yet the Italians were equally adamant that the buttresses were sufficient. Neither side did more than assert the correctness of their views, and there is no sign that anyone was capable of computing thrusts, even in the rough-and-ready way prescribed in the earliest surviving account of thrusts compiled by a European architect, the tract written c. 1530 by the Spaniard Rodrigo Gil de Hontañón. In 1400 the Parisian architect Jean Mignot declared that the buttresses at Milan ought to be three times as deep as the piers inside were wide, but he gave no indication of whether this was an unvarying rule-of-thumb or whether it was his considered estimate of the specific needs of Milan. The former is the more likely, since Mignot regarded as absolute errors the many things at Milan which were at variance with the long established practices of the northern French lodges; for him there was no question of making allowances for the difference of milieu.

In fact Mignot and all the other Northern critics of the structural design were wrong, for the cathedral has proved to be perfectly stable. Like the Northerners, the Milanese had an intuitive grasp of structural parameters which very rarely failed them. Moveover, they were right to point out that

205 Milan Cathedral, choir from the south-east, begun 1386. Debts to German Gothic include the general format of the apse windows [cf. *168*], the blind tracery panelling crowned by gablets [cf. *100*] and the gap between the buttress statues and their canopies (cf. Ulrich von Ensingen's north-west tower at Strasbourg, begun 1399).

their Northern adversaries were forgetting the greater strength of marble and granite relative to the limestone traditionally employed for French Gothic churches. They might have added that the use of heavy materials for the wall structure at Milan improved its ability to resist the lateral thrusts from the vaults, especially as the webs of the latter were made comparatively light by being constructed of brick, the traditional Lombard building material. It is odd that no-one mentioned the exposed abutting walls which make so important a contribution to the stability of the vaults over the three inner vessels. Almost the only comment on structure made by either side which is cogent by modern standards is the Milanese defence that their five vessels of staggered heights were stronger than the Cologne-inspired scheme submitted by Heinrich Parler in 1392. The sense of this must be that the relatively small differences in height between the vessels enabled the lower vaults to function as abutments for the adjacent higher vaults.

Undoubtedly the Northern architects thought that much of what they saw at Milan was ugly. However, in the records of the meeting held to discuss Parler's criticisms, the precise nature of his objections was not revealed, presumably in the hope of keeping tempers down. Instead, the Milanese masters were asked to comment on positive proposals made by Parler or to state their opinion of particular features which by implication he had criticized. Inevitably the Milanese threw out all Parler's suggestions and declared themselves satisfied with their design. Parler's most effective argument would have been not words but a large and enticingly detailed drawing of his alternative scheme. The Milanese shrewdly avoided countering Parler's proposals with aesthetic arguments, for they must have realized that this terrain was a morass. They concentrated instead on practicalities, dismissing the triforium as a waste of money and arguing that the double aisles of equal height would be dark because the inner aisle lacked a direct light source. They chose to forget that the latter would have been more than compensated for by the high clearstorey of the main vessel.

Apart from structural design, the most controversial topics at Milan were the status and proper application of geometrical and arithmetical proportions. In the scheme preserved in Antonio di Vincenzo's drawing of 1390 [206a], the overall internal width and the height of the main vessel appear to be the same – 96 Milanese braccia or 67m. This idea of building 'to the square' – ad quadratum as the Milanese documents call it – was quite common in the North, but whereas it was used there to generate many secondary proportional relationships (see pp. 172–3), in the 1390 scheme for Milan the heights of the main features are fixed by a grid whose vertical intervals of 10 braccia were obviously unrelated to the 96 braccia of the total height. This lack of coordination appears to have been attacked by Nicolas de Bonaventure or the next foreigner consulted, Johann von Freiburg, for in 1391 a mathematician from Piacenza, Gabriele Stornaloco, was asked to devise a scheme in which a grid such as the Milanese insisted on (apparently because it facilitated the use of measuring rods of standard lengths) was combined with a section based on an equilateral triangle [206b]. This figure, which Johann von Freiburg had recommended in 1391, was even more widely used in the North than the square, no doubt because lower central vessels resulted from its use and on account of its value as a symbol of the equal persons of the Trinity. An equilateral triangle based on the 96-braccia-wide nave already laid out would have risen 83.138 braccia, a dimension which was not only incommensurable but indivisible into whole-number units. Stornaloco therefore rounded up the height to 84 braccia and so made it divisible into six units of 14, the same number of 16-braccia units as are contained in the width. To this extent the grid formed by the 14-by-16-braccia rectangles approximated to a square. Probably because its height of 50m was excessive (cf. Beauvais's 48m), Stornaloco's scheme was rejected by the Milanese masters, although it must be admitted that no such anxiety is mentioned in the minutes of the discussion of the much higher scheme submitted soon afterwards, probably by Heinrich Parler [206c]. The latter was in part an attempt to solve the same problem but without Stornaloco's deviation from strict geometry, for it combines the square of 96 braccia proposed in 1390 with a regular grid of 16-braccia squares. The grid was undoubtedly a concession to the Milanese, for most Northern architects

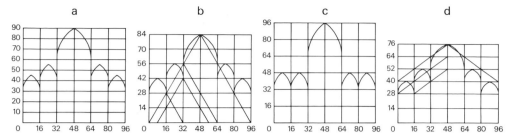

206 Milan Cathedral, proportional systems for determining the heights of major elements in the design: (a) project of 1390 preserved in a sketch and notes by Antonio di Vincenzo; (b) project of 1391 devised by Gabriele Stornaloco; (c) project of 1392 probably by Heinrich Parler; (d) project accepted in 1392. The dimensions are in Milanese *braccia*.

went out of their way to use far less obvious ratios (see pp. 172–3). Despite its attempt to combine Northern and Italian usages, Parler's design was doomed because the Milanese had become determined to use a curious scheme (of unknown authorship) which produced a central vessel somewhat lower than Stornaloco's and which corresponds closely to the existing building [*206d*]. This consists of two layers of Stornaloco's 14-by-16-braccia units surmounted by four layers of units 12 braccia high. The part of the section which contains arches fits into a framework of overlapping Pythagorean triangles but no single geometrical figure governs the whole section.

This clumsy hybrid earned the contempt of Mignot, who insisted that the section conform to an equilateral triangle. The gulf which divided him from the Milanese on the question of proportional relationships is best illustrated by their comments on the design of the capitals. No doubt this design appeared as grotesque to Mignot as it had to Ulrich von Ensingen, who quit in 1395 rather than execute it, but instead of expressing his disapproval in aesthetic terms, Mignot declared that the capitals violated a rule that bases and capitals be of equal height. He cited no authority for this rule. The Milanese replied with a hasty formulation of their own, according to which capitals should be four times higher than bases, but readily admitted breaking this rule and using a capital-to-base ratio of 5:1 because it facilitated the inclusion of statues and niches. During discussion of some problem of this order (the context is unfortunately not stated in the rather inadequate minutes) Mignot had told the Milanese that their proposals were wilful and contrary to good rules. When the Milanese replied that knowledge (*scientia*) of geometry was irrelevant and that a solution could be arrived at simply by the application of practical skill (*ars*), Mignot uttered a famous retort, written in the minutes as 'ars sine scientia nihil est' – skill is nothing without [theoretical] knowledge. This is a clear echo of what had been written by St Augustine almost a thousand years earlier in his *De Musica*, the most influential aesthetic treatise of the Middle Ages. For Augustine, music and architecture were the noblest arts because they embodied the same mathematical proportions as the universe itself; hence they transcended their earthly nature by leading the mind away from the world of appearances towards the contemplation of the divine order. In failing to give due weight to the mathematical basis of their art, the Milanese were not merely failing to conform to Mignot's professional standards: they were undermining the religious basis of great church architecture.

Spain

The earliest Gothic great church in Spain whose design cannot be classed as a French importation is the cathedral begun in 1298 at Barcelona, the chief city of Catalonia [*207, 208*]. Barcelona in the late 13th century was a rapidly expanding commercial centre whose trading links extended throughout the Mediterranean and into the Atlantic. In many ways it resembled the mercantile cities of northern Italy, yet it differed from them fundamentally in being part of a kingdom. In fact Barcelona was very visibly a royal place, for the kings had a palace sited in the centre of the city and close to the cathedral. The mutually advantageous relations between the kings of Aragon and Barcelona's merchants were the motor behind the phenomenal growth of Aragonese commercial and military power during the 13th century: the kings gave the merchants protection from the depredations of the nobles; taxes from the merchants enabled the king to conquer Sicily in 1282; the acquisition of Sicily gave the merchants an invaluable base for further commercial expansion . . . The mercantile and royal aspects of Barcelona's distinctive binary culture are both documented in the architecture of the cathedral, whose main sources were the mendicant churches erected in the city largely under bourgeois patronage, and Toledo Cathedral, seat of the Spanish primate and most important church associated with the rival kingdom of Castile. Confirmation that the borrowings from Toledo were ideologically inspired comes from Lisbon, chief city of another of the Iberian kingdoms, where the choir of the cathedral begun before 1345 by Alfonso IV of Portugal is even more obviously Toledan than Barcelona.

 Apart from its exceptional darkness, the predominant characteristic of the interior of Barcelona Cathedral is its lateral expansiveness. This is generated by the unique two-tier arrangement of deep cellular chapels opening out of the aisles, by the broad proportioning of the central vessel, by the great height and openness of the arcades, and not least by the remarkable shortness of the church. Short, wide naves were already familiar in Catalonia from modest basilican cathedrals of the Lérida type [*117*] as well as from mendicant churches such as those of the Dominicans and Franciscans in Barcelona. The latter, both destroyed in the 19th century, were Barcelona's introduction to Gothic architecture and also the source of two of the cathedral's most distinctive features: its omission of transepts and the arrangement whereby the walls dividing its lateral chapels function as internalized buttresses. At the mendicant churches the chapels rose only half as high as the naves, so the upper halves of their buttresses were visible externally, but at the cathedral

207 Barcelona Cathedral, west end of the nave, showing the arches of the early 15th-century west tower. The cubic external massing and flat terraces above the vaults are typical of Spanish Late Gothic [cf. *214*].

the two tiers of chapels absorbed the full height of the buttresses [*207*]. Internalized buttresses which double as chapel-separating walls were common at French cathedrals by this date, yet it is fairly certain that the main inspiration for their use at the cathedral was the mendicant churches, as only these anticipated the absolute flatness of the exterior lateral elevations. Further proof of indebtedness to what in most parts of Western Europe would have been an unlikely source of inspiration for a cathedral is the exactly equal height – 25.5m – of the main vessels here and at the Barcelona friars' church whose dimensions are known, that of the Dominicans. The height of the Franciscan church, which was consecrated in 1297, is not recorded. The bishop of Barcelona in 1298 was a Franciscan, and perhaps it was he who stipulated this modest height.

Despite its mendicant borrowings, Barcelona remains firmly within the sphere of cathedral architecture. This is evident in the apsidal plan of the lower lateral chapels, which derives from those of Narbonne Cathedral. There may have been a competitive element in the imitation, as it was only in the previous century that Catalonia had been wrested from the ecclesiastical province of Narbonne. The inclusion of two ground-level chapels per bay was certainly an expression of rivalry, since the only earlier example of this curious arrangement occurs in the chevet of the much smaller cathedral begun in 1262 at Valencia, Barcelona's main competitor among the cities of the eastern seaboard. The link is reinforced by a further shared rarity, the windows over the chapels, although at Barcelona the openings are much larger and serve the unique end of providing a dramatic and symbolically apt contrast with the dim light in the rest of the church. The only Spanish antecedents of the Valencia windows are at Toledo Cathedral [*116*].

The influence of Toledo on Barcelona has generally been played down by writers on Catalan Gothic, most of whom have been concerned to stress the political and cultural distinctness of Catalonia within Spain. However, there

208 Barcelona Cathedral, interior looking north-east, begun 1298. The choir enclosure occupying the east part of the nave is a characteristic feature of Spanish cathedrals.

Opposite
209 Barcelona, S. Maria del Mar, interior looking east, begun 1324. The central vessel is 32m high, 6.5m higher than that of Barcelona Cathedral.

210 Palma de Mallorca Cathedral, interior looking south-east, begun 1306. The nave has a lower ratio of pier mass to volume than any other vaulted Gothic basilica.

is very little in the central vessel at Barcelona which cannot be understood as a critical response to Toledo and to other members of the Bourges 'family' of designs, the latter perhaps accessible to the Barcelona master in the form of drawings housed in the Toledo lodge. The modelling of the upper storeys on the triforium and oculi in the inner aisles at Toledo was only part of a radical rethinking of the main vessel of the Toledo choir [115], whose most important innovation was the raising of the main arcades at the expense of the other storeys. Barcelona also reproduces the bulky transverse arches of Toledo's high vaults, the unusually wide spacing of the piers and the obtuse pitch of the arcade arches; but whereas at Toledo these elements generate a slow and heavy bay rhythm, the much taller and slimmer piers used at Barcelona produce an altogether livelier effect. Their elongated proportions, the overall shape of their capitals and the richness of the arcade arches they carry are all reminiscent of the piers in Toledo's fellow 'follower' of Bourges, the choir of Le Mans Cathedral. The continuous band of capitals and the separation they effect between piers and arches may have been a conscious enhancement of these aspects of Le Mans, but their main significance is that they and the stilting of the transverse arches in the high vault represent a rejection of Bourges's.and Toledo's 'split' piers, which if used here would have resulted in high vault responds extending an uncomfortably short distance above the main arcade capitals. The fact that the high vaults and aisle vaults spring from the same group of capitals, together with the small difference in height between the three vessels, makes it tempting to regard Barcelona as an approximation to a hall church. However, it is very unlikely that such a classification bears any relation to the actual creative processes involved, for large-scale hall churches were not being built in Catalonia at

this date. The hall church-like qualities of the design are probably best regarded as an attempt to invest a basilican church with some of the spatial amplitude and clarity possessed by the wide aisleless naves of the friary churches. The finest of the great churches inspired by Barcelona Cathedral show a continuing dependence on mendicant architecture.

The dedication of the parish church of S. Maria del Mar (Our Lady of the Sea) in the port area of Barcelona commemorates the source of the wealth which enabled it to be rebuilt from 1324 on the model of the cathedral [209]. There is a possibility that its greater height has to do not just with bourgeois self-assertion but with pride in the fact that for a long period in the early Middle Ages the church had housed the relics of the cathedral's patron, St Eulalia. S. Maria is in fact significantly simpler than the cathedral, but the simplifications result in a design of greater concentration and power. The most basic changes are the substitution of windows for the cathedral's ill-lit upper tier of lateral chapels and the increase in the length of the bays to the point where those of the central vessel become square in plan. Both adjustments can be seen as evidence of a conscious attempt to revert to Catalan precedent, since the components of the aisle elevations are the same as those of the lateral elevations of the Barcelona mendicant churches, and the division of the central vessel into square bays follows the nave of Valencia Cathedral, begun in 1303. What is certainly not derived from any earlier building is the idea of a continuous band of high-level windows seen through very wide and very simply detailed arcades. Only the Bourges group of designs anticipates the impression that a low and very wide basilican church has been split apart by the insertion of another which is high and narrow. The sexpartite vaulting of Bourges itself comes closest to foreshadowing the sense of colossal scale conveyed by the four great square bays of the main vessel. Nevertheless, the Bourges concept is diluted here by the many differences between the lateral elevations of the main vessels and aisles, differences which are worked into a subtle system of visual balances. Whereas in the main vessel the length of the straight bays is accentuated by contrast with the inordinately close spacing of the apse supports, in the outer elevations we find wide arches opening into the radiating chapels and much narrower lateral chapel entrances, three to a bay. Continuity is provided by the even size of the windows above all the chapel openings. As well as embodying a singular artistic vision, the elevations of S. Maria exemplify what later became a general characteristic of the Gothic great church in Spain, namely the frank acceptance of small windows such as had long been the normal means of excluding heat and glare from less ambitious churches. The round windows in the clearstorey of Barcelona Cathedral are admittedly also small, but most of the wall surface below them is voided by the triforium arcade. At S. Maria sheer unbroken wall surface comes into its own as a major component of the design and acquires a distinctively Gothic membranous quality through its association with extremely thin arch mouldings and tracery.

At various times during their protracted construction periods, both S. Maria del Mar and Barcelona Cathedral enjoyed the support and patronage of the kings of Aragon. However, the only major church in the Catalan Gothic style which owed its inception to royal patronage was the cathedral of Palma, chief city of the short–lived kingdom of Mallorca [*210, 211*]. When James I of Aragon captured Mallorca from the Moors in 1229 he followed the tradition established by earlier Spanish kings who conquered new territory, and immediately had the main mosque turned into a cathedral. His son, James I of Mallorca, was no less conscious of Spanish royal tradition when in 1306 he ordered the building of a funerary chapel comparable to those which kings of Castile had earlier added onto the east ends of the converted mosques at Toledo and Seville. It is very probable that the royal chapel at Palma was always conceived as the first phase of a new cathedral on the lines of the existing building; certainly the chapel and the aisleless choir into whose east wall it opens look as if they belong to a single unified scheme. Structural evidence at the west end of the choir shows that the original plan for the nave consisted of a main vessel no higher than the choir, with aisles of the same height as the chapels flanking the choir and cellular lateral chapels of apsidal plan. As in the present nave [*210*], the piers were to be octagonal, a form new to Spanish great church architecture but later widely diffused on account of its use at S. Maria del Mar. Given the readiness of Mallorca and Catalonia to recruit Tuscan painters, sculptors and stained glass artists, imitation of the octagonal piers at S. Croce in Florence [*200*] or the original 1294 project for Florence Cathedral becomes a distinct possibility. The masonry of the east responds of the Palma arcades provides clear evidence that the piers were always to have resembled those of the existing nave in employing the

211 Palma de Mallorca Cathedral from the south-east, begun 1306. At the far right is the funerary chapel of the kings of Mallorca. As at many Spanish cathedrals, no towers are integrated into the main façade (the west turrets are 19th-century).

Bourges principle of 'splitting', according to which upper extensions form high vault responds and the remainder, the greater part, receive the aisle vaults and main arcades.

Some time around 1360 it was decided to build the main vessel and aisles 15m higher than had been at first envisaged. The central vessel rose to 44m, a height exceeded only by Beauvais, Milan and Cologne, and at 29m the aisles were virtually as high as the central vessels at Westminster Abbey, the tallest Gothic church in England. Since the lateral chapels were built to the height originally intended, the result is a steeply stepped five-part section reminiscent of five-aisled churches like Bourges and Toledo. But at Palma, even more than in any High Gothic church, verticality triumphs over the laws of statics. The astoundingly slender piers are no fewer than sixteen times higher than they are thick – a record for a large vaulted basilican church – and their extension as responds rising beyond the main capitals has the effect of making them seem even slighter than they are. The walls, which look and actually are extremely thin, occupy much more surface area than the windows. Glazing predominates only in the east wall, where three huge roses come close to voiding most of the solid masonry. By virtue of their positioning, the roses reinforce the orientation of the nave towards the brilliantly lit choir and royal chapel. In this respect they are an improvement on the transept roses of French Gothic churches, which outshine the windows in the symbolically and liturgically more important chevets.

The gravity-defying vision of Gothic presented by the Palma nave depended for its realization on the most massive external buttressing to be found at any major medieval church [211]. The main buttresses are in effect the walls between the lateral chapels continued the whole way up the aisle walls and ending as freestanding buttress piers half as high as the clearstorey.

212 Gerona Cathedral, choir 1312–47, nave begun 1416. The triforium is virtually the only element of conventional great church architecture present in the nave.

213 Seville Cathedral, nave looking north-west from the outer south aisle, begun 1402. The nave was built first because royal permission to rebuild the funerary chapel of Ferdinand III at the east end of the 12th-century mosque was not given until 1443.

Their depth almost equals the clear span of the aisles. The two tiers of flyers which spring from these immovable masses ought to have been more than adequate to abut the 19.5m-wide vault of the main vessel; and it seems that the partial collapse of the latter in the 17th and 18th centuries was due to poor workmanship rather than to any flaw in the design, for the rebuilt vaults have endured. The outward thrusts from the apsidal vaults over the lateral chapels are probably adequately contained by the wedge-shaped masses of masonry between the canted sides of adjacent apses, but perhaps out of a sense of occasion due to the splendid setting of the cathedral high above the harbour, it was decided to make the buttresses on the lateral chapels uniform with those receiving the flyers. The presence of windows lighting the chapels is indicated only by the wider intervals between the buttresses that flank them, but the variation is not enough to soften the extraordinary palisade effect produced by the close spacing and uniformity of the buttresses. This effect would have been still more powerful if the redesigning of the nave in the 1360s had not entailed adding towering masses of plain masonry above the pinnacles of the flyer-receiving buttresses.

The swansong of Catalan great church Gothic is the nave of Gerona Cathedral [*212*]. Replacement of the Romanesque nave was not put in hand until 1416, almost seventy years after the completion of the choir, a slightly simplifed version of that at Barcelona Cathedral. The architect, Guillermo Boffiy, proposed that the nave be a single room equal in width to all three vessels of the choir. Not surprisingly, Boffiy's proposal proved controversial, and in order to evaluate it the chapter convened a twelve-man *junta* of senior architects, all from within the kingdom of Aragon except the architect of Narbonne Cathedral. Although seven spoke against the single-span nave and only five were in favour, the chapter decided to adopt Boffiy's design. The record of their decision shows that the main advantages of the single span were perceived as its comparative cheapness and speed of execution. No one seems to have argued that because the aisleless nave was only a somewhat enlarged copy of the functional preaching naves built for the Catalan mendicants it was unworthy of a cathedral; and if there was disquiet on that account it would perhaps have been quelled by satisfaction that the 23m clear span gave Gerona the widest vaulted nave built in the Middle Ages. In fact Gerona is less impressive technically than Palma, whose central vessel it exceeds by about 3m, since the omission of aisles enables the vault to be abutted directly by 5m-deep buttresses sitting on the walls between the lateral chapels. Aesthetically the Gerona nave is interesting mainly by virtue of its unexpected juxtaposition with the basilican choir and the strange 'cutaway section' view it affords of the latter. Even these effects were anticipated more than a century earlier at the very large Franciscan church of Naples, S. Lorenzo, although a direct connection is less likely than common descent from southern French Cistercian churches where wide naves are combined with narrow chancels flanked by low transept chapels.

When work began on the nave of Gerona the economy of Catalonia and Aragon generally was in steep decline owing to the southward shift in the main maritime trade routes. The clearing of the Straits of Gibraltar which accompanied the Castilian reconquest of Andalusia in the mid-13th century opened up a direct link between the Mediterranean and Atlantic economies and paved the way for the emergence of Seville as the richest and largest city in Spain. However, it was not until the last quarter of the 14th century that the Seville chapter began to give serious consideration to replacing their earthquake-damaged former mosque by a church 'of a magnificence appropriate to this city and to the authority of this cathedral'. The minutes of the meeting of 8 March 1401 preserve a remark made by one of the chapter in the spirit of megalomania that must have launched many great church building projects: 'we shall have a church [so great and] of such a kind that those who see it built will think we were mad.'

Seville Cathedral is in fact the largest of all medieval cathedrals, whether one reckons size in terms of floor area or of volume [*213, 214*]. The plan is an immense 76 by 115m rectangle symbolically swallowing up the whole site of the mosque. The north and south walls occupy the same positions as those of the mosque, but the east and west walls are set a few metres further out than their predecessors, apparently for no other reason than to ensure that the length of the main interior space minus the chapels be equal to the 108m of Toledo Cathedral. Among several other borrowings from the church which served as a yardstick of ambition for the cathedral builders of medieval Spain the most obvious is the concept of the seven-part cross section comprising a main vessel flanked by double aisles and cellular lateral chapels. Nevertheless, the character of these spaces and the relationships between them are unique to Seville.

Many Spanish churches earlier than Seville have long bays which allow comparatively unimpeded views between the aisles and main vessels, but given the similarity of Seville's main elevations to Toledo's it seems reasonable to see this feature as specifically Toledan [115]. The inner and outer aisles, of equal height rather than staggered as at Toledo, are notable for their exceptional amplitude. In fact each bay of the aisles has approximately

214 Seville Cathedral from the south-west: nave, begun 1402; crossing tower, 1515–18, by Juan Gil de Hontañón; bell tower (former minaret), 12th- and 16th-century; south transept façade, late 15th-century (portal 19th- and 20th-century). The projections at the base of the clearstorey contain semicircular passages linking the internal walkways in front of the clearstorey windows [213]. This avoids hollowing out and thereby weakening the wall immediately behind the springings of the high vault. The chapels projecting from the west wall are probably based on those at S. Maria del Mar in Barcelona.

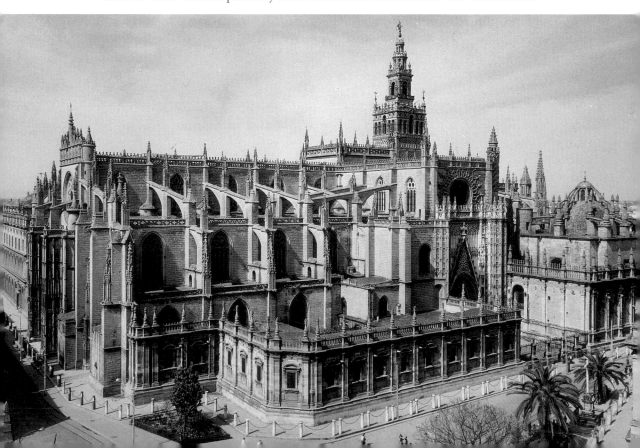

half the volume of one bay of the main vessel, as against the quarter which is the norm for basilican churches. At Toledo the staggered heights and fairly even lighting of the five parallel vessels allow their form and extent to be clearly perceived from practically all viewpoints, but when one stands in the central vessel at Seville the gloom created by the lack of direct lighting in the inner aisles combines with the extreme remoteness of the outer walls to create uncertainty about the lateral boundaries of the church. Possibly the Seville designer's inspiration came from the scarcely less shadowy and indeterminate spaces which open out beyond the great arcades at Barcelona Cathedral [208]. There is no real kinship with the sense of infinity generated in low, many-aisled mosques such as that which preceded the cathedral, for any spatial movement within the aisles is effectively frozen by the piers. Combining the bulk of Toledo's piers with the linearity of Barcelona's, these mighty supports present a series of broad angled surfaces which, like those of the comparably massive diamond-plan supports used in some first-generation Gothic buildings [24], emphasize the autonomy of each bay.

In the main vessel there is evidence of a parallel preoccupation with containing what would normally be the predominant sense of movement, in this case vertical movement generated by the steep proportioning and the powerful vault responds. The boundary between responds and piers is fixed at the level of the arcade capitals by a substantial moulded band, an awkward cross between the capital-level string courses on the nave piers at Toledo and the continuous capitals at Barcelona Cathedral. A more important counter to verticality is the balustrade running along the base of the clearstorey. Its widely spaced vertical bars and the way in which it cuts across the outer ribs leave little doubt that the model was the triforium balustrade in the western bays of Prague Cathedral, where it impinges only on the outer shafts [167]. Despite its remoteness from Seville, Prague is a perfectly likely source of inspiration for an architect charged with designing a church of European ambition situated in a region with no previous tradition of cathedral building. What is true of Prague is true also of Florence Cathedral [202], the only earlier major church whose high vault ribs are traversed by a balustrade. Like its precursors at Florence and Prague, the Seville balustrade is part of a design in which a major objective was the subordination of verticality to the longitudinal integrity of the main vessel. The other most important device which serves this end, the longitudinal ridge rib, has no counterpart at Prague or Florence. Derived ultimately from Burgos, the ridge rib is the one feature of Seville apparently drawn from a local source, for exactly similar ribs occur in the high vaults of what is practically the only earlier Gothic church of any ambition in the whole of Andalusia, the late 13th-century parish church of S. Ana in Seville. The detailed handling of the design is basically French Flamboyant in character. The identity of the original designer of Seville is uncertain, but whoever he was, his horizons were as wide as those of the community in whose midst he worked.

215 Seville Cathedral, reredos of the high altar, begun 1482, by Pieter Dankaert and others. The pierced onion-dome canopies and the fanciful arch forms are typical of the Brabant Florid style.

Opposite
216 Burgos Cathedral, Chapel of the Constable of Castile, begun soon after 1482. The chapel documents the intense rivalry between the monarchy and the leading aristocratic families in late medieval Spain, for it is richer than the intended burial church of King Ferdinand and Queen Isabella (S. Juan de los Reyes, Toledo) begun a few years earlier. The top-lighting coming through the pierced tracery of the vault is a 20th-century alteration effected by glazing the outer roof.

217 Granada Cathedral, interior looking north-west, begun 1528. Part of the domed sanctuary-cum-royal funerary chapel is visible in the foreground.

Few other complete cathedrals were built in 15th-century Spain, and of these none represents a major artistic initiative. Most are minimally modernized versions of the simple two-storey type established as the norm for Spanish cathedrals during the 12th and 13th centuries [*117*]. The one element of French great church design which achieved a wider currency in the Late Gothic period than it had during the 13th century was the ambulatoried chevet. That ambulatories never became *de rigueur* in the 15th and early 16th centuries was probably due largely to the vogue for gigantic wooden high altar reredoses (*retablos*) which superseded architecture proper as the visual focus of eastern arms [*115, 215*]. But the refusal of late medieval Spain, especially Castile, to accept foreign notions of the great church was also linked to a variety of cultural factors: the involvement of the bishops in the political turmoil resulting from weak royal rule during the 14th and early 15th centuries; the restriction of the economic growth of many northern towns by the drift of an already sparse population towards the recently reconquered southern territories; the traditionally inward-looking character of Castilian national life resulting from centuries of preoccupation with the reconquest and recolonization of a vast land. Yet the Spanish resistance to the

great church concept must also have been a major cause of the influx of foreign architects. The paradox is more apparent than real, since it was the restricted scope of 15th-century Spanish church building projects which put native architects at a disadvantage compared to foreigners whenever the need arose for some specially magnificent piece of work.

As elsewhere in the late Middle Ages, many of the most impressive works of 15th-century cathedral architecture were towers and funerary chapels. A Spanish tradition of circular and octagonal lantern towers, in continuous existence since the Romanesque period, culminated in the tall two-stage examples built onto earlier crossings at Valencia (late 14th century) and Burgos (c. 1466–1502). The latter, by the German Juan de Colonia, collapsed in 1539, but its low-pitched roof, bold angle turrets, two-tier windows and squinches making the transition from the square to the octagon are perpetuated both in its mid-16th-century replacement and in the tower-like Constable's Chapel added to the east end of the cathedral by Juan's son Simón from 1482 [216]. Juan had come to Burgos in 1442 at the invitation of the bishop, who wished that the 13th-century western towers of the cathedral should be crowned with openwork tracery spires like those he had seen while travelling in Germany. The Burgos spires were imitated poorly at León and belatedly at Oviedo, and the fact that their impact was so slight is symptomatic of the ephemeral nature of German stylistic influences as well as of Spain's marked lack of enthusiasm for the very high steeples which were a normal adjunct of Northern Gothic churches. Evidently the tradition of compact, cubic massing had become too deeply rooted during the Romanesque period to be dislodged; and in any case, by the late medieval period Spanish cathedrals were becoming so hemmed in by ancillary buildings that, with the exception of terminal façades, their exteriors had ceased to be major foci for architectural invention.

Foremost among these various 'parasite' structures were octagonal funerary chapels, a distinctively Iberian building type whose development culminated in the 15th century. The origins of the type are complex, but it is clear that the single-bay-plus-apse plan of the lower part of the finest example, the Burgos Constable's Chapel, derives from the royal chapel formed within the eastern arm at Toledo Cathedral (see p. 158) and that projected for Seville but superseded by the present larger chapel. The combination of a longitudinally planned lower part with an octagonal upper part [216] derives from two chapels added to the east end of Toledo, one of which houses the tomb of an earlier constable of Castile. The Burgos Constable's Chapel has a bearing on the history of Spanish great church design since it exemplifies certain stylistic trends which appeared in 'private' religious architecture before achieving general currency. Most fundamental of these is the treatment of the chapel as a rather loosely related series of rich passages of decoration, although the looseness is less extreme here than in the central monument of the floridity which became general after the union of Castile and Aragon in 1474. This is S. Juan de los Reyes in Toledo, the intended funerary church of the founders of the union, Ferdinand and Isabella (begun c. 1480). S. Juan was designed by a Frenchman and the Constable's Chapel by the son of a German architect, yet both typify their period in including a very large admixture of the fantastic Brabant Florid forms introduced into Spain by the invading army of Low Countries artists responsible for the reredoses and choir stalls commissioned by practically every important church during the late 15th century. The main Low Countries elements in the upper part of the Constable's Chapel are the complex tracery 'frills' to the recesses and the parapet under the windows, the latter an undulating pattern used again in a vastly enlarged form as a frame for the circular window in the south transept front at Seville [214]. Like the huge sculptured heraldic shields found on the lower walls at Burgos, the Seville window decoration is juxtaposed with broad areas of plain ashlar walling. Such extremes of severity and richness are very characteristic of Spanish Late Gothic architecture, and may have originated in the dramatic contrasts generated when simply treated interiors became receptacles for spectacularly elaborate fittings. Certainly there are considerable numbers of

218 Salamanca Cathedral, west front, begun 1512. The tendency to use small windows and the lack of a strong tradition of towered fronts were the main preconditions favourable to the development of the reredos-like façade in late medieval Spain.

late 15th- and early 16th-century churches whose exteriors are starkly simple except for terminal façades modelled on sculptured wooden reredoses [218].

The vault in the Constable's Chapel at Burgos is the only part of the design which betrays Simón de Colonia's German background. It is a variant of the apse vault at Prague [167, 172w], and the openwork tracery filling the central star – a unique feature at the time – looks like a flattened version of the traceried spires added by Simón's father to the west towers at Burgos. Far more typical of Spanish latest Gothic vaults are those in the early 16th-century cathedrals of Salamanca and Segovia, both designed by the prolific Juan Gil de Hontañón [219, 220]. The curved ribs may derive ultimately from German sources, but whereas in Germany long curving ribs seem to have

219 Salamanca Cathedral, south nave aisle looking north-east, begun 1512. The mannered detail of the pier shafts overshooting the capitals derives, like much else, from Seville Cathedral [213]. Among minor modifications made during the course of building are the Renaissance busts in the spandrels of the main arcades.

220 Segovia Cathedral, south nave aisle looking north-east, 1525–58.

been valued for the sense of movement they generate and for their capacity to soften bay divisions, the much shorter ribs at Salamanca and Segovia are worked into dense, approximately diamond-shaped areas of pattern which emphasize the centre of each vaulting compartment and so complement the centuries-old Spanish usage of few and powerfully stressed bays.

The bay design at Salamanca and Segovia derives from Seville, and it is the successful marriage of the most ambitious cathedral scheme of the 15th century with the rich new vault types which entitles Juan Gil's two great churches to be considered the crowning achievements of Spanish cathedral Gothic. At Salamanca [219], begun in 1512, the diamond-plan Sevilian piers have been made approximately circular, a revision possibly prompted by awareness of Seville's debt to Toledo or even of the latter's to Bourges. The shape of the piers is nicely echoed in the patterning of the aisle vaults, especially in those compartments where two sets of concentric liernes suggest the convexity of fan vaults. That this correspondence between piers and vaults was not fortuitous is apparent from the different but parallel concern evidenced at Segovia [220]. Here, more strictly Sevilian piers with shafts boldly projecting from the centre of concave angled faces are combined with areas of rib pattern whose overall diamond shape is indented at the centre of the sides. To emphasize the connection between projecting shafts and indented vault patterning, the diagonal ribs which link the two are given a bolder gauge than the other ribs, a variation not present at Salamanca. In general, Segovia embodies a more convincing expression of the relation between supports and arched elements than Salamanca, where the piers look disproportionately bulky relative to their loads. Moreover, the suppression of the continuous capital bands which at Seville and Salamanca encircle the piers at the springing level of the main arcade arches allows a stronger upward movement from the verticals of the piers to the ribs and arches. It also promotes a greater sense that the piers are self-effacing carriers for the vaults, the real glory of the interior.

Salamanca was built because the small Romanesque cathedral had been deemed unworthy of the city and its university, the second largest in Europe after Paris. At Segovia the Romanesque cathedral had been destroyed in a revolt of the Castilian towns in 1521 which was essentially a protest against the absorption of Spain into Charles V's Habsburg Empire. It fell to the townspeople of Segovia to pay for the new building, so the close imitation of the cathedral of neighbouring Salamanca is perhaps partly explicable as a conscious affirmation of Castilian identity. However, the greatest opening for cathedral building in early 16th-century Spain was at Granada, capital of the last part of the peninsula to be retaken from the Moors. A first Gothic project of 1523 was superseded in 1528 by the earliest designs in the Renaissance style to be used at any Spanish cathedral [217]. The archbishop was evidently an enthusiast for architecture 'a lo Romano', but because Charles V was worried lest a new church in this style would impair the recently completed Gothic tomb chapel of Ferdinand and Isabella, the architect, Diego de Siloé, was summoned to court 'to defend his work and intention'. No record exists of what was said at this meeting, but it is likely that Siloé would have pointed out that he had higher authority than mere fashion for the most Roman-looking feature of his design, the domed chevet-cum-royal tomb chapel, for this was a much closer approximation than any of the earlier axial tomb chapels at Spanish cathedrals to their ultimate source, the 4th-century rotunda of the Holy Sepulchre in Jerusalem. Apart from its domed east end, Granada is only a very superficially classicized compound of elements taken from Toledo and Seville, the two standards of cathedral ambition in Spain; and it was this eminently traditional scheme which formed the basis for the succession of giant cathedrals erected during the next two centuries in Andalusia and in the New World.

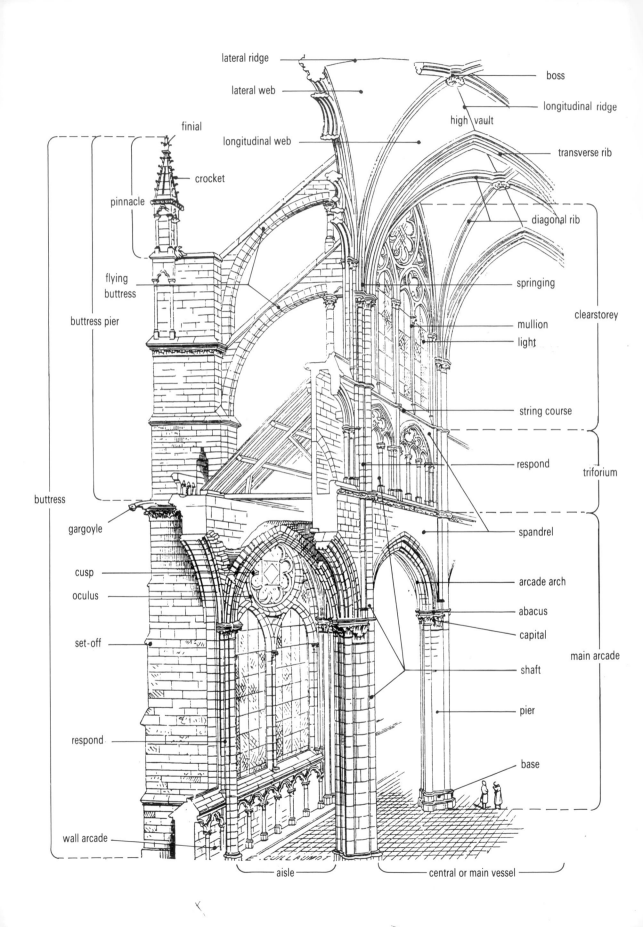

lateral ridge

lateral web

finial

crocket

pinnacle

longitudinal web

flying
buttress

buttress pier

boss

longitudinal ridge

high vault

transverse rib

diagonal rib

springing

clearstorey

mullion

light

string course

respond

triforium

buttress

gargoyle

cusp

oculus

set-off

respond

wall arcade

spandrel

arcade arch

abacus

capital

shaft

pier

main arcade

base

E. GUILLAUMOT

aisle

central or main vessel

Glossary

abacus   See diagram.

aedicule   See *canopy*.

aisle   See diagram.

ambulatory   An *aisle* or passageway connecting the side aisles of a *choir* and running behind the east end of its *central vessel* [*19,27*].

apse   A termination of semicircular or half-polygonal plan, usually to a *central vessel*, chapel or *aisle*.

arcade arch   See diagram.

architect   A word seldom used in the Middle Ages but preferable to the authentic but now inappropriately humble-sounding 'master mason'. The wooden parts of medieval churches were normally the responsibility of a master carpenter, so in this sense most churches had two architects.

archivolt   A *moulding* decorating the face of an arch and following its profile. On Gothic portals, frequently decorated with figure sculpture [*91*].

arch order   One of several arches making up a compound arch of stepped section [*52, 125*].

ashlar   Masonry blocks cut to a smooth face and with more or less regular joints.

axial   On the main east-west axis of a church.

bar tracery   Thin stone bars forming a decorative pattern within an arched window opening. Except for *plate tracery* all tracery is of this kind [*80*].

base   See diagram.

basilica   A church with side *aisles* and a *central vessel* lit by a *clearstorey*.

bay   In its fullest sense, a longitudinal spatial compartment defined externally by *buttresses* and internally by *piers*, *responds* and the *transverse ribs* of the vault. Also used of the major compartments in an elevation.

blind tracery   Dummy *tracery* constructed as part of a solid surface [*86,177*].

boss   See diagram.

buttress   See diagram.

buttress pier   See diagram.

canopy   An arched, open-sided structure standing over an altar, image or person, usually carried on columns or thin *piers* if freestanding [*137*].

centering   Wooden support for the building of an arch or vault, removed after completion [*16*].

central vessel   See diagram.

chapter house   The room off the east side of a cloister used by monks or canons for formal assemblies and the transaction of business.

choir   The eastern arm of a *cruciform* church, sometimes but not always housing the *liturgical choir*.

clearstorey   See diagram.

conoid   In Gothic *vaults*, the inverted cone-like configuration of *ribs* and *webs* [*137*].

corbel   A projecting bracket supporting a statue or architectural member.

coursed   Constructed as part of the horizontal rows of stones (courses) in a wall.

crocket   See diagram.

crocket capital   A capital decorated with *crockets* in the form of broad ridged leaves ending in curled, hook-like tips [*39*].

crossing   The intersection of the four arms of a cruciform church, sometimes supporting a tower.

cruciform   Cross-shaped, pre-eminently in plan.

cusp   See diagram.

diagonal rib   See diagram.

dosseret   A shallow strip-like projection behind a shaft.

eastern arm   See *choir*.

edge bedding   A method of setting stone blocks so that the stratification planes of the stone as it lay in the quarry are set on edge relative to the horizontal beds of mortar. (Confusingly, the stratification planes are also often referred to as 'beds'.) The French term *en délit* is applied to this technique in much recent art historical writing.

elevation   A vertical face of a building or part of a building.

false bearing   The carrying of the upper walls or arches of a structure on thinner supports arranged so that the upper level overhangs the lower on one side [*41a*].

false gallery   A middle storey resembling a *gallery* but lacking a windowed outer wall [*31*].

fan vault   A *vault*, its purest form consisting of concave-sided half- or quarter-cones built of *ashlar* and decorated with *blind tracery*. A feature of English Perpendicular Gothic [*155*].

fillet   A raised strip applied to arch mouldings [*125e*] or shafts [*128*].

finial   See diagram.

flowing tracery   Tracery composed predominantly of *ogees* [*143*].

flying buttress   See diagram.

four-centred arch   A *pointed arch* formed of four arcs, the lower pair of smaller radius than the upper [*162*].

gallery   In medieval churches, the space above an *aisle*, with openings into the *central vessel* and a windowed outer wall [*33*].

gargoyle   See diagram. (Sometimes a dummy, lacking a water channel.)

hall church   A church with *aisles* equal in height to the *central vessel* and hence lacking a *clearstorey* [*112*].

haunch   The part of an arch or *vault* directly above the *springing*.

high vault   See diagram.

lady chapel   A chapel dedicated to the Virgin Mary.

lancet   A single window opening with a *pointed-arched* head [*38*].

lantern tower   A tower with windows shedding light into the *crossing* [*38*].

lateral ridge   See diagram.

lateral web   See diagram.

Latin cross   A cross with one arm longer than the others.

lierne   A decorative *rib* not connected to the corner of a *vault* compartment [*147*].

light   See diagram.

liturgical choir   The enclosed area occupied by choir stalls for the clergy serving the church [133].

longitudinal ridge   See diagram.

longitudinal web   See diagram.

main arcade   See diagram.

main vessel   See diagram.

mouchette   An asymmetrical version of a *soufflet* [143].

moulding   The profiling of projecting and recessed architectural members, notably arches [125].

mullion   See diagram.

nave   The part of a church west of the *sanctuary* and *crossing*.

net vault   A *vault* with a net-like configuration of *ribs*. A feature of German Late Gothic [174].

oculus   See diagram.

ogee   An S-curved profile often used in arches during the late medieval period.

panelling   Repeating units of glazed, open or blind *tracery*, the basic unit being an arch enclosed in an upright rectangle. A feature pre-eminently of English Perpendicular Gothic [162].

pendant   A vault *conoid* not supported by a wall or *pier* and often constructed as an elongated *boss* or *voussoir* [163, 170, 195].

penetration   A fragmentary transverse *tunnel vault* penetrating the lower part of a higher longitudinal tunnel vault [151, 167].

pier   See diagram.

pinnacle   See diagram.

plate tracery   A series of closely spaced but distinct window openings consisting of *lights* and *oculi*, giving the impression of having been punched through a sheet or plate of stone [60].

pointed arch   An arch formed of two arcs of equal radius.

Purbeck marble   A fossiliferous limestone – not true marble – quarried on the coast of southern England and treated as marble in the Middle Ages on account of its capacity to take a polish [124].

quatrefoil   A decoration formed of four lobes or part-circles.

radiating chapel   A chapel opening out of an *ambulatory* and planned so that its central axis radiates from the centre of the main *apse* [66].

rear arch   An arch at the inner edge of a window or door opening.

relieving arch   An arch built into the masonry of a wall to relieve downward pressure on an opening beneath.

reredos   A high screen or wall behind an altar, usually incorporating sculpture [159, 215].

respond   See diagram.

reticulation   An all-over pattern like the mesh of a net [148].

rib   An arch of thin section in a *vault*.

ridge rib   A horizontal *rib* at the *lateral* or *longitudinal ridge* of a *vault* [124].

roundel   A decoration of circular format [79, 219].

sanctuary   The area round and particularly in front of a high altar.

segmental arch   An arch formed of an arc which is less than half a circle.

set-off   See diagram.

sexpartite vault   A *vault* with six divisions, its *springings* including alternately three *ribs* and one rib. Usually used over two bays [5].

shaft   See diagram.

shaft ring   A ring-shaped feature masking joints in *edge-bedded shafts* and attaching them to a wall or *pier*.

soufflet   A symmetrical leaf-like form used in *flowing tracery* [143].

spandrel   See diagram.

springing   See diagram.

squinch   A half-conical niche placed in the corners of a rectangular structure to form the base for the support of a dome or polygonal vault [216].

stilted arch   An arch which rises vertically for some distance above its supports.

string course   See diagram.

tabernacle   See *canopy*.

template   Full-size pattern cut from thin wooden sheets (nowadays metal) to enable masons to check that the profiling of the stones they were cutting conformed to the architect's design.

tierceron   A decorative *rib* extending between no more than one corner of a *vault* compartment and one of the ridges [124].

tracery   See *bar tracery*, *plate tracery* and *blind tracery*.

transept   The north or south arm of a *cruciform* church.

transom   A horizontal member in a *tracery* window [151].

transverse rib   See diagram.

trefoil   A decoration formed of three lobes or part-circles.

triforium   A storey below the *clearstorey*, usually incorporating arches opening towards the *central vessel*, a *wall passage* (either continuous or running only the length of each *bay*), and a rear wall concealing the roof space above the *aisle* [44, 45]. See diagram.

triumphal arch   The arch at the entrance to a main *apse* [7].

tunnel vault   A longitudinal arched tunnel, the simplest kind of *vault* in terms of its three-dimensional form. In Gothic architecture its surface is often decorated with *ribs* [128, 157].

tympanum   A vertical surface defined by an arch and often decorated with sculpture when used above an important doorway [97].

vault   An arched covering of masonry, or occasionally of wood imitating masonry.

voussoirs   The wedge-shaped stones making up an arch or *rib*.

wall arcade   See diagram.

wall head   The top of a wall.

wall passage   A passage running lengthwise through a wall, often open to the interior through arches [47].

wall rib   A *rib* separating the *lateral web* of a *vault* from the wall of the supporting structure [202].

web   See diagram.

walk   A covered way forming one side of a cloister [155].

Select Bibliography

AB   *Art Bulletin*
BAA CT   *British Archaeological Association Conference Transactions*
BM   *Bulletin Monumental*
G   *Gesta*
JSAH   *Journal, Society of Architectural Historians*
JWCI   *Journal of the Warburg and Courtauld Institutes*

General Surveys

DEHIO, G., & G. VON BEZOLD, *Die kirchliche Baukunst des Abendlandes*, II (Stuttgart 1901)

FRANKL, P., *Gothic architecture* (Harmondsworth 1962)

GRODECKI, L., A. PRACHE & R. RECHT, *Gothic architecture* (London 1986)

GROSS, W., *Die abendländische Architektur um 1300* (Stuttgart 1948)

Structural Design

DENEUX, H., 'De la construction en tas-de-charge . . .', *BM*, 102 (1943–4), 241–56

HEYMAN, J., 'The stone skeleton' *International Journal of Solids and Structures*, 2 (1966), 249–80

MARK, R., *Experiments in Gothic structure* (Cambridge, Mass. 1982)

SANABRIA, S. L., 'The mechanization of design in the 16th century: the structural formulae of Rodrigo Gil de Hontañón', *JSAH*, 41 (1982), 281–93

TAYLOR, W., & R. MARK, 'The technology of transition: sexpartite to quadripartite vaulting in High Gothic architecture', *AB*, 54 (1982), 579–87

WILLIS, R., 'On the construction of the vaults of the Middle Ages', *Transactions, Royal Institute of British Architects*, I, pt 2 (1842), 1–69; reprinted in R. Willis, *Architectural history of some English cathedrals*, II (Chicheley 1972)

Building and Masonry Techniques

BINDING, G., & N. NUSSBAUM, *Die mittelalterliche Baubetrieb . . .* (Darmstadt 1978)

CHAPELOT, O. & P. BENOÎT (eds), *Pierre et métal dans le bâtiment au Moyen Age* (Paris 1985)

JAMES, J., *Chartres, the masons who built a legend* (London 1982)

KIMPEL, D., 'Le développement de la taille en série . . .', *BM*, 135 (1977), 195–222

SANFAÇON, R., 'Le rôle des techniques dans les principales mutations de l'architecture gothique', *Cahiers d'Etudes Médiévales*, 7 (1982), 93–129

SHELBY, L. R., 'Medieval masons' tools . . .', *Technology and Culture*, 2 (1961), 127–30; 4 (1965), 127–30

WOLFF, A., 'Chronologie der ersten Bauzeit des Kölner Domes', *Kölner Domblatt*, new ser., 28–9 (1968), 9–229

Drawing and Geometry

BARNES, C. F., *Villard de Honnecourt, the architect and his drawings. A critical bibliography* (Boston 1982)

BRANNER, R., 'Villard de Honnecourt, Reims and the origin of Gothic architectural drawing', *Gazette des Beaux-Arts*, 6th ser., 61 (1963), 129–46

BUCHER, F., 'Medieval architectural design methods 800–1560', *G*, 11 (1972), 37–51.

—, 'The Dresden sketch-book of vault projection', *Actes du XXIIᵉ Congrès International d'Histoire de l'Art* (Budapest 1973), 527–37

COLCHESTER, L. S., & J. H. HARVEY, 'The Wells tracing floor', *Archaeological Journal*, 131 (1974), 210–14

HAHNLOSER, H., *Villard de Honnecourt . . .* (Graz 1972)

LALBAT, C., G. MARGUERITTE & J. MARTIN, 'De la stéréotomie médiévale: la coupe des pierres chez Villard de Honnecourt', *BM*, 145 (1987), 387–406; 147 (1989), 11–34

MORRIS, R. K., 'The development of later Gothic mouldings in England c.1250–1400', *Architectural History*, 21 (1978), 18–57; 22 (1979), 1–48

MURRAY, S., 'The Gothic façade drawings in the Reims Palimpsest', *G*, 17 (1978), 51–5

RECHT, R., 'Sur le dessin d'architecture gothique', *Etudes d'art médiéval offertes à Louis Grodecki* (Strasbourg 1981), 167–79

SHELBY, L. R., 'Setting out the keystones of pointed arches . . .', *Technology and Culture*, 10 (1965), 236–48

—, 'Medieval masons' templates', *JSAH*, 30 (1971), 140–54

—, 'The practical geometry of medieval masons', *Studies in Medieval Culture*, 5 (1975), 133–44

Architects and Masons

BAUCHAL, C., *Nouveau dictionnaire biographique et critique des architectes français* (Paris 1887)

COLOMBIER, P. DU, *Les chantiers des cathédrales* (Paris 1973)

HARVEY, J. H., *The medieval architect* (London 1972)

—, *English medieval architects. A biographical dictionary down to 1550* (Gloucester 1984)

KIMPEL, D., 'La sociogenèse de l'architecte moderne', in X. Barral i Altet (ed.), *Artistes, artisans et production artistique au Moyen Age*, I (Paris 1986), 135–49

KNOOP, D., & G. P. JONES, *The medieval mason* (Manchester 1967)

THIEME, U., & F. BECKER, *Allgemeines Lexikon der bildenden Künstler*, 37 vols (Leipzig 1907–50)

Symbolism, Meanings

BANDMANN, G., *Mittelalterliche Architektur als Bedeutungsträger* (Berlin 1951)

BUCHER, F., 'Micro-architecture as the "idea" of Gothic theory and style', *G*, 15 (1976), 71–89

BÜCHSEL, M., 'Ecclesiae symbolorum cursus completus', *Städel-Jahrbuch*, new ser., 9 (1983), 69–88

CROSSLEY, P., 'Medieval architecture and meaning: the limits of iconography', *Burlington Magazine*, 130 (1988), 116–21

KRAUTHEIMER, R., 'Introduction to an iconography of medieval architecture', *JWCI*, 5 (1942), 1–33

NEALE, J. M. & B. WEBB, *William Durandus, Bishop of Mende, on the Symbolism of Churches and Church Ornaments* (London 1843)

PANOFSKY, E., *Gothic Architecture and Scholasticism* (New York 1951)

SAUER, J., *Symbolik des Kirchengebäudes* (Freiburg-im-Breisgau 1924)

SIMSON, O. VON, *The Gothic cathedral* (Princeton 1988)

Liturgical Uses of Great Churches

BLUM, P. Z., 'Liturgical influence on the design of the west front at Wells and Salisbury', *G*, 25 (1986), 145–50

FOWLER, J. T. (ed.), *The rites of Durham* (Durham 1914)

HAMILTON, B., *Religion in the medieval West* (London 1986)

HOPE, W. H. ST J., 'Quire screens in English churches', *Archaeologia*, 68 (1917), 43–110

KLUKAS, A. W., 'The *Liber Ruber* and the rebuilding of the east end at Wells', *BAA CT*, Wells and Glastonbury 1978 (1981), 30–35

KROOS, R., 'Liturgische Quellen zum Kölner Domchor', *Kölner Domblatt*, new ser., 44–5, (1979–80), 35–202

ORME, N., *Exeter Cathedral as it was, 1050–1550* (Exeter 1986)

Building Records

CANTÙ, C., *Annali della fabbrica del duomo di Milano*, 8 vols (Milan 1877–85)

CHAPMAN, F. R., *Sacrist rolls of Ely*, 2 vols (Cambridge 1907)

COLVIN, H. M. (ed.), *Building accounts of King Henry III* (Oxford 1971)

—, *et al.*, *The History of the King's Works: the Middle Ages*, 2 vols (London 1963)

ERSKINE, A. M., 'The accounts of the fabric of Exeter Cathedral, 1279–1353', *Devon & Cornwall Record Society Publications*, new ser., 24 (1981); 26 (1983)

GUASTI, C., *S. Maria del Fiore, la costruzione . . . secondo i documenti* (Florence 1887)

MURRAY, S., *Building Troyes Cathedral: the Late Gothic campaigns* (Bloomington & Indianapolis 1987)

NEUWIRTH, J., *Die Wochenrechnungen und der Betrieb des Prager Dombaues 1372–1378* (Prague 1890)

Documentary Evidence

FRISCH, T. G., *Gothic art 1140–c.1450. Sources and Documents* (Toronto 1987)

GRINTEN, E. F. VAN DER, *Elements of art historiography in medieval texts* (The Hague 1969)

HOLT, E. G. (ed.), *A documentary history of art, I: the Middle Ages and the Renaissance* (New York 1957)

LEHMANN-BROCKHAUS, O., *Lateinische Schriftquellen zur Kunst in England . . . 901 . . . 1307*, 5 vols (Munich 1955–60)

MORTET, V., & P. DESCHAMPS, *Recueil de textes relatifs à l'histoire de l'architecture . . . en France, XIIe–XIIIe siècles* (Paris 1929)

SALZMAN, L. F., *Building in England down to 1540. A documentary history* (Oxford 1967)

SCHLOSSER, J. VON., *Materialien zur Quellenkunde der Kunstgeschichte, I: Mittelalter* (Vienna 1914)

Economic Aspects

BIGET, J.-L., 'Recherches sur le financement des cathédrales du Midi au XIIIe siècle', *La naissance et l'essor du gothique méridional au XIIIe siècle* (Cahiers de Fanjeaux, 9) Toulouse 1974

KRAUS, H., *Gold was the mortar* (London 1979)

KIMPEL, D., 'Ökonomie, Technik und Form in der hochgotischen Architektur', in K. Clausberg *et al.* (eds), *Bauwerk und Bildwerk im Hochmittelalter* (Giessen 1981), 103–25

LOPEZ, R., 'Economie et architecture médiévales, cela aurait-il tué ceci?', *Annales*, 7 (1952), 433–8

VROOM, W. H., *De financiering van de kathedraalbouw . . .* (Maarssen 1981) [with English summary]

WARNKE, M., *Bau und Überbau, Soziologie der mittelalterlichen Architektur . . .* (Frankfurt 1976)

France, general

BIDEAULT, M. & C. LAUTIER, *Ile-de-France gothique*, I (Paris 1987) [first volume in series planned to cover Gothic architecture throughout France]

BONY, J., *French Gothic architecture of the 12th and 13th centuries* (Berkeley 1983)

BROSSE, J. (ed.), *Dictionnaire des églises de France*, 5 vols (Paris 1966–71) [includes Belgium and Switzerland]

KIMPEL, D., & R. SUCKALE, *Die gotische Kirchenbaukunst in Frankreich 1130–1270* (Munich 1985)

VIOLLET-LE-DUC, E., *Dictionnaire raisonné de l'architecture française du XIe au XVIe siècles*, 10 vols (Paris 1858–68)

England, general

ALEXANDER, J., & P. BINSKI (eds), *Age of Chivalry. Art in Plantagenet England 1200–1400*, exh. cat. (London 1987)

KIDSON, P., P. MURRAY & P. THOMPSON, *A history of English architecture* (Harmondsworth 1979)

PEVSNER, N., *et al.*, *The Buildings of England*, 46 vols & revised edns (Harmondsworth 1951–)

Germany, general

DEHIO, G., *et al.*, *Handbuch der deutschen Kunstdenkmäler*, 20 vols & revised edns (Munich 1964–)

NUSSBAUM, N., *Deutsche Kirchenbaukunst der Gotik* (Cologne 1985)

Low Countries, general

GELDER, H. E. VAN & J. DUVERGER (eds), *Kunstgeschiedenis der Nederlanden*, I (Utrecht 1954)

OZINGA, M. D., & R. MEISCHKE, *Gothische kerkelijke bouwkunst* (Amsterdam 1953)

Italy, general

WAGNER-RIEGER, R., *Die italienische Baukunst zu Beginn der Gotik*, 2 vols (Graz 1956–7)

WHITE, J., *Art and architecture in Italy 1250–1400* (Harmondsworth 1987)

Spain, general

LAMBERT, E., *L'art gothique en Espagne aux XIIe et XIIIe siècles* (Paris 1931)

TORRES BALBÁS, L., *Arquitectura gótica* (Ars Hispaniae, VII) (Madrid 1952)

CHAPTER I *Early Gothic*
Origins

AUBERT, M., 'Les plus anciennes croisées d'ogives, leur rôle dans la construction', *BM*, 113 (1934), 5–67, 137–237

BILSON, J., 'Durham Cathedral and the chronology of its vaults', *Archaeological Journal*, 79 (1922), 101–60

BONY, J., 'Diagonality and centrality in early rib-vaulted architectures', *G*, 15 (1976), 15–25

HENRIET, J., 'St-Lucien de Beauvais: mythe ou réalité?', *BM*, 141 (1983), 273–94

—, 'St-Germer-de-Fly . . .', *BM*, 143 (1985), 94–142

PRACHE, A., *Ile-de-France romane* (La Pierre-qui-Vire 1983)

France

BRANNER, R., 'Gothic architecture 1160–80 and its Romanesque sources', *Acts of 20th International Congress of the History of Art*, I, (Princeton 1963), 92–104

BRUZELIUS, C.A., 'The construction of Notre-Dame in Paris', *AB*, 69 (1987), 540–69

CLARK, W. W., 'The first flying buttresses: a new reconstruction of the nave of Notre-Dame de Paris', *AB*, 66 (1984), 47–65

—, & R. KING, *Laon Cathedral, architecture* 1, 2 (*Courtauld Institute Illustration Archives, companion texts* 1, 2) (London 1983–7)

CROSBY, S. MCK., *The royal abbey of Saint-Denis . . .* (New Haven 1987)

GARDNER, S., 'Two campaigns in Suger's western block at St-Denis', *AB*, 66 (1984), 574–87

GERSON, P. L. (ed.), *Abbot Suger and Saint-Denis* (New York 1986)

HENRIET, J., 'La cathédrale de St-Etienne de Sens . . .', *BM*, 140 (1982), 81–174

KIDSON, P., 'Panofsky, Suger and St-Denis', *JWCI*, 50 (1987), 1–17

PANOFSKY, E., *Abbot Suger on the abbey church of St.-Denis and its art treasures* (Princeton 1979)

PRACHE, A., 'Les arcs-boutants au XIIᵉ siècle', *G*, 15 (1976), 31–42

—, *St-Remi de Reims* (Geneva 1978)

SEYMOUR, C., *Notre-Dame of Noyon in the twelfth century* (New York 1968)

VERMAND, D., *La cathédrale . . . de Senlis . . . au XIIᵉ siècle . . .* (Senlis 1987)

England

BILSON, J., 'Notes on the earlier architectural history of Wells Cathedral', *Archaeological Journal*, 85 (1928), 23–68

BONY, J., 'French influences on the origins of English Gothic architecture', *JWCI*, 12 (1949), 1–15

COLCHESTER, L. S. (ed.), *Wells Cathedral. A history* (Shepton Mallet 1982)

DRAPER, P., 'William of Sens and . . . the original design of the choir termination of Canterbury Cathedral 1175–1179', *JSAH*, 42 (1983), 238–48

—, 'Recherches récentes sur l'architecture dans les Iles britanniques à la fin de l'époque romane et au début du Gothique', *BM*, 144 (1986), 305–28

HEARN, M. F., 'Ripon Minster and the beginning of the Gothic style in England', *Transactions, American Philosophical Society*, 73, pt 6 (1983), 1–196

WILLIS, R., *The architectural history of Canterbury Cathedral* (London 1845); reprinted in R. Willis, *Architectural history of some English cathedrals*, I (Chicheley 1972)

WILSON, C., 'The sources of the late 12th-century work at Worcester Cathedral', *BAA CT*, Worcester 1975 (1978), 80–90

—, 'The Cistercians as "missionaries of Gothic" in Northern England', in C. Norton & D. Park (eds), *Cistercian art and architecture in the British Isles* (Cambridge 1986), 86–116

WOODMAN, F., *The architectural history of Canterbury Cathedral* (London 1981)

CHAPTER II *Thirteenth-Century Gothic*
French High Gothic

BRANNER, R., *The cathedral of Bourges . . .* (Cambridge, Mass. 1989)

— (ed.) *Chartres Cathedral* (New York 1969)

DURAND, G., *Monographie de l'église cathédrale Notre-Dame d'Amiens*, 2 vols (Amiens 1901–3)

KLEIN, B., 'Chartres und Soissons. Überlegungen zur gotischen Architektur um 1200', *Zeitschrift für Kunstgeschichte*, 49 (1986), 437–66

MEULEN, J. VAN DER, *Chartres: Biographie der Kathedrale* (Cologne 1984)

MURRAY, S., 'The choir of the . . . cathedral of Beauvais . . .', *AB*, 62 (1980), 533–51

RAVAUX, J.-P., 'Les campagnes de construction de la cathédrale de Reims au XIIᵉ siècle', *BM*, 137 (1979), 7–66

REINHARDT, H., *La cathédrale de Reims* (Paris 1963)

Early thirteenth-century regional styles in northern France

BRANNER, R., *Burgundian Gothic architecture* (London 1960)

BONY, J., 'The resistance to Chartres in early thirteenth-century architecture', *Journal, British Archaeological Assoc.*, 3rd ser., 20–21 (1957–8), 35–52

DEVLIEGHER, L., 'De opkomst van de kerkelijke gothische bouwkunst in West-Vlaanderen gedurende de XIIIᵉ eeuw', *Bull. de la Commission royale des monuments et des sites*, 5 (1954), 177–345; 7 (1956), 7–121

TITUS, H. B., 'The Auxerre Cathedral chevet . . .', *JSAH*, 47 (1988), 45–56

Rayonnant

BRANNER, R., *St Louis and the court style in Gothic architecture* (London 1965)

BRUZELIUS, C. A., *The 13th-century church at St-Denis* (New Haven 1985)

DAVIS, M. T., 'The choir of the cathedral of Clermont-Ferrand . . .', *JSAH*, 40 (1981), 181–202

—, 'On the threshold of Flamboyant: the second campaign of construction of St-Urbain, Troyes', *Speculum*, 59 (1984), 847–84

RECHT, R., *La cathédrale de Strasbourg* (Stuttgart 1984)

REY, R., *L'art gothique dans le Midi de la France* (Paris 1934)

Germany

ADAM, E., *Das Freiburger Münster* (Stuttgart 1981)
CLEMEN, P., *Der Dom zu Köln* (Düsseldorf 1937)
HASSE, M., *Die Marienkirche zu Lübeck* (Munich 1983)
KUBACH, H. E., & A. VERBEEK, *Romanische Baukunst am Rhein und Maas*, 3 vols (Berlin 1976)
KUNST, H.-J., 'Die Entstehung des Hallenumgangchores. Der Dom zu Verden an der Aller . . .', *Marburger Jahrbuch für Kunstwissenschaft*, 18 (1969), 1–104
SAUERLÄNDER, W., 'Style or transition. The fallacies of classification discussed in the light of German architecture 1190–1220', *Architectural History*, 30 (1987), 1–13
SCHUBERT, E., *Der Magdeburger Dom* (Frankfurt 1984)
WINTERFELD, D. VON, *Der Dom in Bamberg*, 2 vols (Berlin 1979)
—, 'Zum Stande der Baugeschichtsforschung', in W. Nicol (ed.), *Der Dom zu Limburg* (Mainz 1985), 41–84

Spain

BRANNER, R., 'The movements of Gothic architects between France and Spain in the early thirteenth century', *Actes du XIXᵉ Congrès International d'Histoire de l'Art* (Paris 1959), 44–8
LORENTE JUNQUERA, M., 'El ábside de la catedral de Toledo y sus precedentes', *Archivo Español de Arte y Arqueologia*, 13 (1937), 25–36
PUENTE MIGUEZ, J. A., 'La catedral gótica de Santiago de Compostela . . .', *Compostellanum*, 30 (1985), 245–75

England

BRANNER, R., 'Westminster Abbey and the French court style', *JSAH*, 23 (1964), 3–16
KIDSON, P., 'St Hugh's Choir', *BAA CT*, Lincoln 1982 (1986), 29–42
WILSON, C., et al., *Westminster Abbey (New Bell's Cathedral Guide)* (London 1986)

CHAPTER III   Late Gothic

England

BOCK, H., *Der Decorated Style* (Heidelberg 1962)
BONY, J., *The English Decorated Style . . .* (Oxford 1979)
DRAPER, P., 'The sequence and dating of the Decorated work at Wells', *BAA CT*, Wells and Glastonbury 1978 (1981), 18–29
GIBB, J. H. P., 'The fire of 1437 and the rebuilding of Sherborne Abbey', *Journal, British Archaeological Assoc.*, 138 (1985), 101–24
HARVEY, J. H., *The Perpendicular style* (London 1978)
KIDSON, P., 'The architecture of St George's Chapel' in M. Bond (ed.), *The Saint George's Chapel quincentenary handbook* (Windsor 1975), 29–39
LEEDY, W. C., *Fan vaulting: a study of form, technology and meaning* (London 1980)

Central Europe

CLASEN, K. H., *Deutsche Gewölbe der Spätgotik* (Berlin 1958)
CROSSLEY, P., 'Wells, the West Country, and Central European Late Gothic', *BAA CT*, Wells and Glastonbury 1978 (1981), 81–109

LEGNER, A. (ed.), *Die Parler . . . 1350–1400*, exh. cat., 5 vols (Cologne 1978–80)
SWOBODA, K. M., *Peter Parler: der Baukünstler und Bildhauer* (Vienna 1943)
WORTMANN, R., *Das Ulmer Münster* (Stuttgart 1981)

Low Countries

LEEMANS, H., *De Sint-Gummaruskerk te Lier* (Antwerp & Utrecht 1972)
HASLINGHUIS, E., & C. PEETERS, *De dom van Utrecht* (The Hague 1965)
MOSSELVELD, J. H. VAN (ed.), *Keldermans. Een architektonisch netwerk in der Nederlanden* (The Hague 1987)
PEETERS, C., *De Sint-Janskathedraal te 's-Hertogenbosch* (The Hague 1985)
PHILIPP, K. J., 'Sainte-Waudru in Mons . . . Planungsgeschichte einer Stiftskirche 1449–1450', *Zeitschrift für Kunstgeschichte*, 51 (1988), 372–413
ROGGEN, D., & J. WITHOF, 'Grondleggers en grootmeesters der Brabantse Gothiek', *Gentsche Bijdragen tot de Kunstgeschiedenis*, 10 (1944), 83–209

France

MURRAY, S., 'The choir of St-Etienne at Beauvais', *JSAH*, 36 (1977), 111–21
NEAGLEY, L. E., 'The Flamboyant architecture of St-Maclou, Rouen . . .', *JSAH*, 47 (1988), 374–96
SANFAÇON, R., *L'architecture flamboyante en France* (Quebec 1971)
TAMIR, M. M., 'The English origin of the Flamboyant style', *Gazette des Beaux-Arts*, 6th ser., 29 (1946), 257–68
VACHON, M., *Une famille parisienne d'architectes et maîtres-maçons, les Chambiges 1490–1643* (Paris 1907)

Italy

ACKERMAN, J., ' "Ars sine scientia nihil est". Gothic theory of architecture at the cathedral of Milan', *AB*, 31 (1949), 84–111
MIDDELDORF-KOSEGARTEN, A., 'Zur Bedeutung der Sieneser Domkuppel', *Münchner Jahrbuch der bildenden Kunst*, 3rd ser., 21 (1970), 73–98
ROMANINI, A. M., 'Architettura', *Il duomo di Milano* (Milan 1973), 97–232
SAALMAN, H., 'S. Maria del Fiore: 1294–1418', *AB*, 46 (1964), 478–500
TOKER, F., 'Florence Cathedral: the design stage', *AB*, 60 (1978), 214–31
—, 'Arnolfo's S. Maria del Fiore: a working hypothesis', *JSAH*, 42 (1983), 101–20
TRACHTENBERG, M., *The campanile of Florence Cathedral. "Giotto's Tower"* (New York 1971)

Spain

CHUECA, F., *La catedral nueva de Salamanca* (Salamanca 1951)
DURÁN SANPERE, A., 'La cathédrale de Barcelone', *Congrès Archéologique de France (Catalogne)*, 117 (1959), 28–36
DURLIAT, M., *L'art dans le royaume de Majorque* (Toulouse 1962)
FALCON MÁRQUEZ, T., *La catedral de Sevilla. Estudio arquitectónico* (Seville 1980)
LAVEDAN, P., *L'architecture religieuse en Catalogne, Valence et Baléares* (Paris 1935)

Index of persons and works

Numbers in *italics* refer to illustrations. Italicized numbers in brackets indicate mentions in captions. Numbers in **bold** type indicate the principal references to a subject.

A. Augustinian abbey or priory
a. architect or architecturally active artist
B. Benedictine abbey or priory
C. Cistercian abbey
co. collegiate foundation
D. Dominican friary
F. Franciscan friary
p. parish church
p., co. parish church raised to collegiate rank before or during the building period discussed in this book
Pr. Premonstratensian abbey

Acknowledgments

I wish to record my thanks to those who helped me during the writing of this book. Paul Crossley read and criticized the sections on Central Europe; Caroline Bruzelius, Joanna Cannon, Peter Fergusson, Lindy Grant, Peter Kidson and Anne Prache answered queries relating to their fields of specialization; Victor Schmidt sent me photocopies from Dutch publications not traceable in British libraries; my fellow members of the History of Art Department of Westfield College – David Bindman, Caroline Elam and Catherine Reynolds – showed forbearance towards an obsessed and occasionally overwrought colleague; Pauline Baines, the designer, was exceptionally willing to take account of the expository functions of the illustrations; John Hutchinson drew fig. 28 specially for this book; Shirley Prager Branner, Stuart Harrison and Stephen Murray made available to me images which are their copyright; the staff of Westfield College Library and of the Conway Library in the Courtauld Institute of Art were unfailingly helpful; Joyce Jayes and Angela Rose patiently word-processed several versions of the text; the Faculty of Arts of Westfield College awarded me a grant from the Jane Herbert Memorial Fund which, together with David McLees's driving, enabled me to visit Rhenish and Swabian churches; Sebastian Birch's and Yvette Vanden Bemden's hospitality in Brussels and Jill Kerr's driving made possible two Belgian study trips. My greatest debt is to Emily Lane, who took a very fine-toothed critical comb through two drafts.

In preparing drawings for this book use has been made of illustrations published by other writers, and in some cases changes have been made to bring them into conformity with my own interpretations. I should like to acknowledge the following debts to 20th-century scholars, while making clear that any departures from the originals are entirely my responsibility: J. S. Ackerman 206; J. Bilson 125f, h; J. Bony 37; R. Branner 66b, 73b; S. McK. Crosby 28, 36; H. Deneux 20; G. Durand 66d, 73d, 125c; C. Seymour 41a; F. Toker 201a.

CW
London, 1989

For illustrations, acknowledgment is due to the following: A.C.L., Brussels 40, 178, 181; Aerofilms Ltd 53, 56, 62, 63, 64, 119, 130; Alinari 200, 203; Alinari/Brogi 204; Archives Photographiques, Paris/S.P.A.D.E.M. 16, 21, 23; James Austin 2, 26, 27, 71, 72, 90, 193; Bibliothèque Nationale, Paris 94; Robert Branner 80; Jutta Brüdern 103, 114; Courtauld Institute of Art, University of London 5, 25, 52, 54, 59, 60, 82, 115, 116, 141, 145, 147, 156, 158, 168, 169, 170, 173, 187, 188, 189, 192, 196, 198, 199; Malcolm Crowthers 133, 134, 163; Fitzwilliam Museum, University of Cambridge 7; Vladimir Fyman 167; Foto Grassi 1; Stuart Harrison 51; Hirmer Fotoarchiv 22, 24, 33, 35, 89, 91, 92, 95, 97; Ingeborg Limmer 102; A.F. Kersting 34, 55, 61, 78, 124, 126, 131, 132, 135, 161, 162, 166, 202, 213, 214, 219; Mansell/Alinari 205; Bildarchiv Foto Marburg 4, 15, 48, 65, 68, 86, 98, 106, 108, 111, 112, 113, 174, 175; Mas, Barcelona 117, 208, 209, 210, 211, 215, 216, 217, 220; Stephen Murray 190; Werner Neumeister 171; Rheinisches Bildarchiv, Cologne 84; Rijksdienst voor de Monumentenzorg, Zeist 180, 182; Helga Schmidt-Glassner 107, 110; Society of Antiquaries of London 140; Collection Viollet 191; Christopher Wilson 6, 8, 9, 11–14, 17–20, 28–32, 36, 37–39, 41–47, 49, 50, 57, 58, 66, 67, 69, 73, 74, 76, 77, 81, 83, 85, 87, 88, 93, 96, 100, 101, 104, 118, 120–123, 125, 127, 129, 136–138, 142–144, 146, 148–155, 157, 159, 160, 164, 172, 176, 177, 179, 184, 194, 195, 201, 206, 218.

Illustrations have also been reproduced from the following publications: J. Bentham, *The history and antiquities of the conventual cathedral church of Ely . . .* (Cambridge 1771) 145; R. W. Billings, *Baronial and ecclesiastical antiquities of Scotland* (Edinburgh & London 1842–52) 128; G. van Caster, 'Le vrai plan de la tour de St.-Rombaut à Malines', *Cercle archéologique, littéraire et artistique de Malines*, 8 (1898) 186; K. J. Conant, *Carolingian and Romanesque architecture 800–1200* (Penguin Books, Harmondsworth 1959) 3; A. Cremer, *Die Herstellung der Domkirche in Limburg-an-der-Lahn* (Berlin 1874) 105; G. Durand, *Monographie de l'église cathédrale Notre-Dame d'Amiens* (Amiens 1901–3) 70; E. van Even, *Louvain monumental* (Louvain 1860) 185; F. Mackenzic, *The architectural antiquities of the collegiate chapel of St. Stephen, Westminster . . .* (London 1844) 139; J. Puig i Cadafalch, 'El problema de la transformació de la catedral del Nord, importada a Catalunya . . .', *Miscel·lania Prat de la Riba* (Barcelona 1921) 207; G. E. Street, *Some account of Gothic architecture in Spain* (London 1865) 212; E. Viollet-le-Duc, *Dictionnaire raisonné de l'architecture française du XIe au XVIe siècle* (Paris 1858–68) 75 and p. 292; R. Willis, 'On the construction of the vaults of the Middle Ages', *Transactions, Royal Institute of British Architects*, I, pt 2 (1842) 165.